We live in a broken world, evidenced by every morning newspaper. Dr. Ruth Hetzendorfer not only takes on the subject but also exposes the root issues and paints a path of restoration. Anyone can present evidence, but rare is the gift that finds solutions.

—Glenn Burris Jr.
General Supervisor, The Foursquare Church

Dr H., as she is known on our campus, has without question given her life to helping the hurting. Her book has captured the heart of a caring professional adapted to a layperson's world. In my opinion this resource will bring hope to many that find their way to churches, centers, and ministries that provide friendship/lay counseling.

—Dan Stewart
President of Life Pacific College, 2003-08
Overseer to a Healing Ministry Center and a Former Pastor

Dr. Hetzendorfer gives us a systematic guide to pastoral care. She defines the seven root problems people face and the five most common ways these problems express themselves and then provides us with solid practical steps to help. This book is a great resource to turn to when we need fresh ideas or as a text for teaching others to give pastoral care.

—Dr. Steve Schell
Senior Pastor, Northwest Foursquare Church
Chairman, Doctrine Committee of the Foursquare Board of Directors
Chairman, Education Committee
Chairman, Governance Committee

THE PASTORAL COUNSELING HANDBOOK

A Guide to Helping the Hurting

Ruth Hetzendorfer

This book is published in association with
Patti M. Hummel, President & Agent
The Benchmark Group LLC
Nashville
benchmarkgroup1@aol.com
benchmarkgroup1@bellsouth.net

BEACON HILL PRESS
OF KANSAS CITY

Copyright 2009 by Ruth Hetzendorfer and Beacon Hill Press of Kansas City

ISBN 978-0-8341-2465-3

Cover Design: Kevin Williamson
Interior Design: Sharon Page

Disclaimer: The author of *The Pastoral Counseling Handbook* and Beacon Hill Press of Kansas City are not engaged in rendering medical, psychiatric, psychological, legal, or other professional services or advice. Such services and advice should be secured from a member of the relevant profession. Where appropriate, state and local laws and requirements should be consulted.

The author and Beacon Hill Press of Kansas City disclaim any liability, loss, or risk—personal or otherwise—incurred as a consequence, directly or indirectly, of the use or application of any contents of this work.

All Scripture quotations not otherwise designated are from the *Holy Bible, New International Version®* (NIV®). Copyright © 1973, 1978, 1984 by International Bible Society. Used by permission of Zondervan Publishing House. All rights reserved.

Scripture quotations marked NLT are from the *Holy Bible, New Living Translation*, copyright © 1996, 2004. Used by permission of Tyndale House Publishers, Inc., Carol Stream, IL 60188. All rights reserved.

Scripture quotations marked TM are from *The Message*. Copyright © 1993. Used by permission of NavPress Publishing Group.

Library of Congress Cataloging-in-Publication Date

Hetzendorfer, Ruth, 1950-
 The pastoral counseling handbook : a guide to helping the hurting / Ruth Hetzendorfer.
   p. cm.
 Includes bibliographical references.
 ISBN 978-0-8341-2465-3 (pbk.)
 1. Pastoral counseling—Handbooks, manuals, etc. I. Title.
 BV4012.2.H44 2009
 253.5—dc22

2009029932

CONTENTS

Dedication	6
Introduction	7

Part I
The Helping Process — 17
   1. The Power of Listening and the Stages of Helping — 19

Part II
Most Common Roots — 33
   2. Root of Rejection — 35
   3. Root of Unforgiveness — 49
   4. Root of Pride — 61
   5. Root of Perfectionism — 71
   6. Root of Rebellion — 83
   7. Root of Sexual Abuse — 93
   8. Root of Dysfunction — 109

Part III
Most Common (Negative) Fruits — 123
   9. Fruit of Depression — 125
   10. Fruit of Anxiety (Worry and Fear) — 135
   11. Fruit of Low Self-Esteem — 143
   12. Fruit of Anger — 153
   13. Fruit of Shame and Guilt — 163

Part IV
Common Problems — 175
   14. Grief and Loss — 177
   15. Divorce — 187
   16. Affairs — 201
   17. Stepparenting — 213
   18. Sexual Addiction — 223

Part V
Supplemental Topics — 237
   19. Engagement — 239
   20. Marital Helps — 253
   21. Legal and Ethical Issues — 269
   22. Supplements — 277

Bibliography — 285

I would like to dedicate this book to my amazing daughters, Heather and Vanessa, for their undying love and support through this process. I would especially like to thank Vanessa for the endless hours she took to keep me organized and correctly formatted.

Also, a huge thanks to Joy Moyal, a wonderful friend, who has given me hours of guidance and ideas.

INTRODUCTION

The first time I went to counseling was the last time. Years ago before I became a licensed counselor, I went to see a Christian counselor about some issues in my life. The person was not gentle or authentic and, worse, didn't seem to understand my situation. I told myself that one day when I counseled I would make every effort to understand a counselee's inner world and help him or her feel comfortable in the healing process. This is what most helpers want to do but don't always know how.

When I first started counseling, I was amazed at how many men and women had been sexually abused. I soon realized that all my education did not prepare me adequately to deal with this issue. I started searching through books and reading everything I could to help me understand what life was like for a person who has been sexually abused. This was the beginning of a lifelong search for knowledge and wisdom of many kinds of personal hurts. This book will give you some of that knowledge and wisdom to aid you in helping others.

If you have ever wanted to help someone but felt as if you did not know what to do or where to start, then take heart. This book carries a message of hope to the hurting and to those who desire to help them. The basis of this message is healing through the work of the Lord Jesus Christ in a person's life. Healing from past wounds requires hard work that involves examining an individual's past as well as conscious changes in his or her present behavior, thinking, and spiritual life.

Whether you are a pastor or layperson with a desire to help others, this handbook will enable you to counsel or help more effectively. Many of the steps and ideas written have come from years of counseling. Most of what I learned in the practical sense was through God's direction and experience. This handbook will give you that understanding also.

I need to point out that some people will come to you with problems that are actually symptoms of a deeper, older issue. If you help them get rid of the symptoms but do not tackle the real problem, the symptoms will continue to return. Often people are unaware of the issue behind their current problems. In this handbook, we will refer to this process as the "root to fruit" process, with the *root* being the big problem, or deep issue, and the *fruit* being the symptom or effect of the problem. (See illustration and list on pages 8-9.)

Tree of Stress-Producing Fruit

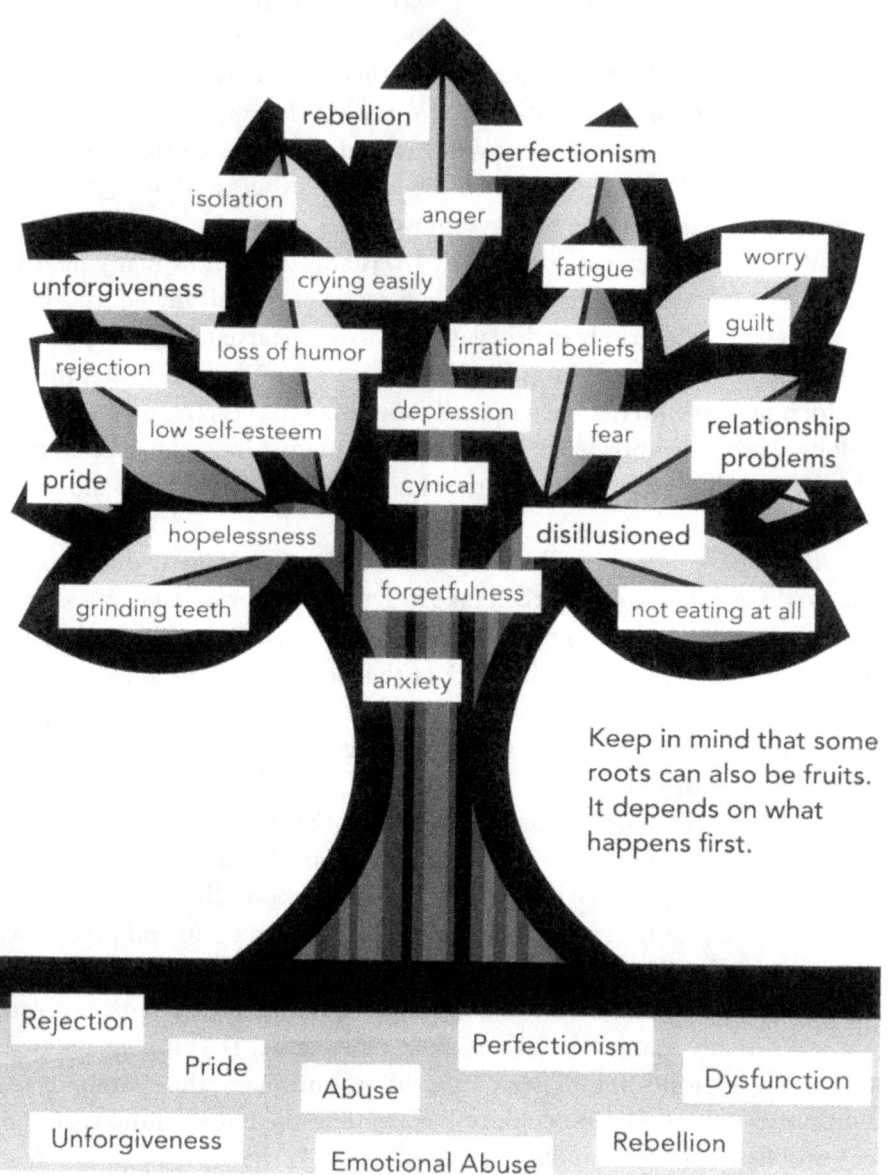

The Following Are Fruits That Can Develop from Roots

FEELINGS
- Agitation
- Irritability
- Anxiety
- Fear
- Boredom
- Unreality
- Nervousness
- Dread
- Hopelessness
- Hostility
- "No one cares"
- Little joy
- Frustration
- Weepy
- Guilt
- Repression
- Denial
- Mood swings
- Crying spells
- Depression
- Anxiousness
- Anger
- Like a failure
- Not good enough

BEHAVIOR
- Nonsmiling
- Giddy
- Boisterous
- Foot tapping
- Finger drumming
- Less productivity
- Insomnia
- Impulsive/reckless
- Accident prone
- Talking fast
- Aggressive/angry
- Excessive drinking/eating
- Withdrawn
- Not as able to work

COGNITIVE/THOUGHTS
- Excessive worry
- Inattentive
- Forgetful
- Nightmares
- Fear of death
- Repetitive thinking
- Putting self down
- Obsession with unwanted thoughts
- Compulsions
- Perfectionism
- Negative thinking/self-talk
- Confusion
- Dull senses
- Irritable
- Cynicism
- Loss of humor
- Less motivated
- Lowered self-esteem
- Boredom
- Spacing out
- Poor concentration
- Disliking free time

RELATIONAL
- Isolation
- Intolerance
- Resentment
- Loneliness
- Lashing out
- Hiding
- Clamming up
- Lowered sex drive
- Nagging
- Distrust
- Less contact with friends
- Lack of intimacy
- Using people
- Selfish

SPIRITUAL
- Emptiness
- Loss of meaning in life
- Doubt in God
- Unforgiving of God or others
- Not forgiving self
- Excessive guilt
- Loss of direction
- Cynicism
- Apathy
- Lack of faith and trust
- Lack of inner peace
- Needing to prove self
- Manipulating God
- Angry at God
- Confused about life in Christ
- Critical gossip
- Self-centered
- Giving up
- Inability to see faults
- Loss of hope
- Rejecting self
- Fearful

PHYSICAL BODY
- Fatigue
- Muscular tension
- Shakiness
- Easily startled
- Clumsiness
- Cold hands or sweaty palms
- Tightness in back/neck
- Sighing
- Feeling immobilized
- Heart "skipping beats"
- Less resistance to colds/flu
- Chest pain
- Rapid heart rate
- Dizziness
- Grinding teeth
- Nausea
- Indigestion
- No energy
- Tense
- Appetite change
- Restlessness
- High blood pressure
- Coronary heart disease
- Headaches
- Ulcers
- Neckache
- Colitis
- Chronic fatigue
- Stomach upsets
- Skin problems
- Digestive upsets
- Anxiety attacks
- Difficulty swallowing
- Hair loss
- Sleep problems
- Vomiting
- Constipation
- Weight change
- Tension
- Rash

For example, rejection is the most common root. From this root, a person may have a fruit of unforgiveness as a result of others' actions. Other fruits of rejection could be rebellion or pride, which would serve to protect the person from rejection. Both rebellion and pride are also roots, but in this case they are fruits because rejection happened first. The pride and rebellion evolved as ways to cope with the hurt of rejection. If those attributes stay there long enough, they can become rooted and will be more difficult to remove. They can also start producing fruits of their own.

It is important to understand and discover in helpees which issue came first in their lives. Were they prideful and then others rejected them? Did they feel rejection from someone and then became prideful? The key to helping the helpee is to discover, or root out, the origination point. You can chop off the fruits of the root by giving the helpee behavioral exercises, but those fruits will return unless the root is dug up. To dig up the root, prayer and forgiveness of others and self are essential steps. Of course, helpees always need God's forgiveness. These steps, as well as many others, are included in each "root" chapter of this handbook.

How Can You Put This Book to Work for You?

Reading this book in its entirety will give you a whole picture of genuine caring and fundamental helping. If you can listen and care about people's feelings, you are already on your way to helping them. This book will be a valuable resource each time you listen to helpees as they discuss their issues. You can assist them in making the needed connections in their lives so that they can focus on the areas that will enable their healing to begin.

This book will be of more value to you if you first use it in your own life. If you make connections from your own life experiences and deal with your own roots and fruits, then it will be easier to guide another person toward healing.

As the author, I need to point out that the material in this book has come through years of experiences from counseling others as well as from life in general. These ideas have been substantiated through a collaboration of research and life experience.

The church has become very cautious about counseling correctness with the rise of legal attacks against and within it. Thus this book acts as a guide to help you through the dangerous waters of ministry in the helping field. Because many who work in this field are not legally licensed counselors, the terminology in this book will be broad. Thus the term *helping* will take the place of the well-known and used word *counseling*. The counselee is the *helpee*, and you, the ministering one, are the *helper*. It is vital for you to read the ethics and legalities chapter. Always remember that if you cannot easily aid the helpee, you need to refer that person to a professional in-the-field counselor. It is vital to know when something is over your head and you need to refer.

How This Handbook Is Laid Out

The handbook is divided into five main parts: (1) The Helping Process, (2) Most Common Roots (the basis of problems), (3) Most Common (Negative) Fruits (the effects of the roots), (4) Common Problems, and (5) Supplemental Topics (marriage, engagement, legalities, and additional matters).

The Helping Process part lays out a clear picture of a typical session. Skills are given that will help you know how to listen in a caring and helpful manner. Step-by-step analysis is laid out to guide you through a session, including specific suggestions of what to ask.

In the next three parts of the book, each root, fruit, and common problem is broken down into an explanation, the steps to healing, homework ideas, and Scripture to encourage and guide the helpee. This process equips the helper with tools to guide the helpee to wholeness.

The last part of the book has a chapter of helps for marriage problems. This chapter will give couples ways to talk through problems. There is also a chapter with details for seven complete premarital sessions. These session guides also include problems to look for, issues to discuss, and homework ideas. This last part of the book also includes a chapter on the legalities of helping people, a must for everyone to read.

The Value of Being a Warm, Genuine Person

Your demeanor of acceptance and respect goes a long way toward providing an emotionally safe place for people. The hurting person needs a warm environment to speak out of his or her heart. If we, the church, cannot be safe and nonjudgmental, where will he or she go? Psychiatrist Dwight L. Carlson, upon his return from an overseas ministry trip among missionaries, expressed this idea best when he said, "The only army that shoots its wounded is the Christian army."

Dr. Carlson summed up the philosophy of the group he worked with:
1. We don't have emotional problems. If any emotional difficulties appear to arise, simply deny having them.

2. If we fail to achieve this first ideal and can't ignore a problem, strive to keep it from family members and never breathe a word of it outside the family.
3. If both of the first two steps fail, still don't seek professional help.

I have been a Christian for 50 years, a physician for 29, and a psychiatrist for 15. Over this time I have observed these same attitudes throughout the church—among lay leaders, pastors, priests, charismatics, fundamentalists, and evangelicals alike. I have also found that many not only deny their problems but are intolerant of those with emotional difficulties. Many judge that others' emotional problems are the direct result of personal sin. This is a harmful view. At any one time, up to 15 percent of our population is experiencing significant emotional problems. For them our churches need to be sanctuaries of healing, not places where they must hide their wounds.[1]

Although I think that Christians on the whole have improved this picture tremendously, we still need to be aware of our attitudes, our judgments, and our words. Sometimes the best thing we can do is just listen, care, and pray. God is the ultimate healer, not us.

Six Elements Necessary to Counsel

As a pastor or layperson, you understand that hurting people do not come to you for psychoanalysis. They need healing that only God can do. But to offer pat answers or packaged Scripture phrases can sometimes do more harm than good. So how can you effectively minister to the hurting? The following six elements are necessary for the healing process and will help you understand the essentials of helping others:

1. Validation

The heartbeat of our culture today seems to be fixed on solving problems and moving on to accomplish more. It is not the process, but the result that matters. Unfortunately, this sometimes becomes the mode of operation for relationships and even for ministry. It is tempting to offer solutions or advice, but it does not best serve the one who is hurting. The essential element to open the door to healing is *validation*. This simple but critical element assures helpees that you hear them and understand what they are telling you. It also builds a foundation of trust. People need to identify and state their pain to begin the process of restoration. Validating the feelings of helpees shows that you want to truly walk alongside them to find healing and peace.

Do not skip this step and jump to advice (e.g., "I think you should just give it to God and move on . . .") or else the helpee will get the impression that what you have to say is more important than his or her feelings. By validating a helpee's pain, the door is opened to the path that will lead to healing.

I experienced a powerful example of the effects of validation when I was helping an older lady a couple of years ago. She had talked continually about her hurt and anger for over forty-five minutes without seeming to take a breath. Her thirty years of hurt in her marriage had been bottled up, and it seemed as though she was releasing her anger on me. As I was listening, I knew that only God could intervene. No one could give her back the thirty years she felt she had lost. I realized the afternoon was getting long, so I finally interrupted her, which I rarely do. "I can see you have been through unbelievable pain and many years of hardship. Nothing can ever make up for that," I said. Amazingly, her face softened, tears rolled down her cheeks, and her countenance changed. Did that heal her? Is it that simple? A foolproof formula? No, of course not, but it was a beginning. No one had ever acknowledged her pain. People had listened but not verbally acknowledged that they really heard her pain.

2. Understanding the Inner World of the Hurting

Once you have heard and validated the feelings of the helpee, you must make every effort to understand the *inner world* of this person. We certainly cannot experience everything a person goes through, but we can grasp a working knowledge of what his or her life has been like.

Another woman I'll call Melody lived in the inner world of the sexually abused, a world different from anything some could imagine. As I listened to her story, I realized I was not prepared to truly understand her world. It took a few months of reading everything I could find on sexual abuse to bring clarity to this kind of pain. Yes, I could care and I could listen, but the key came from knowing about her world and what God had to say on this issue.

To understand the inner world of the hurting, you must gather resources that will broaden your understanding. Do everything possible to take yourself outside of your own paradigm and attempt to authentically see the world through the eyes of your helpees. Try to gather resources to encourage them with the knowledge that they are not alone. Chances are that you have never been through what they are going through. Statements such as, "I understand exactly how you feel," can sound very hollow if the helpee suspects that you have not had a similar life experience. Even if some similar experience has occurred in your life, it is essential that you understand that his or her reaction may be very different.

Seeking out resources is a way to communicate to the hurting that you care and empathize with them. Doing so displays that though you cannot possibly understand how they are feeling as a result of this great pain, you can still be there with them as they walk through it. It will also empower them to take some control in their own healing process.

3. Recognition Is Half the Battle

The turning point in the healing journey comes when helpees are able to reach a point of recognition about themselves, their pain, and their experiences. Be aware that it may take some time for a helpee to recognize the root of his or her situation. As you gently guide a helpee to a place of understanding, the helpee's pain may seem worse. A person always feels more pain as he or she recognizes and accepts the impact of his or her situation. It is only then, however, that real healing can take place. A person cannot change what he or she cannot acknowledge. Even as a helpee sees the truth, it may take time to process the big picture before choosing to change.

With grief and loss issues, it is important for you, the helper, to keep in mind that it generally takes *one year to heal for every five years* the helpee had a relationship with the deceased (or person divorced). Several kinds of grief can similarly be devastating, such as losing a job or moving to another state or country.

4. Helping the Helpee Forgive

Guiding the hurting to forgive is always necessary for complete healing. Perhaps they need to forgive a person who has betrayed them, or they may even feel God is the one who has inflicted pain. Hurt is commonly the result of rejection or purposeful infliction. It would be easy for someone like Melody to try to skip this step. Even when a person has made the decision to forgive, it is still a tough road to travel. The "feelings" of forgiveness toward the perpetrator may take nine to twelve months to catch up to the cognitive decision. The need to forgive again may resurface over time. This does not mean that the initial decision to forgive was invalid.

Forgiveness is an issue of the heart wherein we must educate the hurting to extend grace toward the one who has hurt them again and again. Only this will bring true freedom. How true is the statement of S. I. McMillen, M.D.: "I have found that the moment I start hating a man, I become his slave."[2] It will be of vital importance that you walk helpees through this process without condemning them or trivializing their problems.

5. Leading the Helpee to Change Behavior

Although a person can recognize his or her situation and even forgive and feel that freedom, he or she can still carry over some of the same behaviors. These behaviors, which once were reactions to hurt, are now habits or even a lifestyle. For example, Melody's self-talk was very negative. She constantly told herself she was a dirty and worthless person. Changing behaviors and even a lifestyle is very difficult. This is the time you often lose a person's interest. It is a lot of work to change behavior, and it is often uncomfortable. It is easier to keep life the same. Your helpee's determination to change will demonstrate that he or she is committed to putting away the past and becoming whole.

6. Giving Unconditional Love, Acceptance, and Hope

Your countenance of acceptance toward helpees, regardless of what has happened to them, is of utmost importance to the outcome. Your helpees need to see Jesus in you. They need to see a model of acceptance and gentleness and a person who gives value to others. I believe this portrayal is really what Paul meant when he spoke about the importance of love in 1 Cor. 13:13: "Trust steadily in God, hope unswervingly, love extravagantly. And the best of the three is love" (TM).

We must lead helpees to Christ by our example and give them hope that life can be better. We must know that the process will make the difference and believe in our hearts that no matter how difficult the situation seems, *there is always hope.* If we don't have hope, we will not be able to give it. We must always remember that God is the ultimate healer—not us. "For nothing is impossible with God" (Luke 1:37).

Important Disclaimer!

Suggestions, comments, and opinions provided are general information and are not intended to substitute for medical, psychiatric, psychological, legal, or other professional advice. This book does not endorse laypeople or pastors helping people who have issues requiring an ongoing counselor. This book is intended to serve as a guide to help the hurting when possible. See chapter 21, "Legal and Ethical Issues." Check with your county and state for specific regulations on suicide, child and elder abuse, AIDS, and domestic violence.

Notes

1. Dwight L. Carlson, M.D., *Christianity Today*, Vol. 42, No. 2 (February 9, 1998), 48.

2. S. I. McMillen and David E. Stern, *None of These Diseases* (Old Tappan, N.J.: Fleming H. Revell Company, 1984), 116.

PART I
THE HELPING PROCESS

*The LORD is close to the brokenhearted
and saves those who are crushed in spirit.*
—Ps. 34:18

How do you help?
    How do you incorporate listening skills?
    How do you work on the issue?

The next few pages are designed to help you get a view of what a helping session could look like.

1— THE POWER OF LISTENING AND THE STAGES OF HELPING

He who answers before listening—that is his folly and his shame (Prov. 18:13).

A key to the helping process is being a good listener. Few people seem to have natural listening skills. We tend to think about how a conversation relates to us rather than the other person. Putting ourselves in the shoes of someone else can be difficult.

As a helper, the more you practice the listening skills introduced in the first part of this chapter, the more aware you will become of the needs of others. Learning these skills means, for a short time, letting go of your own needs. Once you can focus on what another person is going through, you will be able to guide him or her through the helping process, as described in this chapter's second part.

Begin by asking yourself these questions:
- Am I tuning in to what a person is saying, or am I relating it to myself?
- Am I assuming I know what a person is going to say and stop listening?
- Do I concentrate on the meaning of the message?
- Do I watch verbal and nonverbal behavior?
- Do I consider the best way to respond?
- Do I practice these skills with others to sharpen my ability to really hear what a person is saying?

Basic Listening Skills for All Helpers

If you are talking more than the helpee, you are not helping and you are certainly not listening. Listening is a unique skill that few people master. The art of listening comes by much patience, compassion, and care. We will examine basic active listening skills.

1. Validating—a Skill All to Itself

People need to identify and state their pain to begin the process of restoration. Validating the helpee's feelings shows that you want to truly walk alongside the helpee to help him or her find healing and peace.

Skipping this step and jumping to advice (i.e., "I think you should just give it to God and move on") indicates to the helpee that what you have to say is more important than what he or she is saying. Instead, by validating the helpee's pain, the door is opened to the path that will lead to healing.

Examples of validation include statements such as the following:

"I can see that you feel hurt when you think about it."

"It sounds like you have been in a lot of pain over this."

"I can't imagine what you have been through."

"I can see you are hurting."

You do not need to have all of the answers, but simply as James put it, "be quick to listen [and] slow to speak" (James 1:19).

As a counseling professor I have found the most difficult thing for students to remember is to reflect the helpee's pain by verbally validating before asking the next question or, worse yet, thinking they need to give a quick fix. Validation is essential for healing.

Ask Yourself the Following

What is the depth of the helpee's pain?

How often is it interwoven in the story?

Have I acknowledged his or her pain verbally each time pain is demonstrated?

Example

HELPEE: It has been very hard for me the past three weeks. My aunt—who I was close to—died, my job role is changing daily, and now because of finances I am having to take my children out of private school and put them in public school. I have little energy and life seems so bleak now.

HELPER: You have certainly gone through a lot of change. That would be very difficult to experience all at once.

Or

HELPER: Wow, that has to be overwhelming. I can see why you would have little energy. That is a lot to go through.

2. Paraphrasing

This skill involves saying the same thing as the helpee but in fewer words. This assures the helpee that you are listening and know what he or she is saying.

Ask Yourself the Following

What is his or her basic message?
How do I restate it in less words?
Did the helpee feel that I heard him or her?

Example

HELPEE: I don't know about him. One moment he's nice as can be. The next moment he lashes out and says hurtful things about me. I am always so upset that I either walk away or lash out myself. Then it really becomes ugly.

HELPER: So he changes from one moment to the next.

3. Clarifying

This skill guides the helper into a better understanding of what the helpee is saying. This method of questioning brings the content into a sharper focus. What does the helpee really mean?

Ask Yourself the Following

What doesn't seem to make sense?
What part needs more information?
What parts am I not putting together?

Example

HELPEE: I don't understand why I get so upset with my husband. He is such a wonderful guy. He just annoys me. He thinks he always knows what is right to do. He always ends up with the last word. This frustrates me. It doesn't matter what I say. Sometimes I say how I feel. Then he gets upset.

(Examples of clarifying responses)

HELPER: He gets upset at what kind of feelings?
HELPER: I'm not sure I understand. Could you tell me more?
HELPER: Give me an example of what you mean.
HELPER: Let me state what I think you mean to see if I understand.

4. Reflecting Feelings

This skill can show an understanding of the helpee's feelings. It can bring reflection to the helpee on ideas or thoughts he or she hadn't realized or understood.

Ask Yourself the Following

What is the overall feeling?
What does the helpee's tone suggest?
Is the helpee's body language saying something different from his or her words?
Does the helpee concur that the identified feeling is correct?

Example

HELPEE: I'm wondering if you can help me find a new way of responding to my wife. I spend most of my time listening and not saying much. What is the use of saying anything? She will just get upset anyway.
(Examples of reflecting responses)
HELPER: You seem to feel frustrated. Do you think you feel like giving up?
HELPER: It really hurts to be rejected by someone you love. You seem to feel angry in this situation.

Example

(Here is an example of reflection of inconsistencies between verbal and nonverbal.)
HELPEE: I feel like I am doing well. I have plenty to do each day, and I am sure I am feeling better about my marriage.
HELPER: You are smiling, but I sense you are really hurting inside.
HELPER: You say you really care about your wife, but when you talk about her, you clench your fists.

5. Confrontation

This skill can aid several areas. A safe environment must first be established if confrontation is to take place. Always use a noninvasive method of confronting. Learn to soften your words. This skill is used to tell the helpee about his or her discrepancies, lack of awareness of self or perhaps recognition of fear and/or anger.

Ask Yourself the Following

What appears to be inconsistent in what the helpee is saying?

Is there something the helpee fails to recognize in his or her life?
Is the helpee blind to the hurt he or she may be causing another person?

Example

HELPEE: I feel really hurt by my mom. She spends all her time at work. Everything is more important to her than me and my sister. When she comes home, she never has anything nice to say. She just says she is tired and doesn't want to be bothered with us. She always had an excuse when we asked her to go to school events. Not that my family is bad or anything—my parents really love me. They always did the best they could. My mom is really a good mother. Our family always had a lot of love.

HELPER: There seems to be some real hurt with you and your mother. You seem to have difficulty talking about that hurt. Do you feel you need to be protective of your mom?

HELPEE: I feel bad saying anything bad and who wants their family to sound awful? We are just a normal family.

HELPER: I can see this is difficult for you. It is OK to talk with someone about things that have hurt you. No one has gone without at least some hurt in his or her family. Most parents are trying to be the best parents they can be. But in order for you to heal, we have to look at the whole truth about all that has happened. Let's look at this a little more.

6. Summarizing

This skill involves listening to all parts of the message (thus far) and bringing them all together. This method has a variety of purposes, one being to bring the content to closure and another to demonstrate to the helpee all that has been discussed.

Ask Yourself the Following

What are the main issues and emotions that have been discussed?
Would it be more meaningful for me (the helper) to sum up this information or for the helpee to do it? In deciding, consider your purpose. Was it to
- Warm up the helpee at the beginning?
- Focus scattered thoughts and feelings?
- Close discussion on a particular theme?
- Check your understanding of the helpee's progress?
- Encourage the helpee to explore themes more completely?

- Terminate the relationship with a progress summary?
- Assure the helpee that the sessions are moving along well?

Or was it to

- Test your own understanding of what has been said?
- Evaluate how the helpee is feeling at the end of the session?
- Evaluate the importance of the topics discussed?

In the first group of questions, the helpee hears you summarize; in the second, the helpee summarizes.

Example

Here is a scenario. A young college girl has just discussed her fear of her boyfriend breaking up with her. There doesn't seem to be much reason for her to worry continually about this. The helper has asked her also about her parents. She has explained that her dad was never at home and that when he did come home, he was busy and distracted. She never remembers sitting down and talking to him about her life. Once, when she asked her dad for help with some hurt she was experiencing with her friends, he told her the problem was her fault and what else could she expect.

HELPER: We have talked about your relationship with your boyfriend and how you worry a lot about him breaking up with you. We've looked at that from several angles but didn't come up with anything concrete that could substantiate that fear. The fear of breaking up is definitely there. We also discussed the hurt you had with your dad and how he seemed to never be there for you. You seem to have a difficult time talking about your dad and the things you missed. You even mentioned that he isn't here for you now. There is a lot of hurt in these relationships, and I would like us to look at the possibility that there could be a link between them. Do you think you fear rejection from your dad? From your boyfriend?

The above is just a sample of the summarization of a session.

Now that we have surveyed the necessary listening skills, we will examine what a counseling (helping) session is like.

Diagram of a Helping Session

1. Prepare yourself	2. Ask: How can I be of help to this person?	3. What does the helpee need to recognize?	4. What is the issue? How can the helpee work on it?
Keep yourself in the Word of God.	A. Compassion is your main tool—feel *with* helpee.	Incorporate listening skills to promote listening. These do not need to be in this order. These are skills to be used when needed.	A. What Is the Issue? Have you connected the fruits to a root?
Ask the Holy Spirit to guide you.	B. Respect Being nonjudgmental	How does helpee feel? What is his or her understanding?	B. Solving the Issue What does God say? Is there an issue to solve? Connecting the fruits to the root—if so, see "Steps to Assist the Helpee . . ." in the chapter for the root.
Be aware of your own personal issues of sexuality and burnout.	C. Care about what is happening in helpee's life.	A. Validation Use this when pain is expressed. This skill is vital to healing.	C. Work on the Issue Help the helpee think of ways to resolve his or her issue and make any needed decisions. This may mean looking more at the "root" chapters in the book and the questions given. There may not be a decision to make.
A. Time to Listen How are your listening skills?	D. Genuineness If you are real, the helpee will feel free to open up. Carl Rogers states that being genuine, respectful, and showing empathy is foremost in this process.[1]	B. Paraphrasing Be sure you are understanding what helpee is saying. This also helps helpee see you are listening. This may be used when necessary to show understanding.	D. Information Gathering Sometimes the most helpful solution can be having the helpee read information on the issue to bring further understanding. Is forgiveness a part of solving this issue? If so, look at the unforgiveness chapter.

1. Prepare yourself (continued)	2. Ask: How can I be of help to this person? (continued)	3. What does the helpee need to recognize? (continued)	4. What is the issue? How can the helpee work on it? (continued)
B. Begin with Prayer	E. Being Culturally Sensitive Carl Rogers emphasizes the need to understand the inner world of the person you are seeing.	C. Clarification Clarify what you don't understand—tune in to what helpee is saying. Does helpee have a goal? This helps bring clarification.	Is the helpee serious about changing? Make sure helpee is committed to the process. Give him or her materials to work on. See homework sections.
	It is vital to be aware of family values and issues that relate particularly to other groups.	D. Reflecting Feelings How is the helpee feeling? Is helpee aware of his or her feelings?	E. Ending a Session Make sure you have brought God and His Word into this.
		E. Confrontation Use if needed—that is, if there is a discrepancy in what helpee says and does. Are you seeing the fruits? Is what helpee came in for really the issue?	F. Pray with Helpee See Scripture sections. Give helpee scriptures to take home and study.
		F. Summarizing State briefly what has been discussed, bringing all parts together. See summarization in the listening skills section.	
As a result of your preparation, you will be ready to help helpee become involved.	As a result, the helpee will be open to speak from his or her heart.	As a result of this process, the helpee should be experiencing some clarity.	As a result of this process, the helpee should be learning new behaviors.

Explanation of the Helping Process

To start with, keep in mind that if you're talking more than the helpee, you are not helping; you are probably giving advice, teaching, or talking about yourself. The homework you assign is what teaches helpees more about the issue and helps them work on their behavior. See "Understanding Self" in chapter 22, on pages 277-78, to aid you in this process.

What follows are the stages of the helping process with their explanations. (An overview of the process is also found in the diagram beginning on page 25.) Some adaptation will be needed, but these are the general steps.

First, You Need to Be Prepared

- Keep yourself in the Word of God.
- Ask the Holy Spirit to guide you.
- Be aware of your own personal issues of sexuality and possibility of burnout from too much counseling.

A. Time to Listen

- See the active listening skills in previous pages.
- Notice verbal and nonverbal cues.
- Attend to the helpee's feelings as well as the content—what the helpee is saying.

B. Open in Prayer

Second, Ask the Helpee, "How Can I Be of Help?"

Or ask, "How can I help you today?" Let the helpee tell you his or her story.

A. Compassion. Answer with meaning, feeling, and compassion.

B. Respect. Are you showing value to the helpee?

C. Care. Are you caring in your responses? What does your body language say? Are you in a rush?

Make sure you understand the helpee's story. Be sure to ask the helpee what he or she means. Do not interrupt with your own stories, opinions, or reflections. Reflect how the helpee feels. Always keep an attitude of acceptance. Use only the information he or she has given you. Carl Rogers, founder of Person-Centered Counseling, says the most important technique is the helper's attitude toward people: "congruence (genuineness), unconditional positive regard (respect), and empathy."[2]

D. **Genuineness.** Are you real? Carl Rogers says being real, warm, transparent, and caring will facilitate the process.

E. **Culturally Sensitive.** It is vital to be aware of family values and issues that relate particularly to other groups.

Third, You Need to Help the Helpee Recognize and Understand His or Her Issue

The helpee needs to know how his or her feelings affect his or her content (the issue) so he or she can start understanding the issue.

Use empathy but add insight into the problem: "You feel _____ because _____ and you want _____."[3]

Using the skills listed below (when needed) you will be able to guide the helpee toward recognition of the issue and eventually healing.

A. **Validating the Helpee.** Validating pain and hurt is essential to the healing process:
- "I can see why you feel so hurt."
- "You have been through a lot."
- "I can't imagine how much that would hurt."

Validating needs to be spoken every time a significant pain is expressed—especially before the next question. This is essential for most people. Some men feel better being validated by a nod or expression of acceptance than words of validation.

B. **Paraphrasing.** At times it may be necessary to paraphrase what a helpee says to show you understand his or her problem. This could be anywhere in the session.

C. **Clarification.** Clarify by recognizing uniqueness and generalities and helping the helpee become specific. What is it you don't understand about the helpee's story?

D. **Reflecting Feelings.** What does the helpee need to understand about his or her own feelings? Is the helpee aware enough of his or her feelings to put words to them?

E. **Confrontation.** Confronting a helpee might be necessary in several situations. Seeing a discrepancy between what the helpee says and other actions the helpee shows you in the session could prompt a need for confrontation. It might also be necessary when you observe the helpee changing his or her words or being inconsistent in his or her stories.

The right to confront must be earned by your relationship with the helpee. You also must know from God that it is necessary to confront.

Confrontation could have a harsh tone, but you can confront in a gentle, kind manner. Preface your words by saying, "I want to ask you a question about something I have noticed in what you said . . ."

F. Summarizing. Summarizing goes a step further than paraphrasing. Summarize the whole discussion of the session—the key points. This helps you as well as the helpee see clarity and progress. You need to attend to everything the helpee has said—the content as well as the way it was said, or the feeling.

Put the content and feeling together: "In this session we have talked about _____." Describe the content and feelings, bringing in the important details. Ask if the helpee sees the same things in the summary. This helps you and the helpee see clarity.

Fourth, What Is the Issue? How Can the Helpee Work on It

Consider what God says on the issue, and bring the Word of God into the matter. Approach sin if that is the issue.

Never use words such as, "You have a problem." Some words we use can be very discouraging.

A. "What Is Really the Issue at Hand?" It might be a matter of goal setting or working on behaviors. It might be a problem-solving issue. This is a good time to look at the symptoms (fruits that have been identified) and decide what possibly could be the root(s). It is often necessary to see if forgiveness is a part of solving the issue? Unforgiveness is common to many issues.

B. Solving the Issue. This may not be possible at the moment. Remember the decision about what to do always belongs to the helpee. The helpee may already know what to do and just needed validation of his or her hurt. Maybe the issue is one the helpee must work out over time, or it may be an issue dealing with choices. This is when you should be considering what possible fruits you are seeing and what root is present. Study the questions in the chapters of this handbook corresponding to the different roots: rejection, unforgiveness, pride, perfectionism, rebellion, sexual abuse, and/or dysfunction.

Example

"From what you say, you seem to be allowing anger (fruit) to control part of your life. Perhaps we need to look closer at your relationship with your mother (possible dysfunctional family root) as you mentioned earlier." Ask yourself, "Where does God fit into this? What biblical character experienced the same issue? Or what does God's Word say in response to the issue?" See what you can contribute to this issue to bring clarity.

C. Work on the Issue. You can say to the helpee, "We will come up with a way to work on this," or "What do you see as a way to help you through this anger?" Or if you have established a root, see the Steps to Assist the Helpee in the chapter of this handbook covering that specific root.

D. Information Gathering. What could you give the helpee to do from the homework sections to help him or her throughout the week?

There are several ways a helpee could work on an issue. For example, the helpee could write a letter expressing the anger he or she feels toward another person but not send the letter. You could also ask the helpee what he or she has already done to work on an issue. Or if it is an issue such as a young girl breaking up with her boyfriend, having her list the pros and cons of the situation might help. Ultimately, any decision has to be made by the helpee. See the homework assignments under the root(s) if needed.

Ask the helpee, "What have you done that hasn't worked?" If the helpee is still angry or unforgiving, ask him or her if he or she would like to try something else. Give the helpee suggestions. For example, the helpee could consider talking to the person who caused the hurt.

In many ways, you suggest the kinds of homework and ask the questions that have been described earlier, including asking the helpee if there is a decision that needs to be made. Again, if you have found the root, go ahead and start on the Steps to Assist for the root. This helps the helpee see potential results so that he or she can really commit to the process. For example, have the helpee pray about forgiving his or her mother. Pray blessings on her. Read *The Art of Forgiving by* Lewis B. Smedes (Ballantine Books, 1997). For the next week, ask the helpee to fill out the "Understanding Self" exercise in chapter 22 of this book.

Knowledge about the issue can bring more light to understanding. See the list of books in each root, fruit, and problem chapter. This can help the helpee learn ways to change or work on his or her behavior. What materials could you give the helpee to help him or her learn about this issue over the next few weeks?

E. Ending of Session. Here are some steps to help you bring a session to a close:

1. Let the helpee know what you have covered and again what he or she is to do.
2. Review with the helpee and make sure he or she knows what you are expecting in the next week or two.
3. Make sure you talk to the helpee about establishing prayer and Bible reading each day—even if for a short time.

4. Be sure to give the helpee specific scriptures appropriate for the issue.
5. Make a referral if needed. Know when something is over your head.

F. Pray with the Helpee. Give the helpee hope though the Word.

The Don'ts of Helping

When interacting with a helpee, you must know not only what to do but also what not to do. The following list will help you with the things to avoid in a helping session.

1. Don't look shocked when a helpee gives you information.
2. Don't say, "I know just how you feel."
3. Don't disclose experiences in your own life unless it is done rarely and then only briefly.
4. Don't make life-changing decisions for the person you are helping.
5. Don't minimize the helpee's issue.
6. Don't say, "If you just trusted God more, you would be OK," or "If you would pray more, you wouldn't be depressed."
7. Don't lecture, "Be glad it isn't worse."
8. Don't be too sympathetic: "You poor thing."

Notes

1. Quoted in Charles Thompson and Linda Rudolph, *Counseling Children*, 5th ed. (Belmont, Calif.: Wadsworth Brooks/Cole, 2000), 145.
2. Ibid., 119.
3. Ibid., 123.

PART II
MOST COMMON ROOTS

Rejection
Unforgiveness
Pride
Perfectionism
Rebellion
Sexual Abuse
Dysfunctional Family/Emotional Abuse

CONTEXT
Each root chapter first explains the context of the root. Some of the fruits of the root are also listed and explained.

STEPS TO ASSIST HELPEE
Steps are given to help you progress through ways to guide the helpee to healing.

HOMEWORK FOR HELPEE
Homework is strongly suggested for each helpee. Use all the ideas listed, or tailor the ideas to the helpee's need.

BOOKS FOR HELPEE
Suggested books for the helpee to read

SCRIPTURES FOR HELPEE
Scriptures are suggested for the helpee.

2 – ROOT OF REJECTION

Rejection is the most common root. Most everyone has been rejected at some time in his or her life. To know if rejection is a problem in a person's life, you will need to know the significance of the relationship of the one who rejected the person and how long and severely the person was treated.

Context of the Root of Rejection

Rejection is a deep wound that erodes the whole person. It is the most common root of problems. The three most common sources of rejection are parent-child, peers, and male-female relationships.

Common Sources of Rejection

Parents

Parents who do not communicate love contribute to this root. This may be parents who do not know how to give love, having never received it. It may be parents who have learned to give love by overindulgence or even parents who are so angry they are loving one minute and hostile the next. It is no wonder that some people have neither heard the words "I love you" nor received daily or at least weekly hugs.

Parents who do not evaluate their source of rejection and find healing will usually repeat the same process in their children.

Parents that cause the root of rejection can also be any of the following:[1]

- Alcoholics or even workaholics. Parents who have difficulty emotionally attaching to their children due to their own hurt may find other ways to deal with their pain, such as alcohol.
- Parents who substitute giving gifts for love. The child often grows up not knowing how to give love to his or her own children and is emotionally empty.
- Critical parents (possibly perfectionist). A harsh or hostile parent often creates a picture of God as a distant and uncaring being who is ready to whack a person on the head. It is difficult for a person to grow up feeling he or she can never truly please his or her parent or God. Attachment or lack of attachment can create a view of God for life.
- Parents who expect the child to follow their own goals or desires.

Parental problems are most often the source of rejection. Seldom does a person continue to suffer rejection from peers in the adult years. The pain of parental rejection, however, can pervade a person's entire life.

Peers

Growing up isn't easy. Difficulty fitting in at school, academic problems, social problems, not fitting in a group, and a general lack of acceptance can affect a child as he or she grows up. If a child feels total acceptance, value, and love at home, he or she will be able to endure rejection at school without too much difficulty. Peer rejection rarely affects a person in adulthood. I have known people who were convinced their rejection was from their peers earlier in life until they understood the dynamics in their own family. See "Symptoms of the Dysfunctional Home" in chapter 8.

Male-Female Relationships

The rejection experiences in these relationships strip away the emotional need to be whole. These are the basic emotional needs: love, security, approval, acceptance, and identity. Look for patterns of rejection in previous dating relationships or marriage. When did the helpee first begin to feel rejected? Did rejection from the past damage his or her relationships, or did a rejected relationship permeate other areas of life? (See chapter 15, "Divorce.")

Other Sources of Rejection

The Media. The media causes a sense of rejection by what it displays. Beauty and talent are displayed as the norm, bringing a sense of inadequacy to many people. No one is exempt. Beauty and thinness seem like such priorities in our society that without them we feel we have no value.

God. Because of sin, guilt develops and brings a sense of rejection. If a person has never known the true acceptance of a father, he or she may have a difficult time understanding the depth of God's love and acceptance.

Results of Rejection

A hole in the personality describes a person who has a hole so big that nothing can fill it. No matter how someone may try to fill this hole by receiving compliments and acceptance, nothing will help until the hole is healed.

This type of person usually overwhelms friends, a spouse, and even relatives because so much is demanded from them. An empty person needs constant attention from everyone around.

This person may try to fill the void through achievement, career, education, or success, but these things cannot fill the vacuum. The person will still feel empty and will search even harder to fill the void left from rejection.

When people are not seeking God in their life, it is like constructing a wall that prohibits fellowship with Him. The effects of rejection hurt people's faith in God. Many times people try to fill this by being busy for Jesus. This only makes them feel more and more empty.

Rejection, especially from parents, can keep a person from giving love to others. People who have not been taught how to express love learn how to reject others.

Additional Fruits of Rejection

A person doesn't have to have all of these to have the root of rejection:

1. **Rebellion.** A rebellious person hates being under submission to authority. Because of this unwillingness to submit to others he or she becomes unteachable. His or her pride becomes the major stumbling block. This individual also may display attitudes of defiance, stubbornness, and selfishness.[2]
2. **Bitterness/unforgiveness.** Bitterness is a part of unforgiveness growing deeper.
3. **Pride/perfectionism.** This fruit could develop as a way to cope with rejection.
4. **Depression.** Inward self-pity, sleep irregularities, nervousness, mood swings, lashing out, isolation, fatigue, apathy, cynicism. Depression is common for all the roots.
5. **Anxiety.** This fruit generally affects all of us to some degree.

6. **Low self-esteem.** This fruit often develops from being rejected. Unless someone is taught a lot of positive self-worth, feeling low about self would be normal.
7. **Anger.** This fruit results from frustration at being rejected. Related to this is anger at God. Rejected persons might begin to be angry with God for allowing all their hurts to happen. They might begin to harden their hearts toward others and reject those who do show them God's love, because they resent even having to go through the hurtful experience.
8. **Guilt.** A person who struggles with guilt feels he or she deserves rejection. Such a person feels his or her rejection is a result of an action he or she was responsible for, but it is really a result of being continually belittled and blamed. The person begins to never feel right about his or her actions or statements, and the process of guilt takes over.[3]
9. **Competition and jealousy.** These are also destructive results of rejection.[4] Sometimes we react to these feelings of rejection by becoming a perfectionist or by becoming a workaholic, trying to earn self-worth. (See chapter 5, "Root of Perfectionism.")
10. **Defensiveness.** Defensive persons may be very critical. They might justify judging others who have hurt them or who judge them in return. Defensive persons can see the faults in others but little in their own lives.
11. **Insecurity.** An insecure person might hang on too long and hard in relationships. When there is a lack of love from those closest to him or her, there is a higher likelihood of insecurity. An insecure person may have a hard time putting complete trust in God.[5]
12. **Putting walls up.** A person who puts up walls has an extreme fear of rejection. Because of this, he or she tries to reject others before having to face rejection.
13. **Distrust.** Because of previous abandonment, being left behind, being violated, and/or being hurt in numerous other ways, a person having this fruit has a hard time trusting other people.
14. **Hardness of heart.** People who are hard of heart are so tired that they no longer care about their relationships. Their wounds go so deep that they become harder to heal. Another sign of a hardened heart is a life without emotion. Usually these people do not show signs of their deep hurts and also do not feel joy. This is called a flat affect. This can be healed if a person is willing to go back and

experience the pain he or she never felt and work on forgiving. The younger a person develops this lack of emotion, the more difficult it is to change.

15. **Hopelessness.** A hopeless person will see no prospect for being loved or having the desires of his or her heart come true. This is displayed in Prov. 13:12: "Hope deferred makes the heart sick, but a longing fulfilled is a tree of life."
16. **Poverty.** "Many people live in physical poverty simply because they have a poverty image. They don't feel they're worthy of having anything even though Jesus died so we could prosper and have our needs met."[6]
17. **Memory recall.** Bitterness produced by unwillingness to forgive brings the curse of being tormented by memories or hurts. This is almost like a tape player in one's head repeating back the painful experience.
18. **Self-pity.** A person with the fruit of self-pity rejects others the moment he or she feels rejected or disapproved of by them. Inwardly this person toils over words of rejection until he or she no longer accepts the one doing the rejecting.[7]

Steps to Assist the Helpee Heal from Rejection

Initial Sessions

First Session

1. What is the problem (root)? What are the fruits? What is the helpee's relationship with God like? Does he or she spend time in prayer each day?
2. How are the fruits affecting the helpee's life? What is the prevalent fruit? Examine the helpee's behavior. How much of a self-esteem issue has this created?
3. Have we uncovered all those who have hurt the helpee? Are there hidden issues?
4. What biblical principles does the helpee need to understand?
5. What is the best book for the helpee?

Second Session

1. Has the helpee diligently worked on his or her homework? What has the helpee done to work on forgiveness? Does he or she understand that forgiveness may take some time?

2. Does the helpee still have spewing issues he or she wants to discuss? How hard is the helpee working on his or her behavior?
3. Have I gone far enough into the helpee's background? Does the helpee understand his or her family dynamics?
4. Is the helpee inconsistent at times in what he or she says about a family member? Is the helpee angry?
5. What patterns are we looking at? Do we see clearly the patterns that have been formed throughout the years?
6. What is the helpee's belief system? In self? In God? In life?
7. What are the behavioral things the helpee needs to do while he or she is healing?

What Does the Helpee Need to Know Biblically?

Understand how Christ suffered: "He was despised and rejected by men, a man of sorrows, and familiar with suffering. Like one from whom men hide their faces he was despised, and we esteemed him not" (Isa. 53:3).

Recall God's promise to us: "Do not be afraid; you will not suffer shame. Do not fear disgrace; you will not be humiliated. You will forget the shame of your youth and remember no more the reproach of your widowhood. For your Maker is your husband—the LORD Almighty is his name—the Holy One of Israel is your Redeemer; he is called the God of all the earth" (Isa. 54:4-5).

Questions to Ask the Helpee

- Do you feel you have forgiven those who have hurt you? (Helper asks self, "Am I sure about the helpee's response? You can't always go by what a helpee says. What evidence do I have? Is there another root? What questions do I need to ask?")
- Could you please describe your family background?
- What do you feel is the major source of your pain?
- How often did your parents encourage you?
- Do you feel your parents totally accept you as you are?
- Did you ever feel your siblings were favored over you?
- How busy were your parents growing up?
- Did you feel your efforts growing up were accepted by your parents?
- What were the expectations your parents placed on you?
- Did you feel you met their expectations?
- Could you check off a list of feelings that you are experiencing?
- Do you ever feel you have barriers or walls up?

- How easy is it for you to make friends?
- How did you feel the last time you were hurt?
- How often do you compare yourself to others?
- What evidence can you give that you have forgiven?

Homework for the Helpee

1. Ask God to give you confidence in the abilities He has given you.
2. Pray each day. If you need to, work on forgiving yourself. Use a sample prayer if you have difficulty praying. (See "Prayers for Helpees" in chapter 22, "Supplements.")
3. Read a Psalm and Proverb chapter every day. Start reading in one of the Gospels.
4. Pray for those you feel have rejected you. See homework for unforgiveness in chapter 3 if necessary.
5. Be conscious of your self-talk. Write down what you say to yourself in a day. Go back and evaluate it. Tell why it is right or wrong thinking.
6. Journal your thoughts each time you begin to feel doubt in your abilities or when you beat yourself up mentally.
7. Do something good for yourself every day.
8. Look in the mirror and say five positive things about yourself each day.
9. Remember, repetition is the key to learning. This applies to learning new behaviors. Be positive toward others.
10. Make a list of the people that you feel have rejected you, and include a specific action with each person that shows how you feel that person rejected you.
11. Confront (if you think it will help) those who you feel have rejected you in the past, and choose to forgive them.

Books for the Helpee

Backus, William, and Marie Chapian. *Telling Yourself the Truth*. Minneapolis: Bethany House Publishers, 1980.

Dimarco, Hayley. *The Art of Rejection*. Grand Rapids: Revell, 2006.

Eldredge, John. *Waking the Dead*. Nashville: Thomas Nelson Publishers, 2003.

Hagin, Kenneth. *In Him* (Booklet). Tulsa: Faith Library Publications, 1975.

Hicks, Roy. *Healing Your Insecurities*. Tulsa: Harrison House, 1982.

Jackson, John Paul. *Breaking Free of Rejection*. North Sutton, N.H.: Streams Ministries Int'l, 2004.

McGee, Robert. *The Search for Significance*. Nashville: W Publishing Group, 1998.

Meyer, Joyce. *The Root of Rejection*. Tulsa: Harrison House, 1994.

Powell, John. *Why I Am Afraid to Love: Overcoming Rejection and Indifferences*. Allen, Tex.: Resources for Christian Living, 1999.

Prince, Derek. *God's Remedy for Rejection*. Kensington, Pa.: Whitaker House Publishers, 2002.

Scriptures for the Helpee

Job 5:20-25
In famine he will ransom you from death, and in battle from the stroke of the sword. You will be protected from the lash of the tongue, and need not fear when destruction comes. You will laugh at destruction and famine, and need not fear the beasts of the earth. For you will have a covenant with the stones of the field, and the wild animals will be at peace with you. You will know that your tent is secure; you will take stock of your property and find nothing missing. You will know that your children will be many, and your descendants like the grass of the earth.

Joel 2:25-26
I will repay you for the years the locusts have eaten—the great locust and the young locust, the other locusts and the locust swarm—my great army that I sent among you. You will have plenty to eat, until you are full, and you will praise the name of the LORD your God, who has worked wonders for you; never again will my people be shamed.

Habakkuk 2:3
For the revelation awaits an appointed time; it speaks of the end and will not prove false. Though it linger, wait for it; it will certainly come and will not delay.

Habakkuk 3:17-19
Though the fig tree does not bud and there are no grapes on the vines, though the olive crop fails and the fields produce no food, though there are no sheep in the pen and no cattle in the stalls, yet I will rejoice in the LORD, I will be joyful in God my Savior. The Sovereign LORD is my strength; he makes my feet like the feet of a deer, he enables me to go on the heights.

Psalm 139:1-18
O LORD, you have searched me and you know me. You know when I sit and when I rise; you perceive my thoughts from afar. You discern my going out and my lying down; you are familiar with all my ways. Before a word is on my tongue you know it completely, O LORD. You hem me in—behind and before; you have laid your hand upon me. Such knowledge is too wonderful for me, too lofty for me to attain. Where can I go from your Spirit? Where can I flee from your presence? If I go up to the heavens, you are there; if I make my bed in the depths, you are there. If I rise on the wings of the dawn, if I settle on the far side of the sea, even there your hand will guide me; your right hand will hold me fast. If I say, "Surely the darkness will hide me and the light become night around me," even the darkness will not be dark to you; the night will shine like the day, for darkness is as light to you. For you created my inmost being; you knit me together in my mother's womb. I praise you because I am fearfully and wonderfully made; your works are wonderful, I know that full well. My frame was not hidden from you when I was made in the secret place. When I was woven together in the depths of the earth, your eyes saw my unformed body. All the days ordained for me were written in your book before one of them came to be. How precious to me are your thoughts, O God! How vast is the sum of them!

Were I to count them, they would outnumber the grains of sand. When I awake, I am still with you.

Matthew 10:29-32
Are not two sparrows sold for a penny? Yet not one of them will fall to the ground apart from the will of your Father. And even the very hairs of your head are all numbered. So don't be afraid; you are worth more than many sparrows. Whoever acknowledges me before men, I will also acknowledge him before my Father in heaven.

Psalm 84:11
For the LORD God is a sun and shield; the LORD bestows favor and honor; no good thing does he withhold from those whose walk is blameless.

Psalm 90:17
May the favor of the Lord our God rest upon us; establish the work of our hands for us—yes, establish the work of our hands.

Malachi 3:7
"Ever since the time of your forefathers you have turned away from my decrees and have not kept them. Return to me, and I will return to you," says the LORD Almighty.

Galatians 3:26-29
You are all sons of God through faith in Christ Jesus, for all of you who were baptized into Christ have clothed yourselves with Christ. There is neither Jew nor Greek, slave nor free, male nor female, for you are all one in Christ Jesus. If you belong to Christ, then you are Abraham's seed, and heirs according to the promise.

John 15:16
You did not choose me, but I chose you and appointed you to go and bear fruit—fruit that will last. Then the Father will give you whatever you ask in my name.

Isaiah 29:14
Therefore once more I will astound these people with wonder upon wonder; the wisdom of the wise will perish, the intelligence of the intelligent will vanish.

Jeremiah 29:11-12
"For I know the plans I have for you," declares the LORD, "plans to prosper you and not to harm you, plans to give you hope and a future. Then you will call upon me and come and pray to me, and I will listen to you."

Isaiah 53:3-4
He was despised and rejected by men, a man of sorrows, and familiar with suffering. Like one from whom men hide their faces he was despised, and we esteemed him not. Surely he took up our infirmities and carried our sorrows, yet we considered him stricken by God, smitten by him, and afflicted.

Isaiah 54:10-11

"Though the mountains be shaken and the hills be removed, yet my unfailing love for you will not be shaken nor my covenant of peace be removed," says the Lord, who has compassion on you.

Isaiah 49:14-15

But Zion said, "The Lord has forsaken me, the Lord has forgotten me." "Can a mother forget the baby at her breast and have no compassion on the child she has borne? Though she may forget, I will not forget you!"

1 John 4:18

There is no fear in love. But perfect love drives out fear, because fear has to do with punishment. The one who fears is not made perfect in love.

Psalm 73:23-24

Yet I am always with you; you hold me by my right hand. You guide me with your counsel, and afterward you will take me into glory.

Romans 8:38-39

For I am convinced that neither death nor life, neither angels nor demons, neither the present nor the future, nor any powers, neither height nor depth, nor anything else in all creation, will be able to separate us from the love of God that is in Christ Jesus our Lord.

1 Peter 3:9

Do not repay evil with evil or insult with insult, but with blessing, because to this you were called so that you may inherit a blessing.

Jeremiah 30:16-20

"But all who devour you will be devoured; all your enemies will go into exile. Those who plunder you will be plundered; all who make spoil of you I will despoil. But I will restore you to health and heal your wounds," declares the Lord, "because you are called an outcast, Zion for whom no one cares." This is what the Lord says: "I will restore the fortunes of Jacob's tents and have compassion on his dwellings; the city will be rebuilt on her ruins, and the palace will stand in its proper place. From them will come songs of thanksgiving and the sound of rejoicing. I will add to their numbers, and they will not be decreased; I will bring them honor, and they will not be disdained. Their children will be as in days of old, and their community will be established before me; I will punish all who oppress them."

Isaiah 41:9

I took you from the ends of the earth, from its farthest corners I called you. I said, "You are my servant"; I have chosen you and have not rejected you.

Psalm 103:13

As a father has compassion on his children, so the Lord has compassion on those who fear him.

Isaiah 30:18

Yet the LORD longs to be gracious to you; he rises to show you compassion. For the LORD is a God of justice. Blessed are all who wait for him!

Notes

1. Carroll Thompson, *Possess the Land* (Dallas: Carroll Thompson Ministries, 1994), 29.
2. Cathy Lechner, *I'm Trying to Sit at His Feet: But Who's Going to Cook Dinner* (Orlando: Creation House, 1995), 111-13.
3. Ibid.
4. Joyce Meyer, *The Root of Rejection* (Tulsa: Harrison House, 1987), 28.
5. Lechner, *I'm Trying to Sit at His Feet*, 111-13.
6. Meyer, *Root of Rejection*, 28.
7. Lechner, *I'm Trying to Sit at His Feet*, 111-13.

3 — ROOT OF UNFORGIVENESS

Unforgiveness seems to be very common in helpees. It is very easy to be hurt and then shove the hurt aside mentally, thinking it really wasn't a problem, only to later find resentment growing. I find many people think they have forgiven when they are still harboring hurt. Having a memory of an incident is not a sign of unforgiveness. Rather, it is what a person experiences with a memory that can indicate whether or not forgiveness has occurred.

Anger is a sign or fruit of hurt, fear, and/or frustration. Anger can be a sign of unforgiveness also. There are questions in this chapter to help you discover if the helpee has unforgiveness.

Many issues we face in life require us to forgive in order to let go of them. We all need to be aware of the unforgiveness that could creep into our lives, and we must be prepared to get rid of it before it develops into bitterness. As the Word of God says, bitterness can defile many: "See to it that no one misses the grace of God and that no bitter root grows up to cause trouble and defile many" (Heb. 12:15).

Context of the Root of Unforgiveness

"Be kind and compassionate to one another, forgiving each other, just as in Christ God forgave you" (Eph. 4:32).

Spiritual Aspects of Unforgiveness

In the Lord's Prayer Jesus prayed, "And forgive us our sins, as we have forgiven those who sin against us" (Matt. 6:12, NLT). In Matt. 6:14-15 Jesus says, "If you forgive those who sin against you, your heavenly Father will forgive you. But if you refuse to forgive others, your Father will not forgive your sins" (NLT). Jesus' words speak loud and clear of the spiritual decline that will occur without forgiveness.

Unforgiveness makes it difficult to spend time with God. Often a person will feel as though a wall is between him or her and God. This can be a sign of unforgiveness.

Unforgiveness retains the sins of the past and the present, and if left untreated, it will affect future relationships. John 20:23 says, "If you forgive anyone's sins, they are forgiven. If you do not forgive them, they are not forgiven" (NLT).

It is important for believers to release their unforgiveness, because unforgiveness only hurts them more and not the one who inflicted the pain. We do not have the need, obligation, or ability to judge others. Instead we are to free them from our judgment and give the matter to God.[1]

Unforgiveness alienates the believer from the Body of Christ, causes division, and brings jealousy, envy, and strife into our lives. Satan wants to bring division to the Body of Christ and can because people are much more vulnerable without support. Thus, it is essential to pursue forgiveness in our lives.[2]

Stages and Origin of Bitterness

Bitterness and unforgiveness have a strong tie because bitterness is the outcome of unforgiveness. Bitterness is part of the root of unforgiveness but could be viewed as the part of a root that twists even deeper into the ground than the rest. Bitterness could be defined as strong animosity marked by anguished resentfulness or disdain. The fruits that come from bitterness are anger, wrath, slander, malice, and hate.

Bitterness develops in people from a lack of forgiveness toward those in their lives who have hurt them. These hurts can come from many different relationships. Two examples would be from child-parent relationships and husband-wife relationships. The deepest hurts come from those who are closest to us.

Bitterness begins to infect the whole system. Hurt comes out in a person's speech, is seen in a person's actions, is revealed in a person's attitudes, and begins to break down a person's physical health. Not only does bitterness defile an individual's body, but it also begins to hurt others. Bitterness never helps relationships, only hurts people. It cuts those who are the target of bitterness out of a person's life and brings critical attitudes into the equation.

Bitterness Is Developed Out of Unforgiveness

The development of bitterness from unforgiveness has three parts:

1. *Spiritually*, a bitter person loses the ability to love God. God commands us to forgive each other. When people choose not to forgive, they are putting their will above God's will. This essentially is loving the self above God.[3]
2. *Emotionally*, the person focuses so much on the one who inflicted the pain that he or she begins to unconsciously become just like the one he or she resents.[4] The person is living in the past.
3. *Physically*, some may not realize that bitterness and unforgiveness cause physical ailments as well. In *None of These Diseases* McMillen and Stern discuss how a person's body can start to develop such things as ulcerative colitis; high blood pressure; and excessive secretions from the pituitary, adrenal, and thyroid glands from anger and bitterness.[5]

Recognizing the Hurt

It is not wrong to be hurt, but the way you deal with it makes all the difference in the way it affects you. In order to recognize this hurt, it is important to review some basic characteristics. A bitter person . . .

>cares very little for anyone else
>is very touchy
>is very possessive and has only a few friends
>is ungrateful
>gives harsh criticism
>holds grudges and finds it difficult to forgive
>displays stubbornness or a sulky attitude
>may not want to help anyone

The Destruction of Unforgiveness

Bitterness is the poisonous seed that roots many sinful paths. It is destructive to all people. The antidote is to continually seek to forgive those who have caused harm. By forgiveness the destruction in a person's life can be uprooted so that its toxic potential does not take root. Immediately let go of hurt through forgiveness.

What Does Forgiveness Really Entail?

In the book *The Art of Forgiveness,* Lewis Smedes explains that there are three indicators that a person has truly sought forgiveness. They are the following:

[1.] We rediscover the humanity of the person who hurt us.
[2.] We surrender our right to get even.
[3.] We revise our feelings toward the person we forgive.[6]

Forgiveness is not a feeling. It is an action. Forgiveness is not about waiting for a feeling upon which to act but about an action we choose to take. When we forgive, we need to leave the incident in the past. We are not pretending we have forgotten, but instead we are letting forgiveness draw out the sting of the hurt. The hurt person needs to discover the practicality of forgiveness and avoid the destructiveness of resentment. Forgiveness saves the expense of anger, the cost of hatred, and the waste of a hurt spirit.[7]

What Does Forgiveness Not Include?

Forgiveness does not mean that what a person did is being promoted as *right*. Sometimes people have a hard time forgiving because they feel that if they forgive, it is like condoning the action of the person who hurt them. This is not the case. Forgiveness does not condone the hurt done to them. Instead it frees them.

When a person forgives, he or she is not giving up his or her right to justice. Justice is not the same thing as wanting revenge. For instance, if a woman is raped, she can forgive the perpetrator without asking the court system to drop the case against him. There are usually consequences to sins committed against us. Revenge is wishing despair and pain on the person who hurt us. When it comes to justice, the forgiver needs to submit the hurt and pain to the Lord and ask Him to bring about the justice. As Rom. 12:19 says, "Do not take revenge, my friends, but leave room for God's wrath, for it is written: 'It is mine to avenge; I will repay,' says the Lord."

Forgiveness does not mean that people must open the door to more pain. If there is a person who is continually hurtful, perhaps the hurt one could distance himself or herself away from the hurtful one (if possible). Forgiving does not mean that the forgiver has to bear continual hurts. It would not be wise to consistently be in the presence of a hurtful person (unless it is unavoidable) but to pray for God to change the hurtful person's heart.[8] Distancing oneself from the hurtful person does not apply if that person is a spouse.

Forgiveness is a choice. From my experience, I have observed that it takes six to nine months before feelings of forgiveness catch up to the decision. The helpee needs to be patient with his or her feelings. As Christians we must forgive. With unforgiveness in our heart we become like the person we hate. We can do things that even surprise ourselves. Keeping an open communication with God is more important than holding on to unforgiveness.

Fruits of Unforgiveness

A person doesn't have to have all of these to have unforgiveness in his or her life.

1. **Rejection.** Feeling rejected by the person who has caused the hurt.
2. **Pride.** This fruit may develop as a way of covering the hurt.
3. **Rebellion.** This can be rebellion against authority or whatever the unforgiving represents: "You hurt me therefore I won't listen to you."
4. **Depression.** A feeling of sadness and being overwhelmed with life and people.
5. **Anxiety.** Being overwhelmed and stressed thinking about the one not forgiven.
6. **Low self-esteem.** This fruit can be from guilt, feeling unworthy because of the anger or hate overtaking life.
7. **Continual sarcastic remarks.** These remarks out of anger permeate a person's life.
8. **Guilt/shame.** This fruit can be from feeling guilt from not forgiving or even guilt/shame for his or her part in the situation. This fruit may not be as likely or apparent.
9. **Becoming like the one you haven't forgiven.** Taking on some of that person's behaviors.
10. **Being oversensitive**
11. **Resentment, hurt, frustration.** All part of anger.
12. **Anger when thinking about the person**
13. **Talking against the person who brought the hurt**
14. **Feelings of revenge** (see chapter 6, "Root of Rebellion")

Steps to Assist the Helpee Out of Unforgiveness

Uncovering the Unforgiveness

Even though the helpee may be unconscious of any unforgiveness at this point, help him or her understand that God looks upon our heart.

1. First ask questions to help prepare helpees to see what is in their hearts. Have helpees pray that God would search out their hearts—that He would try them and know their anxious thoughts and show

them any unforgiveness. Have them pray that God will uncover any hidden resentment and hurt that they have been harboring.
2. The helpee may need to list each person who has hurt him or her. Then you as a helper need to discuss the hurt that the helpee has received from each person regardless of the length of the list.
3. Have the helpee confess his or her sins and ask forgiveness from God. The helpee may need to go to the person that he or she is forgiving to make it complete.
4. If the helpee does not feel he or she can pray to forgive a person, pray that God will help the helpee want to forgive. Have the helpee pray every day that he or she will forgive. It will take about nine months for a helpee's feelings to catch up with his or her choice. Remember it is a choice, not a feeling.
5. Have the helpee look at the fruits of unforgiveness and check off his or hers. Go through each one and discuss how it came about. Have the helpee work at changing one behavior (or fruit) at a time.

Questions to Ask the Helpee
- How often do you think of the situation or person?
- How do you think people treat you?
- If you saw this person prosper, how would you feel about it?
- How did you feel when the situation happened and how do you feel about it now?
- How many close friends do you have? And who are they?
- What traumatic experiences have happened with your family?
- What process have you gone through to forgive a person?
- Who do you feel is to blame for the issue you are currently dealing with?
- How do you feel when you talk about the situation?
- Can you think of anything that has happened to you where you do not feel there has been a resolution yet?
- Do you feel you can trust anyone? Who?
- How do you express your feelings?

Homework for the Helpee

1. Set up a time of prayer and reading the Word. Start reading a psalm and a proverb every day. Read the scriptures about forgiveness also.
2. Consider closing your eyes and thinking about the face of someone you need to forgive. Then imagine the face of Jesus next to that person's face, and ask God to help you forgive that person.
3. Read the story of the prodigal son in Luke 15:11-32. Write a one-page response on why you believe the father forgave his son. Include emotions you feel he may have experienced.
4. Make a list of all of the relationships you are in where you are struggling to forgive. Identify specifically how they hurt you and what you need to forgive them.
5. Write a letter to the person you are angry with. Do not send it. Get out all your anger. Then ask the Lord to help you want to forgive this person. Read Matt. 18:22-35 about the rich man who forgave.
6. See "Prayers for Helpees" in chapter 22. Choose one and read it every day.
7. Make a list of things for which God has forgiven you.

Changing Your Behavior to Prevent Future Unforgiveness

1. Let go of this way of life; do not hold on to anger. Be conscious of when your anger starts becoming sinful.
2. Ask the Lord to change your way of thinking. Try these things to help uproot unforgiveness:
   a. Be slow to take offense.
   b. Refuse hurt feelings. Thank God for what you are learning from this situation.
   c. Pray for anyone who spitefully uses you (Matt. 5:44).
   d. Ask yourself whether you are judging another person.
   e. Stay in the Word and feed your spirit.
   f. Take action to forgive those who have hurt you. The choice is yours.
   g. Lastly, pray for your enemies. Pray that God will bless them.

Books for the Helpee

Anderson, Neil. *The Bondage Breaker.* Eugene, Oreg.: Harvest House Publishers, 2006.

Brennan, Patrick J. *The Way of Forgiveness.* Cincinnati: St. Anthony Messenger Press, 2000.

Cook, Jerry, with Stanley Baldwin. *Love, Acceptance, and Forgiveness.* Ventura, Calif.: Regal Books, 1979.

Lilly, Gene. *God Is Calling His People to Forgiveness.* Kingwood, Tex.: Hunter Books, 1977.

MacArthur, John. *The Freedom and Power of Forgiveness.* Wheaton, Ill.: Good News Publishers, 1998.

Smedes, Lewis B. *The Art of Forgiveness.* Nashville: Moorings, 1996.

———. *Forgive and Forget.* New York: HarperCollins Publishing, 2000.

Scriptures for the Helpee

Ephesians 4:26-27
"In your anger do not sin": Do not let the sun go down while you are still angry, and do not give the devil a foothold.

Ephesians 4:31-32
Get rid of all bitterness, rage and anger, brawling and slander, along with every form of malice. Be kind and compassionate to one another, forgiving each other, just as in Christ God forgave you.

Matthew 5:44-45
But I tell you: Love your enemies and pray for those who persecute you, that you may be sons of your Father in heaven. He causes his sun to rise on the evil and the good, and sends rain on the righteous and the unrighteous.

Galatians 5:15
If you keep on biting and devouring each other, watch out or you will be destroyed by each other.

Hebrews 12:15
See to it that no one misses the grace of God and that no bitter root grows up to cause trouble and defile many.

Isaiah 43:18-19
Forget the former things; do not dwell on the past. See, I am doing a new thing! Now it springs up; do you not perceive it? I am making a way in the desert and streams in the wasteland.

Leviticus 19:16-17
Do not go about spreading slander among your people. Do not do anything that endangers your neighbor's life. I am the LORD. Do not hate your brother in your heart. Rebuke your neighbor frankly so you will not share in his guilt.

1 John 2:9-11
Anyone who claims to be in the light but hates his brother is still in the darkness. Whoever loves his brother lives in the light, and there is nothing in him to make him stumble. But whoever hates his brother is in the darkness and walks around in the darkness; he does not know where he is going, because the darkness has blinded him.

1 John 3:15
Anyone who hates his brother is a murderer, and you know that no murderer has eternal life in him.

Proverbs 10:18
He who conceals his hatred has lying lips, and whoever spreads slander is a fool.

Proverbs 10:12

Hatred stirs up dissension, but love covers over all wrongs.

Ephesians 5:1-2

Be imitators of God, therefore, as dearly loved children and live a life of love, just as Christ loved us and gave himself up for us as a fragrant offering and sacrifice to God.

Mark 11:25

And when you stand praying, if you hold anything against anyone, forgive him, so that your Father in heaven may forgive you your sins.

Matthew 18:22-35

Jesus answered, "I tell you, not seven times, but seventy-seven times. Therefore, the kingdom of heaven is like a king who wanted to settle accounts with his servants. As he began the settlement, a man who owed him ten thousand talents was brought to him. Since he was not able to pay, the master ordered that he and his wife and his children and all that he had be sold to repay the debt. The servant fell on his knees before him, 'Be patient with me,' he begged, 'and I will pay back everything.' The servant's master took pity on him, canceled the debt and let him go. But when that servant went out, he found one of his fellow servants who owed him a hundred denarii. He grabbed him and began to choke him. 'Pay back what you owe me!' he demanded. His fellow servant fell to his knees and begged him, 'Be patient with me, and I will pay you back.' But he refused. Instead, he went off and had the man thrown into prison until he could pay the debt. When the other servants saw what had happened, they were greatly distressed and went and told their master everything that had happened. Then the master called the servant in. 'You wicked servant,' he said, 'I canceled all that debt of yours because you begged me to. Shouldn't you have had mercy on your fellow servant just as I had on you?' In anger his master turned him over to the jailers to be tortured, until he should pay back all he owed. This is how my heavenly Father will treat each of you unless you forgive your brother from your heart."

John 20:23

If you forgive anyone his sins, they are forgiven; if you do not forgive them, they are not forgiven.

Psalm 32:1-2

Blessed is he whose transgressions are forgiven, whose sins are covered. Blessed is the man whose sin the LORD does not count against him and in whose spirit is no deceit.

Romans 12:17-21

Do not repay anyone evil for evil. Be careful to do what is right in the eyes of everybody. If it is possible, as far as it depends on you, live at peace with everyone. Do not take revenge, my friends, but leave room for God's wrath, for it is written: "It is mine to avenge; I will repay," says the Lord. On the contrary: "If your enemy is hungry, feed him; if he is thirsty, give him something to drink. In doing this, you will heap burning coals on his head." Do not be overcome by evil, but overcome evil with good.

Matthew 5:21-24
You have heard that it was said to the people long ago, "Do not murder, and anyone who murders will be subject to judgment." But I tell you that anyone who is angry with his brother will be subject to judgment. Again, anyone who says to his brother, "Raca," is answerable to the Sanhedrin. But anyone who says, "You fool!" will be in danger of the fire of hell. Therefore, if you are offering your gift at the altar and there remember that your brother has something against you, leave your gift there in front of the altar. First go and be reconciled to your brother; then come and offer your gift.

Ephesians 4:2-3
Be completely humble and gentle; be patient, bearing with one another in love. Make every effort to keep the unity of the Spirit through the bond of peace.

2 Corinthians 2:10-11
If you forgive anyone, I also forgive him. And what I have forgiven—if there was anything to forgive—I have forgiven in the sight of Christ for your sake, in order that Satan might not outwit us. For we are not unaware of his schemes.

Matthew 6:12, 14-15
Forgive us our debts, as we also have forgiven our debtors. . . . For if you forgive men when they sin against you, your heavenly Father will also forgive you. But if you do not forgive men their sins, your Father will not forgive your sins.

1 Peter 3:9
Do not repay evil with evil or insult with insult, but with blessing, because to this you were called so that you may inherit a blessing.

Notes

1. Jerry Cook with Stanley C. Baldwin, *Love, Acceptance, and Forgiveness* (Ventura, Calif.: Regal Books, 1986), 38-46, 56-62.
2. Thompson, *Possess the Land*, 25.
3. Ibid., 26.
4. Ibid., 27.
5. S. I. McMillen and David E. Stern, *None of These Diseases* (Old Tappan, N.J.: Fleming H. Revell Company, 1984), 112, 116.
6. Lewis B. Smedes, *The Art of Forgiveness* (Nashville: Moorings, 1996), 5-6.
7. Ibid., 69.
8. Ibid., 150-51.

4 — ROOT OF PRIDE

Most people deny having pride or at least feel they do not have excess pride in their life. Key questions are very important to find the root of pride.

Pride, perfectionism, and rebellion are all very closely related. If a person has one of these roots, he or she may have all of them. Each of these roots may also have the other two roots as fruits.

For example, the root of pride may have the fruits of perfectionism and rebellion. You will need to see which came first in a helpee's life. A helpee's life story can bring clarity in this area. See "Understanding Self" in chapter 22.

Context of the Root of Pride

A glance into the heart of a prideful person shows someone who seeks personal gain and satisfaction over service to the Lord. Pride is the source of wickedness and deception, because it seeks to fulfill humanity's desires instead of God's desires. Lucifer was the prime example of pride, leading a creation of God into wickedness and deception. "Your heart became proud on account of your beauty, and you corrupted your wisdom because of your splendor" (Ezek. 28:17).[1]

Often people say if a person acts prideful, he or she really has low self-esteem and is covering up his or her feelings by acting prideful. Sometimes that is true, and sometimes the person is truly arrogant. How can we know? To decipher this dilemma we can be sure of one thing, which is that very few (if any) really arrogant people come for help unless their husband or wife drags them in. Those that come in on their own have usually developed other issues as a result of their pride.

Different Kinds of Pride

I Must Be Perfect

The pride of trying to be perfect can be the fear of being hurt, covering up low self-esteem, shyness, nervousness, or any other insecurity with a false sense of being better than others. These kinds of people believe that they have an element of greatness no one else has. Many times the more prideful a person is the more inferior he or she feels.[2] This person may think things such as, "I can't have faults. . . . I must be perfect." These people types may display defense mechanisms such as denial. They will probably not see any of their faults, or they will deny them. They also might exhibit anger toward God. Sometimes the prideful person thinks he or she can make it without God.

I Suffer More than Others

This person may really feel he or she is better than others. People who struggle with the pride of suffering believe that they are exclusive in life. They believe that they have experiences that outnumber and outweigh others' sufferings.

The lies of their self-talk might consist of the following:
- "My suffering brings me closer to God."
- "My suffering is worse than yours no matter what has happened to you."

However, anything that makes a person feel superior to others is not humbling. No one is better than anyone else because of the suffering or lack of suffering he or she has experienced.

I Feel Anger When I Am Not in Control

This person may really feel he or she is better than others. Helpees who exhibit the pride of control would experience the inability to tolerate a situation unless they are in control of it. Their anger might start rising in proportion to the amount of authority that is taken away and given to someone else. Anger is evident when they are not given control of a situation. These types of people feel they are always right. Generally, they are argumentative and angry with the person who stands in their way.

The lie that these people tell themselves is, "I have every right to feel the way I do because if I am in control, I can make things better." The antidote for this type of pride is to submit to God and let Him have control.

What Do Others Think of Me?

This person may really feel he or she is better than others. This pride turns people into attention addicts. They seek out attention everywhere they go. They lie when they tell themselves, "What matters is that others think highly of me."

This person probably believes that he or she . . .

> has the ability anyone else has
> is able to do everything
> is always right

Such persons believe these things because they presume they are the best at what they do. These persons are self-focused and have a hard time seeing validity and accomplishment in anyone else but themselves. They often act grandiosely and may exaggerate the facts. Often they have learned to be manipulative to get what they want. Generally, someone has catered to them growing up.

No One Can Tell Me What to Do

This type of pride comes about through great hurt. A person develops a defense mechanism to survive through the rough experiences of life. See chapter 6, "Root of Rebellion."

I Can Take Care of Myself

This type of pride comes about when a person/child has an early need to take care of himself or herself. This often comes through hurt. This could be real arrogance or a need to feel capable of taking care of oneself. Sometimes a person has made an inner vow saying, "I will not let anyone help me again."

Fruits of Pride

A person doesn't have to have all of these to have pride in his or her life.

1. **Rejection of self or others.** Rejection of self and/or others is a way to cope with keeping pride in one's life. This is a protection from more hurt.
2. **Bitterness and unforgiveness.** People who develop the fruit of unforgiveness from their pride tend to display rage, animosity, estrangement, irritability, defensiveness, an accusing attitude, a justification of personal sins based on the pain caused by others, a short fuse, frustration, a judgmental attitude, and anger.
3. **Perfectionism.** This is a common fruit. Carroll Thompson observes that a perfectionist is "a person who sets up standards for

himself beyond the normal requirements. Through achieving these standards, this person places himself/herself above others and becomes critical of those who do not accept the same standards."[3] This fruit makes living full of stress and anxiety.

Perfectionism can start forming out of a lack of love from others. Perfectionists may mistakenly believe they can attain the affection of others through what they do and how well they do it, but this only starts a bigger cycle of self-judgment. As the process of perfectionism develops, perfectionists may begin elevating the need to be perfect above the needs of others. Eventually, they start to be apathetic to even the basic needs of others. Perfectionists might start to measure others by their own unrealistic standards. Because of all their pent-up frustration, they tend to say hurtful things, use sharp words, and give critical assessments.

Perfectionists usually view God as the Supreme Perfectionist and relate to God on the basis of how well they do things, their accomplishments, and their level of success. Since these people put so much energy into attaining their standards, they might easily fall into another deception called legalism. Because they believe that God's acceptance is based on works, perfectionists can end up with a life filled with works while actually feeling quite distant from God.[4]

A believer's relationship with Christ is not based on works but on Christ's atoning sacrifice on the Cross. It is not about what we do, but about what He has done for us. It is hard for prideful people to understand that, because they feel they have the ability to be perfect and they think they can win God's affections through works. They keep trying to do it themselves.

4. **Rebellion.** Rebelliousness can be a way to demonstrate pride. Rebellion comes about through a person's pride being hurt and becomes a way to compensate for the pain. It is an outward way to escape.

5. **Competition.** Competitive people could be described as constantly striving to surpass another, to be the very best, and people who need to be praised for their accomplishments. They desperately want to be recognized. Competitive people place their value on their accomplishments and on the praise they receive.

They tend to be self-centered, headstrong, self-complimentary, motivated, and envious. They put their own will above others because it is the only way they can get what they want at all times. They are ambitious, but for the wrong reasons. They may be upset when others are praised and when others are given attention for excellence instead of them. This would bring them feelings of insecurity, since they must be the best.

Pride has an insatiable appetite for fulfillment. Regular straining against God and others brings an attitude of competition that absorbs people and keeps them from functioning in their full capacity and God-given talents.

6. **Unbelief.** To believe, a person must recognize a deficiency, which makes him or her weak. The demeanor of pride is self-sufficiency, which becomes a hindrance in the way to belief. Self-reliance goes so deep into the prideful person that such a person feels he or she does not need anyone.

   There is a great contradiction or conflict of interest for a prideful person seeking to serve God. Pride sees the attention and blessing of people, not God. Pride is also characterized by refusing to seek God's will.[5]
7. **Inability to admit a fault.** A person having this fruit feels he or she is always right. Blaming himself or herself would be too much to experience.
8. **Critical of others.** Prideful people have to keep working at feeling above others. Sometimes this comes at the expense of others.
9. **The most common fruits.** Depression, anxiety, low self-esteem, anger, and guilt—as outlined in this book, can also be found in the root of pride.
10. **Blindness.** Prideful persons may have a hard time seeing themselves and others accurately because of the unrealistic view of themselves they have created. Prideful people have difficulty receiving advice or help (believers.org).[6]

Steps to Assist the Helpee Out of Pride

1. Ask the helpee to humble himself or herself before God by praying each day and reading scriptures on pride. Have the helpee study a biblical character who became prideful.
2. First determine if the person is really arrogant or has low self-esteem. Ask questions such as the following:
   - What makes you feel good about your accomplishments?
   - What kinds of things hurt your pride?

- What is your self-talk like?

As the helper, ask yourself whether you see the helpee as feeling superior to others?

3. Discover how the helpee was disciplined growing up. What sort of treatment did the helpee receive from his or her parents? Was there criticism in the home? Did family members apologize? Did family members admit faults? Did they see their weaknesses?
4. What other fruits do you as the helper see? Each of the three roots—pride, rebellion, and perfectionism—can often be either a root or a fruit. Do you see rebellion or perfectionism as a root (coming first) or a fruit?
5. Ask the helpee to ask God to show him or her the deceptions of pride. Make sure the helpee is truly seeing what is coming out of his or her pride.
6. Ask the helpee to repent from any sin.
7. Ask the helpee to work on loving others by doing behavioral things. For example, suggest the helpee do something helpful for three people each day. Compliment others. Look for the good in them.

Questions to Ask the Helpee

- What makes you feel good about your accomplishments?
- Describe yourself compared to the people in your workplace.
- Do you feel that you talk or listen more in conversations during the day?
- Fill in the blank: "I am happiest when _____."
- What kinds of things hurt your pride?
- What is your self-talk like?
- Do people say that you brag about yourself?
- Where do you see yourself in five years?
- How do you know if you have achieved success in life?
- What have you accomplished that you are proud of?
- If you would compare yourself with a friend of yours, would you come out better? If so, in which areas?

Homework for the Helpee

1. Spend time in prayer for the needs of other people.
2. Be humble. If you fail, do not make excuses. Accept fault and try to do better next time.
3. Work on studying pride through scripture reading. Read about a biblical character lifted up in pride.
4. Acknowledge the excellence of others without seeking to acknowledge yourself.
5. Periodically write letters of encouragement to friends and family. You may not write anything about your success or your accomplishments, only their successes and accomplishments.
6. Write down critical statements that you made to or about others and reflect on why that was wrong. Put yourself in their shoes. How would you feel?
7. Look for the good in others. Write down the good qualities that you see in two of the people that you have recently criticized.

Books for the Helpee

Backus, William, and Marie Chapian. *Telling Yourself the Truth*. Minneapolis: Bethany House, 1980.

Dyson, Eric. *The Seven Deadly Sins: Pride*. New York: Oxford University, 2006.

McGee, Robert. *The Search for Significance*. Nashville: W Publishing Group, 1998.

Stoop, David. *Hope for the Perfectionist*. Nashville: Thomas Nelson Publisher, 1987.

Scriptures for the Helpee

Proverbs 28:13
He who conceals his sins does not prosper, but whoever confesses and renounces them finds mercy.

Proverbs 12:2
A good man obtains favor from the LORD, but the LORD condemns a crafty man.

1 Corinthians 13:5
[Love] is not rude, it is not self-seeking, it is not easily angered, it keeps no record of wrongs.

1 Corinthians 10:24
Nobody should seek his own good, but the good of others.

Philippians 2:3-5
Do nothing out of selfish ambition or vain conceit, but in humility consider others better than yourselves. Each of you should look not only to your own interests, but also to the interests of others. Your attitude should be the same as that of Christ Jesus.

Psalm 135:14
For the LORD will vindicate his people and have compassion on his servants.

Jonah 4:3-4
"Now, O LORD, take away my life, for it is better for me to die than to live." But the LORD replied, "Have you any right to be angry?"

Romans 12:3
For by the grace given me I say to every one of you: Do not think of yourself more highly than you ought, but rather think of yourself with sober judgment, in accordance with the measure of faith God has given you.

Psalm 46:10-11
"Be still, and know that I am God; I will be exalted among the nations, I will be exalted in the earth." The LORD Almighty is with us; the God of Jacob is our fortress.

Proverbs 16:18
Pride goes before destruction, a haughty spirit before a fall.

Romans 3:23
For all have sinned and fall short of the glory of God.

James 4:6
But he gives us more grace. That is why Scripture says: "God opposes the proud but gives grace to the humble."

Isaiah 44:20
He feeds on ashes, a deluded heart misleads him; he cannot save himself, or say, "Is not this thing in my right hand a lie?"

James 1:26
If anyone considers himself religious and yet does not keep a tight rein on his tongue, he deceives himself and his religion is worthless.

1 John 2:15
Do not love the world or anything in the world. If anyone loves the world, the love of the Father is not in him.

Jeremiah 29:11
"For I know the plans I have for you," declares the LORD, "plans to prosper you and not to harm you, plans to give you hope and a future."

Romans 4:20
Yet he did not waver through unbelief regarding the promise of God, but was strengthened in his faith and gave glory to God.

1 Peter 5:6-7
Humble yourselves, therefore, under God's mighty hand, that he may lift you up in due time. Cast all your anxiety on him because he cares for you.

Hebrews 6:12
We do not want you to become lazy, but to imitate those who through faith and patience inherit what has been promised.

Psalm 25:20-22
Guard my life and rescue me; let me not be put to shame, for I take refuge in you. May integrity and uprightness protect me, because my hope is in you. Redeem Israel, O God, from all their troubles!

Notes

1. Thompson, *Possess the Land*, 40-42.
2. Frank B. Minirth, M.D., and Paul D. Meier, M.D., *Happiness Is a Choice: A Manual on the Symptoms, Causes, and Cures of Depression* (Grand Rapids: Baker Publishing Group, 2007), 186.
3. Thompson, *Possess the Land*, 40.
4. Ibid., 40, 42.
5. Ibid., 42.
6. Believers Organization, http://www.believers.org/believe/bel147.htm

5 – ROOT OF PERFECTIONISM

"At a conscious level, perfectionists believe that mistake-free living is both possible and urgently necessary."[1]

Perfectionism doesn't have to be a negative thing in one's life. It can be a motivating force to improve one's work or self. It can, however, be debilitating, taking over a person's life. Perfectionism is considered part of a personality disorder known as obsessive-compulsive personality. Perfectionism does not have to be totally debilitating to take over a person's life.

Perfectionism in people seems to be on the increase. I believe the influence of the media and society's intense emphasis on looking beautiful, thin, and young has increased the need of many women and men to be physically perfect.

Perfectionism in some instances can be attributed to genetics, but it can also be learned. If everything a child does never meets the household standard and is constantly improved or changed, perfectionism can develop as a way to cope. Almost always if a person has perfectionism, one or both parents do also.

Again, pride and/or rebellion are often a fruit of perfectionism.

Context of the Root of Perfectionism

Perfectionists are those who set up standards for themselves above and beyond the regular requirements. When their unrealistic standards are accomplished, they may elevate themselves above others and become critical of those who do not have the same high standards. Although these people are hard on themselves, they are usually harder on others around them who do not live up to their standards.

Perfectionists usually have a lack of love toward others, are indifferent to the needs of others, are insensitive, are hasty in judgment, are sharp in words, and are critical.[2]

Nine Ways a Person Can Be a Perfectionist

1. Putting unrealistic expectations on self and expecting a level above being human.[3] An example would be feeling that you can't sin or that if you do, it is worse for you. This attitude brings the following:
   - Anger and guilt
   - Self-rejection
   - Anxiety, discouragement, and depression
2. Developing a feeling that one must excel above the average person to be OK. This is a common feeling of preachers' children.
3. Feeling that one's worth is defined by how perfect one looks. This may lead to a compulsion to have the best of everything. This is when pride can start to merge with perfectionism.
4. Having a drive to do the job better or more flawlessly than others. This often leads people to constantly compare themselves to others, which can develop more feelings of anxiety and stress.
5. Feeling that one's home must be perfect in appearance. This might be for several different reasons:
   - Person seeks to avoid anxiety that is produced when the house is a mess.
   - Person has learned that a perfect house is the only way to be good enough.
6. Believing that one must only buy the best. It must be the best name brand no matter how much it costs. It is possible that a person will order from a menu at a restaurant by looking at the prices first.
7. Feeling that meals must be cooked or fixed perfectly. Unless it can be cooked perfectly with sufficient time and look flawless, a person may not even want to fix a meal.
8. Possessing a drive to always be the most kind, thoughtful, and interesting person as possible. A person may actually wear himself or herself out trying so hard to show interest in everyone all the time. Being kind is certainly a good thing to be; however, when this task controls a person's self-talk, causing him or her anxiety to do it perfectly, it is controlling the person.
9. As a Christian, feeling that one cannot have negative emotions or thoughts. To this person, all feelings have a moral element, and this

contributes to the person working harder to do everything right and to avoid looking at his or her flaws.

Many times perfectionists live in denial and do not let themselves see their own mistakes or flaws, because this would allow them, as well as others, to see that they are not perfect. Because of their fear of failure, perfectionists might become defensive when their flaws are pointed out.

If someone has at least three or more of the nine ways to be a perfectionist, that person will evidence this in his or her life, and those closest to that person will be affected by his or her behavior. It is very difficult for a perfectionist spouse to see that his or her way may not be *the right* way. That person's spouse will almost always *feel inferior* because he or she is continually being told how to do things the correct way. The spouse of the perfectionist will end up feeling he or she can never do anything right. When this happens, there has to be a way for each spouse to give up some of his or her desires. Each will have to give in a little to come to a halfway point.

For example, Linda wanted everything picked up all the time. Her husband came home late from work each night and would neatly lay his work pants over the back of the chair in their bedroom. He didn't hang them up because he was going to wear them the next day for work. She couldn't live with the pants hanging over the chair. The only way was to hang them up. A compromise would be for her to let him do that Monday through Thursday and to have him hang them in the closet on Friday, Saturday, and Sunday. Perhaps they could even move the chair to the side of the room so she wouldn't notice it all the time.

Destructive Cycle

Perfectionism almost always goes in a vicious cycle. The cycle begins with great effort toward the goal. When the task cannot be completed in a perfect way, frustration sets in. There is a fear of failure (or at least what is considered failure by the perfectionist). Depression enters the person's life, making it more difficult to work toward the goal. To change this, the person tries harder to achieve perfection, either in the same area or in another. Again, perfection is hard to achieve, and the person will find himself or herself back at the beginning.

The Emotions of a Perfectionist

Control over one's emotions is a part of perfectionism. Those having a considerable degree of perfectionism may go to great lengths to repress, minimize, or deny their emotions. Showing emotion would mean appearing less than perfect. If a person feels the only way to protect the self from criticism or hurt is to be perfect, then nothing less than the best will do. This impossible way of living will ensure for a person a life of anxiety, fear, and worry but without any display of emotion to others for his or her anxieties.

Fruits of Perfectionism

A person doesn't have to have all of these to be a perfectionist.
1. **Rejection of self.** When a person can't live up to his or her own standards, rejection of self and/or others may occur.
2. **Unforgiveness.** Refusing to forgive self or others.
3. **Pride.** Perfectionism breeds pride because a person feels he or she knows the right way to do things.
4. **Rebellion.** This fruit could occur out of a person's need to always do things his or her own way. This may be seen as control.
5. **Depression, anxiety, and low self-worth.** Dysfunction can enter a home and cause these fruits when perfectionism is present in many areas.
6. **Depression.** This fruit occurs through the futility of trying to be perfect.
7. **Anxiety.** There is always anxiety when trying to be perfect, when trying to obtain the unobtainable.
8. **Low self-esteem.** This fruit occurs because perfectionism can be a front for how a person really feels about himself or herself.
9. **Anger.** Often anger occurs through the frustration of not being able to attain goals.
10. **Tremendous guilt.** This fruit occurs because the person can never totally achieve his or her own standard; his or her standard is too high.
11. **Know it all.** A perfectionist may have a great need to tell others how to take care of their lives by always having an answer.
12. **Avoidance of the imperfect.** The person may see a large number of faults in something, such as a relationship, and thus be unwilling to risk his or her involvement. This may include rejecting others.
13. **Critical of self and others**
14. **Taking more time than most to complete projects**
15. **Refusal to see personal faults**
16. **Procrastination.** The person may find it easier not to do a seemingly unattainable task than to do it imperfectly.
17. **Fear of failure and disapproval**
18. **Discontentment with life**

Steps to Assist the Helpee Out of Perfectionism

1. Help the helpee see how God sees him or her. Show the helpee through the Word (see this chapter's Scriptures for the Helpee) what God is really like. Encourage the helpee to have a daily time with God. Give the helpee scripture.
2. First the helpee must see his or her perfectionism and the stress it has caused. Often perfectionists feel that doing everything perfect is the best and only way to live. It is very difficult for them to see where they need to improve. To admit they are not perfect (and naming a flaw) can be overwhelming.
3. Help the helpee set realistic and attainable goals based on his or her current state of affairs and on what he or she has accomplished previously.
4. Determine the areas where perfectionism touches the helpee's life. Discover why the helpee feels the need to be perfect. Where did this come from? How prevalent was this in the helpee's family as he or she grew up?
5. Help the helpee look at unrealistic thinking, false pride, fears, shyness, bitterness, and insecurities.
6. Help the helpee look at the fruits of perfectionism. See which fruits are present in his or her life. After looking at the fruits, have the helpee work on one or two of the fruits, lessening their impact each day.
7. Help the helpee deal with the fruit and change his or her thinking; help the helpee begin to love himself or herself for who he or she is and not what he or she does. The helpee may need to read the *Search for Significance* or other books (see this chapter's Books for the Helpee). Also, look carefully at the scriptures given in this chapter's Scriptures for the Helpee to further assist the helpee.
8. Help the helpee identify any hidden anger. Look at how he or she sees God. Is there anger toward God?
9. Have the helpee try the following for a week: Instead of placing unreasonable expectations on others, including himself or herself, the helpee can adopt an attitude that says, "I would like to . . . ," "I'm going to work toward . . . ," "I'd appreciate it if you could . . ." Help the helpee work at not using the word "should" in his communication with others or in his or her self-talk. Example: "You *should* have done that better."

10. Focus on excellence instead of perfection. Help the helpee to avoid all-or-nothing thinking in relation to his or her goals. Help the helpee look at his or her self-talk.
11. Have the helpee focus on what he or she is doing daily, not just the final outcome. Remind the helpee to enjoy the process. The helpee needs to change his or her lifestyle and way of doing things. This is never easy. Help the helpee be patient with himself or herself.
12. Have the helpee find an accountability partner.
13. Encourage the helpee to celebrate mistakes. Help the helpee to recognize that many positive things can only be learned by making mistakes. After making a mistake, a helpee can ask in his or her self-talk, "What can I learn from this experience?"

Questions to Ask the Helpee
- What are your long-term goals?
- Do you develop standards for yourself?
- Where in your life do you see improvement needed?
- Do you feel pressure by an external source? How do you deal with this?
- Define failure. Do you feel that you have had failure? If so, can you describe it?
- How do you know you are successful in class, work, home, life?
- What are you proud of and not proud of in your life?
- Where does your pressure come from?
- Define failure and success.
- When do you have a hard time accepting other ways of doing things?
- Give a visual description of a room that isn't perfect. How would you feel walking into that room?
- What are you afraid of?
- When you go to someone else's house and something isn't perfect, how do you respond?
- Do you find yourself judging others by your standards?
- How often do you compliment others?
- Describe the praise you received as a child.
- Did your parents show you areas to work on in your life as well as encourage your talents?

Homework for the Helpee

1. Make sure you spend daily time with God. Read from the Word every day. If you don't know where to start, read a psalm and a proverb and start reading in the Book of John. Pray each day that the Lord will help you reach a balance in your daily life with perfectionism.
2. Write out your goals in chronological order so that once one goal is reached, another goal follows in appropriate order. Examine these goals to see if they are realistic and attainable.
3. Write out your self-talk and then refute it.
4. Write out what it means to be human for other people and for you.
5. Do a study on excellence versus perfectionism. We should all reach for excellence but never perfectionism. Excellence is accepting yourself in your entirety as God has made you to be. That means accepting all of your faults and strengths and doing everything for the glory of God instead of the glory of self.
6. List your faults. If you need help, talk with someone you trust and be willing to hear what he or she has to say. Take this list and thank God for your strengths and weaknesses every day.
7. Focus on the process and the successes during that process, not just on the final outcome.
8. When working through a process and feeling the urge for perfectionism, analyze it. Ask yourself questions such as,
   - Where is this fear coming from?
   - What exactly am I afraid of?
   - What is the worst imaginable outcome?
   - What would happen if the worst-case scenario came true?
   - How could I deal with that?
9. Reflect on times that you have failed. In those circumstances, what things can you learn from your failures? Sometimes we can really only learn through failing. Come to the understanding that failures are not entirely bad.
10. Learn to prioritize. Make lists in order of priority. Start things on that list that cannot give way to other priorities. Put those priorities into action. Practice saying, "No!"
11. Go through the list "Nine Ways a Person Can Be a Perfectionist" (on pages 72-73) and see which applies to you.

Books for the Helpee

Greenspoon, Thomas S. *Perfectionism: What's Bad About Being Good?* Minneapolis: Free Spirit Publishing, 2001.

McGee, Robert. *The Search for Significance.* Nashville: W Publishing Group, 1998.

Miller, J. Keith. *Compelled to Control.* Deerfield Beach, Fla.: Health Communications, 1997.

Smith, Ann. *Overcoming Perfectionism: The Super Human Syndrome.* Deerfield Beach, Fla.: Health Communication, 1990.

Stoop, David. *Hope for the Perfectionist.* Nashville: Thomas Nelson Publisher, 1987.

Scriptures for the Helpee

Matthew 11:28-30
Come to me, all you who are weary and burdened, and I will give you rest. Take my yoke upon you and learn from me, for I am gentle and humble in heart, and you will find rest for your souls. For my yoke is easy and my burden is light.

Zephaniah 3:17
The LORD your God is with you, he is mighty to save. He will take great delight in you, he will quiet you with his love, he will rejoice over you with singing.

Psalm 27:4-5
One thing I ask of the LORD, this is what I seek: that I may dwell in the house of the LORD all the days of my life, to gaze upon the beauty of the LORD and to seek him in his temple. For in the day of trouble he will keep me safe in his dwelling; he will hide me in the shelter of his tabernacle and set me high upon a rock.

Hebrews 4:10-15
For anyone who enters God's rest also rests from his own work, just as God did from his. Let us, therefore, make every effort to enter that rest, so that no one will fall by following their example of disobedience. For the word of God is living and active. Sharper than any double-edged sword, it penetrates even to dividing soul and spirit, joints and marrow; it judges the thoughts and attitudes of the heart. Nothing in all creation is hidden from God's sight. Everything is uncovered and laid bare before the eyes of him to whom we must give account. Therefore, since we have a great high priest who has gone through the heavens, Jesus the Son of God, let us hold firmly to the faith we profess. For we do not have a high priest who is unable to sympathize with our weaknesses, but we have one who has been tempted in every way, just as we are—yet was without sin.

Matthew 8:23-27
Then he got into the boat and his disciples followed him. Without warning, a furious storm came up on the lake, so that the waves swept over the boat. But Jesus was sleeping. The disciples went and woke him, saying, "Lord, save us! We're going to drown!" He replied, "You of little faith, why are you so afraid?" Then he got up and rebuked the winds and the waves, and it was completely calm. The men were amazed and asked, "What kind of man is this? Even the winds and the waves obey him!"

John 3:16-17
For God so loved the world that he gave his one and only Son, that whoever believes in him shall not perish but have eternal life. For God did not send his Son into the world to condemn the world, but to save the world through him.

Proverbs 28:13
He who conceals his sins does not prosper, but whoever confesses and renounces them finds mercy.

Proverbs 12:2
A good man obtains favor from the Lord, but the Lord condemns a crafty man.

1 Corinthians 13:5
[Love] is not rude, it is not self-seeking, it is not easily angered, it keeps no record of wrongs.

1 Corinthians 10:24
Nobody should seek his own good, but the good of others.

Philippians 2:3-5
Do nothing out of selfish ambition or vain conceit, but in humility consider others better than yourselves. Each of you should look not only to your own interests, but also to the interests of others. Your attitude should be the same as that of Christ Jesus.

Psalm 135:14
For the Lord will vindicate his people and have compassion on his servants.

Jonah 4:3-4
"Now, O Lord, take away my life, for it is better for me to die than to live." But the Lord replied, "Have you any right to be angry?"

Romans 12:3
For by the grace given me I say to every one of you: Do not think of yourself more highly than you ought, but rather think of yourself with sober judgment, in accordance with the measure of faith God has given you.

Psalm 46:10-11
"Be still, and know that I am God; I will be exalted among the nations, I will be exalted in the earth." The Lord Almighty is with us; the God of Jacob is our fortress.

Proverbs 16:18
Pride goes before destruction, a haughty spirit before a fall.

Romans 3:23
For all have sinned and fall short of the glory of God.

James 4:6
But he gives us more grace. That is why Scripture says: "God opposes the proud but gives grace to the humble."

Isaiah 44:20
He feeds on ashes, a deluded heart misleads him; he cannot save himself, or say, "Is not this thing in my right hand a lie?"

James 1:26
If anyone considers himself religious and yet does not keep a tight rein on his tongue, he deceives himself and his religion is worthless.

1 John 2:15
Do not love the world or anything in the world. If anyone loves the world, the love of the Father is not in him.

Jeremiah 29:11
"For I know the plans I have for you," declares the LORD, "plans to prosper you and not to harm you, plans to give you hope and a future."

Romans 4:20
Yet he did not waver through unbelief regarding the promise of God, but was strengthened in his faith and gave glory to God.

1 Peter 5:6-7
Humble yourselves, therefore, under God's mighty hand, that he may lift you up in due time. Cast all your anxiety on him because he cares for you.

Hebrews 6:12
We do not want you to become lazy, but to imitate those who through faith and patience inherit what has been promised.

Psalm 25:20-22
Guard my life and rescue me; let me not be put to shame, for I take refuge in you. May integrity and uprightness protect me, because my hope is in you. Redeem Israel, O God, from all their troubles!

Notes

1. Allan E. Mallinger, M.D., and Jeannette De Wyze, *Too Perfect: When Being in Control Gets Out of Control* (New York: Clarkson Potter Publishers, 1992), 37.
2. Thompson, *Possess the Land*, 40.
3. Ibid.

6 — ROOT OF REBELLION

Few people acknowledge that they have this root. It is usually when they recognize that their behavior is hurting someone that they know something in their life is wrong. Great hurt and disappointment become resentment and then rebellion. Rebellion isn't always apparent, as when a child yells at a parent. Rebellion could be just doing the opposite of what someone wants you to do. It could be dragging your feet about doing something that will only take you five minutes. The real feeling behind rebellion is, "You hurt me. See if I do what you want." This kind of behavior doesn't always seem like rebellion. It is often called passive-aggressive behavior.

> Passive–aggressive behavior is passive, sometimes obstructionist resistance to following through with expectations in interpersonal or occupational situations. It can manifest itself as learned helplessness, procrastination, stubbornness, resentment, sullenness, or deliberate/repeated failure to accomplish requested tasks for which one is (often explicitly) responsible. It is a defense mechanism, and (more often than not) only partly conscious.[1]

Again, key questions will help you discover if rebellion is part of a person's life. It is very closely related to the root of pride.

Context of the Root of Rebellion

"The earth reels like a drunkard, it sways like a hut in the wind; so heavy upon it is the guilt of its rebellion that it falls—never to rise again" (Isa. 24:20).

God has a divine purpose for His creation, but through the fall of humankind, rebellion was birthed and has plagued humanity and will continue to do so until the Lord's return. Rebellion brings enmity between humankind and God. Scripture tells us that rebellion produces backsliding (Jer. 5:6), death (Jer. 28:16), the discarding of truth (Dan. 8:12), the hardening of hearts (Heb. 3:8, 15), and desolation (Dan. 8:13).

Sources of Rebellion

Rebellion is a false sense of independence or power that begins to create lies in an individual's self-talk. Rebellion comes in opposition to authority because of pride. King Saul provides an excellent example of how pride produced rebellion against God. In 1 Sam. 13:9-14, Saul rebelled against the Lord. The outcome was that he lost his kingdom for himself and his future generations because of rebellion.

Rebellion can develop out of anger about a past hurt that has not been dealt with. This lack of forgiving develops bitterness, which can destructively lead a person to rebel against authority, especially if authority was the source of the pain that was experienced.

How Does Rebellion Develop?

These are the steps laid out by Thompson in the book *Possess the Land.*[2]

1. Hurt to resentment
2. Resentment to bitterness
3. Bitterness to hatred
4. Hatred to rebellion

In this sequence we forget who we are—the created, not the Creator. Hurt is a form of anger—anger for what has happened. We think of ourselves and have an elevated view of self. For example, we may think things such as,

"How dare he (she) do that to me."

"I have a right to do what I want."

"Why did God allow that?"

"Primarily, temptation is powerful and attractive to human existence because it successfully and deceptively gets people to focus on themselves. . . . The more we focus on 'self,' the less we focus on God."[3]

The individual becomes a slave to self. Instead of being mastered by God, he or she becomes the master over self and uses that to try to manipulate and control others or even be revengeful.

Fruits of Rebellion

A person doesn't have to have all of these to have rebellion in his or her life.

1. **Rejection.** This fruit results from the behaviors that rebellion exhibits.
2. **Unforgiveness.** Toward the ones that have hurt the person.
3. **Pride, superiority, selfishness, arrogant attitude.** To protect self from the hurt the person feels.
4. **Perfectionism.** To prove that the person is OK.

Inward Fruits

5. **Depression.** From the rebellious state of mind.
6. **Anxiety or nervousness.** Resulting from frustration.
7. **Development of a low self-worth**
8. **Guilt.** From the rebellious state.
9. **Loneliness.** People start hiding from the angry person.

The Outward Fruits They May Display

10. **Hatred, violence, murder**
11. **Anger.** A frustration that things aren't different, sometimes not knowing whom one is angry at.
12. **Resentment and unforgiveness.** Toward those who have hurt the person.
13. **Control.** A desire to control one's life and often the lives of others.
14. **Manipulation.** A way for the person to cope and still get his or her way.
15. **Procrastination.** A sense of control, not doing something when a person asks.

Outwardly, rebellion is also a sign of having the root of rejection. Keep that in mind when assessing the roots.

Steps to Assist the Helpee Out of Rebellion

1. How is the helpee's devotional life? It is important to establish his or her relationship with God.
2. Find the source of the rebellion. How long has it been going on? Who is the helpee angry at? Who has hurt the helpee? Who has the helpee hurt? Is there bitterness? What is the bitterness about?
3. Is this about an inner vow such as, "I will never let that person hurt me again," or "I will never listen to my parents again"? If so, the root of pride also needs to be examined. In this case, the helpee has been hurt enough to decide that life isn't worth receiving from others.
4. Is there rejection? If so, go through the Steps to Assist in chapter 2. Most likely that would make the rebellion a fruit of rejection.
5. Are there addictions? Deal with these as well as any shame associated with the addictions.
6. Look at how the helpee views authority and how he or she sees God. Can the helpee trust authority figures? Assist the helpee in developing a healthy view of others—we are fallen but forgiven.
7. Help the helpee see why rebellion is wrong and how he or she is damaged by it. Show the helpee scriptures from pages 88-90.
8. Help the helpee make a choice to change, begin submitting to godly authority, deal with trust issues, forgive those who have hurt him or her, and find a way to release anger.

Questions to Ask the Helpee

- Do you feel that there is anyone whom you are submitted to? If so, describe the relationship(s)?
- Do you view rules as concrete or more as guidelines?
- Describe your experience with discipline and boundaries growing up.
- Are you willing to submit to God's Word?
- Whose authority are you under?
- Whose opinion do you respect and why?
- Give the reasons you don't respect the person in question.
- What authority positions do you find yourself disagreeing with?
- What would make a person worthy of your respect?
- How do you feel about your parents?
- How is your relationship with your parents? Do you mainly talk about deep or surface things with them?
- Do you follow the advice of the people you respect?

Homework for the Helpee

1. Take time to pray every day and to ask forgiveness for rebellion. Do a study of Scripture on rebellion. King Saul's life is an example. Study the results of rebellion in his life.
2. Determine areas of rebellion. Write down your fears.
3. Reflect through journaling how rebellion affects other relationships in your life.
4. Reflect upon your view of God through writing. How do you feel about God in your life?
5. After determining the original hurt, pray that God will help you forgive the hurt and/or person.

Books for the Helpee

Berry, Richard. *Angry Kids*. Wheaton, Ill.: Baker Publishing, 2001.

Carter, Les, Ph.D., and Frank Minirth, M.D. *The Anger Workbook—A 13-Step Interactive Plan to Help You*. Nashville: Thompson Nelson, Inc., 1993.

Nee, Watchman. *Authority and Submission*. Anaheim, Calif.: Living Stream Ministry, 1998.

Working, Randal. *From Rebellion to Redemption*. Colorado Springs: NavPress, 2001.

Scriptures for the Helpee

1 Samuel 15:23
For rebellion is like the sin of divination, and arrogance like the evil of idolatry. Because you have rejected the word of the Lord, he has rejected you as king.

Jeremiah 28:16
Therefore, this is what the LORD says: "I am about to remove you from the face of the earth. This very year you are going to die, because you have preached rebellion against the Lord."

Hebrews 3:15
As has just been said: "Today, if you hear his voice, do not harden your hearts as you did in the days of rebellion."

1 Peter 3:8-9
Finally, all of you, live in harmony with one another; be sympathetic, love as brothers, be compassionate and humble. Do not repay evil with evil or insult with insult, but with blessing, because to this you were called so that you may inherit a blessing.

Ezekiel 36:25-27
I will sprinkle clean water on you, and you will be clean; I will cleanse you from all your impurities and from all your idols. I will give you a new heart and put a new spirit in you; I will remove from you your heart of stone and give you a heart of flesh. And I will put my Spirit in you and move you to follow my decrees and be careful to keep my laws.

Romans 8:1-14
Therefore, there is now no condemnation for those who are in Christ Jesus, because through Christ Jesus the law of the Spirit of life set me free from the law of sin and death. For what the law was powerless to do in that it was weakened by the sinful nature, God did by sending his own Son in the likeness of sinful man to be a sin offering. And so he condemned sin in sinful man, in order that the righteous requirements of the law might be fully met in us, who do not live according to the sinful nature but according to the Spirit. Those who live according to the sinful nature have their minds set on what that nature desires; but those who live in accordance with the Spirit have their minds set on what the Spirit desires. The mind of sinful man is death, but the mind controlled by the Spirit is life and peace; the sinful mind is hostile to God. It does not submit to God's law, nor can it do so. Those controlled by the sinful nature cannot please God. You, however, are controlled not by the sinful nature but by the Spirit, if the Spirit of God lives in you. And if anyone does not have the Spirit of Christ, he does not belong to Christ. But if Christ is in you, your body is dead because of sin, yet your spirit is alive because of righteousness. And if the Spirit of him who raised Jesus from the dead is living in you, he who raised Christ from the dead will also give life to your mortal bodies through his Spirit, who lives in you. Therefore, brothers, we have an obligation—but it is not to the

sinful nature, to live according to it. For if you live according to the sinful nature, you will die; but if by the Spirit you put to death the misdeeds of the body, you will live, because those who are led by the Spirit of God are sons of God.

Proverbs 28:13
He who conceals his sins does not prosper, but whoever confesses and renounces them finds mercy.

Proverbs 12:2
A good man obtains favor from the LORD, but the LORD condemns a crafty man.

1 Corinthians 13:5
[Love] is not rude, it is not self-seeking, it is not easily angered, it keeps no record of wrongs.

1 Corinthians 10:24
Nobody should seek his own good, but the good of others.

Philippians 2:3-5
Do nothing out of selfish ambition or vain conceit, but in humility consider others better than yourselves. Each of you should look not only to your own interests, but also to the interests of others. Your attitude should be the same as that of Christ Jesus.

Psalm 135:14
For the LORD will vindicate his people and have compassion on his servants.

Jonah 4:3-4
"Now, O LORD, take away my life, for it is better for me to die than to live." But the LORD replied, "Have you any right to be angry?"

Romans 12:3
For by the grace given me I say to every one of you: Do not think of yourself more highly than you ought, but rather think of yourself with sober judgment, in accordance with the measure of faith God has given you.

Psalm 46:10-11
"Be still, and know that I am God; I will be exalted among the nations, I will be exalted in the earth." The LORD Almighty is with us; the God of Jacob is our fortress.

Proverbs 16:18
Pride goes before destruction, a haughty spirit before a fall.

Psalm 68:5-6
A father to the fatherless, a defender of widows, is God in his holy dwelling. God sets the lonely in families, he leads forth the prisoners with singing; but the rebellious live in a sun-scorched land.

Romans 3:23
For all have sinned and fall short of the glory of God.

James 4:6
But he gives us more grace. That is why Scripture says: "God opposes the proud but gives grace to the humble."

Isaiah 44:20
He feeds on ashes, a deluded heart misleads him; he cannot save himself, or say, "Is not this thing in my right hand a lie?"

James 1:26
If anyone considers himself religious and yet does not keep a tight rein on his tongue, he deceives himself and his religion is worthless.

1 John 2:15
Do not love the world or anything in the world. If anyone loves the world, the love of the Father is not in him.

Jeremiah 29:11
"For I know the plans I have for you," declares the LORD, "plans to prosper you and not to harm you, plans to give you hope and a future."

Romans 4:20
Yet he did not waver through unbelief regarding the promise of God, but was strengthened in his faith and gave glory to God.

1 Peter 5:6-7
Humble yourselves, therefore, under God's mighty hand, that he may lift you up in due time. Cast all your anxiety on him because he cares for you.

Hebrews 6:12
We do not want you to become lazy, but to imitate those who through faith and patience inherit what has been promised.

Psalm 25:20-22
Guard my life and rescue me; let me not be put to shame, for I take refuge in you. May integrity and uprightness protect me, because my hope is in you. Redeem Israel, O God, from all their troubles!

Notes

1. Wikipedia, http://en.wikipedia.org/wiki/Passive-aggressive_behavior (accessed July 7, 2009).

2. Thompson, *Possess the Land*, 37.

3. David W. Chadwell, "The Foundation of Evil," *Repentance: Teacher's Guide*, http://www.westarkchurchofchrist.org/chadwell/repent/teaching/y2004q2l1.htm (accessed July 21, 2009).

7 – ROOT OF SEXUAL ABUSE

Sexual abuse is by far one of the most difficult issues to heal. Sometimes the abused are so enmeshed in a dysfunctional pattern that they don't know what issues are from being sexually abused and which are just a normal part of growing up. It is so difficult for them to see who they are when they heal. Healing would include forgiveness of the perpetrator and release from constant thinking about the abuse and fear because of it. The abused may come close to a place of healing but refuse to go further, saying, "I don't know who I am without the abuse."

CAUTION

If a male or female has been abused by a male, he or she may not want to talk to a male helper. Use discretion. It may be necessary to send the abused to a professional licensed helper. *Know* when something is over your head and don't hesitate to *refer*.

Context of the Root of Sexual Abuse

This information can help guide you with those who can't find comfort from within and are having difficulty facing past experiences of sexual abuse in childhood.

There are several types of sexual abuse. Some children are traumatized for years by a family member or nearby outsider such as a babysitter. Others may have only one experience of abuse. Some are sexually abused by one of their parents. Every case is different, but all of these children are victims, are innocent, and had no responsibility for the sexual abuse. Most of these victims are living in guilt, denial, anger, and/or confusion. These suffering people need a source of help.[1]

In a child's world, parents are the providers. Without them life would be impossible. With no one to judge his or her parents against, a child may assume that he or she has perfect parents. As the world broadens beyond the crib, children cling to the idea that their parents are perfect in order to feel protected and safe.

Abusive parents are not very understanding with their children. From a child's infancy through adolescence, abusive parents tend to view rebellion or even the differences in a child as a personal attack. They defend themselves by reinforcing their child's dependence and helplessness. Instead of helping the child grow and develop in a healthy way, they undermine his or her development.

Victims of childhood sexual abuse have been taught by their parents or abusers to suppress or even deny their feelings. Denial is a very powerful psychological defense. It can help children forget what their parents or abusers did to them. Denial is sometimes the lid on an emotional pressure cooker; it develops more pressure the longer it is left on.

What Is Sexual Abuse?

Below is an abbreviated version of a list that came from the *Handbook of Clinical Intervention in Child Sexual Abuse* by Suzanne M. Sgroi.*

1. *Nudity.* The adult parades around the house in front of all or some of the family members.
2. *Disrobing.* The adult disrobes in front of the child, generally when the child and the adult are alone.
3. *Genital exposure.* The adult exposes his or her genitals to the child.
4. *Observation of the child.* The adult surreptitiously or overtly watches the child undress, bathe, excrete, or urinate.
5. *Kissing.* The adult kisses the child in a lingering or intimate way.
6. *Fondling.* The adult fondles the child's breasts, abdomen, genital area, inner thighs, or buttocks. The child may similarly fondle the adult at his or her request.
7. *Masturbation.* The adult masturbates while the child observes; the adult observes the child masturbating; the adult and child masturbate each other (mutual masturbation).

---

*Adapted with the permission of The Free Press, a Division of Simon and Schuster, Inc., from *Handbook of Clinical Intervention in Child Sexual Abuse* by Suzanne M. Sgroi, M.D., Copyright 1982 by DC Heath and Co. All rights reserved.

8. *Fellatio.* The adult has the child fellate him, or the adult will fellate the child.
9. *Cunnilingus.* This type of oral-genital contact requires either the child to place mouth and tongue on the vulva or in the vaginal area of an adult female or the adult to place his or her mouth on the vulva or in the vaginal area of the female child.
10. *Digital (finger) penetration of the anus or rectal opening.* . . . Perpetrators may thrust inanimate objects such as crayons or pencils inside as well.
11. *Penile penetration of the anus or rectal opening.*
12. *Digital (finger) penetration of the vagina.* Inanimate objects may also be inserted.
13. *"Dry intercourse."* A slang term describing an interaction in which the adult rubs his penis against the child's genital-rectal area or inner thighs or buttocks.
14. *Penile penetration of the vagina.*

The abuser usually has his or her own denial system. A parent who is the sexual abuser may say to the victim, "It wasn't so bad," or "It didn't happen that way," or "It didn't happen at all."[2] Many times when mothers are aware that their partner is abusing their children, they deny it. If the child's story of sexual abuse is not believed, or if the family denies the situation or refuses to talk about it, the child's hurt can be two to three times worse. This is another betrayal.

When sexual abuse begins, usually a child is told that what is happening is not wrong—that it is a natural way to love someone. It is normal for an abuser to use this method. As the abuse continues, a child begins to deny or repress the hurt and physical and emotional pain. A child may learn to dissociate himself or herself from what is happening in order to avoid pain.

Father-Daughter Incest

In a case of father-daughter incest, a father may become obsessed with his daughter and insanely jealous of her boyfriends. Because of the obsession, the daughter is likely to bond more to her father, feeling increasingly dependent. Often the daughter will mistake the obsession for love, which will alter love expectations later in life.[3] A stepfather is six times more likely to be sexually abusive than a biological father.

In many cases a father starts molesting his daughter when she is four or five years old. In some occurrences, a father has molested his infant daughter.

How Is Self-esteem Damaged by Sexual Abuse?

A child will feel that he or she is being used. Sexual abuse causes a child to feel bad about who he or she is. Shame is a tremendous feeling that overtakes a child's self-esteem. If his or her body responds and the child becomes physically aroused, the shame increases. Symptoms include feeling ugly inside, having a sense of worthlessness, feeling like a failure, feeling helpless, and having great guilt. Survivors of sexual abuse need to know that these feelings are very normal.

For boys who are sexually abused, not only their self-esteem but their identity also comes into question. If abused by a man, he may think he is attracting other men based on instinctive physical reactions of his body. The consequences can be even more extreme if he is abused by his mother. A mother is usually the nurturing one in the child's life. Rejection, betrayal, anger, resentment, anguish, and torment are a few of the words that begin to describe the child's feelings.

When a child is sexually abused by someone whom he or she loved and trusted, there is definite betrayal. This betrayal almost inevitably results in fear and humiliation. Because the relationship was based on manipulation, deception, and secrecy, this becomes the basis of other relationships. The symptoms include a difficulty in trusting others, being distant, a tendency to be involved with destructive people, a lack of caring for others, a difficulty with physical affection, a difficulty communicating desires and thoughts, and secrecy in relationships with others.

The Victim's View of Sex

Most often, the first sexual encounter the victim had was sexual abuse. The experience was painful and very frightening. Because his or her initial sexual experience was a desecration, the victim finds it difficult in later years to regard sex as an enjoyable experience. When love has been misrepresented by sex, a person often views love to be just that—sex, nothing more. Most of the time a person who was sexually abused either hates everything about sex or is overly interested in it.

Sexual Symptoms

- Lack of sexual desire or inhibited sexual feelings
- Inability to enjoy sex
- Sexual dysfunctions such as painful vaginal muscles
- Problems with identity
- Disgust with public displays of affection or sexuality
- Sexual addiction
- Promiscuity

Sorting Out the Emotions of the Victim

Victims of childhood sexual abuse have a difficult time acknowledging and understanding their emotions. They may suppress their emotions, which leads to depression. Others may go to the opposite end of the spectrum and become violent and have a difficult time controlling their emotions. Symptoms include intense anger; mood swings from being depressed to being overactive; extreme fears; sleep disturbances; addiction to food, alcohol, or drugs; obsessive behaviors such as gambling, compulsive shopping, overeating, or cleaning; flashbacks of the abuse; self-destructive behavior such as suicide attempts and/or self-mutilation. Dissociation, a "splitting-off" from oneself, is also used as protection from pain and the devastation of emotions. Time blockages (lack of remembrance of various years) are also parts of dissociation. It is the mind's way of protecting the abused from painful memories.

Since the sexual assault was against the body, adults who were sexually abused as children can suffer from psychologically based illnesses. Symptoms include sore throats, a difficulty in swallowing, migraine headaches, unexplained vaginal pain, frequent bladder infections, skin disorders, a tendency to be accident-prone, and numbness in the legs or arms.[4]

Facts the Victim Needs to Know

1. The child is never responsible for sexual abuse. Most victims feel that they are responsible no matter how young they were when the abuse occurred. This is sometimes the most difficult act of forgiveness—forgiving the self.
2. If a child acts in a sexual manner, most often he or she has learned that being sexual brings approval and attention. Rarely does a child run away or even think that he or she can get away. Often, there is nowhere to go. Survival may be living at home with abuse. This may seem safer than living with another family. "Familiarity, however miserable, is preferred over the unknown."[5]
3. Usually a child does not tell anyone about the abuse. He or she may have been threatened not to tell and be too afraid. The experience brings so much shame that it adds to the fear of telling someone. Most of the time children feel that it is their fault—that they did something to cause the abuse. If the perpetrator tells the child that the abuse is the child's fault, it will only add to the trauma.

Sometimes there is a lack of understanding of what abuse is and what is simply children playing "doctor." In most states when there is a five-year span between children, such activity is considered abuse.

Who Is the Anger Directed Toward?

Most sexual-abuse victims focus their anger on their mother first (in the case of brother or father as the perpetrator). Part of this is from fear of the perpetrator and also because they feel betrayed by their mother. Often father-daughter victims are angrier at their mother. Some victims wonder how much their mother knew about the incest. Many abuse victims are convinced that their mother knew something and wondered why she did not protect them.

In some cases it is possible for a mother not to know the truth. However, there are also mothers who wear blinders and ignore the clues while trying to protect themselves and their families. The other type of mother is the one who is told but does nothing about it. "When this happens, the victim is doubly betrayed."[6] This may cause healing to take two to three times as long. Mothers are supposed to protect their children. That is why the truth that a child's mother did not protect or love him or her is so devastating and sometimes as devastating as the sexual abuse itself.[7]

"Many times the silent partners were abused children themselves. They suffer from extremely low self-esteem and may be reenacting the struggles of their own childhood."[8] If the mother was indeed abused as a child, recognizing her daughter as an abuse victim could mean having to face her past and explain her denial, which is something that may be too painful for her to do.

The anger may also be directed toward any of the following:
God
The self
Men or women
Life in general

Characteristics of Sexual Abuse Victims (a Fruit or Symptom)

- Weight gain/loss (try to make themselves nonsexual to protect themselves)
- Wear very loose clothes or clothes that are not flattering
- Abuse themselves/self-mutilation (scars, cutting)
- May talk in a baby-like manner
- Very interested in sex or not interested at all
- Feel that they are very "dirty" inside
- Generally have guilt and feel it is their fault
- A tendency to sabotage their success
- A tendency to be involved with people who are hurtful

- Difficulty trusting others
- Difficulty communicating feelings to others as well as receiving from others
- Extreme fears and nightmares
- Addiction to food, alcohol, or drugs
- Eating disorders

Other Possible Fruits

1. **Rejection.** The sexually abused may feel rejected because they "feel dirty" even if no one rejects them.
2. **Unforgiveness.** The abused may have no desire to forgive the perpetrator and/or those who didn't protect them.
3. **Pride for protection.** Victims of sexual abuse may pretend to be OK as a false front.
4. **Rebellion against others.** The abused may have anger and hurt and then develop rebellion (a common fruit).
5. **Depression.** This is the most common fruit and is part of the process of dealing with sexual abuse and the process of healing.
6. **Anxiety.** Often there is constant anxiety over what might happen.
7. **Low self-esteem.** This is almost an inevitable fruit and is a natural response to how the abused were treated.
8. **Anger.** This fruit is very common and may be inwardly displayed through depression or outwardly displayed through the abused becoming abusers themselves.
9. **Guilt.** Most of the sexually abused feel that they could have done something to stop the abuse no matter what their age when it started.
10. **Shame.** This is definitely a part of the life of the sexually abused.

There are many more possibilities.

Steps to Assist the Helpee Heal from Sexual Abuse

1. Be Sure to Look at the Helpee's Acceptance of God's Love

It is very difficult for a sexually abused person to heal unless that person can accept that God truly loves him or her and has a plan for his or her life.

2. Recognition Is Half the Battle

To get to the truth the sexually abused person needs to break through the layers of denial. The only way to heal is to get past this denial. First, the victim needs to look at the truth. A helper might start the process by having the victim write down all the details of the abuse: where it happened, who did it, how it was done, how many times it was done, how it felt, how the person feels about it now, and how it is affecting the person's life. This process can become a permanent testimony of the truth—the pain, betrayal—and eventually it will be the road to recovery.[9]

It is important to realize that as the memories come back, the pain will come back. Other relationships may be temporarily affected during this time. Not only does the victim need to face the truth about his or her own experience, but the truth about the perpetrator also needs to be faced.

These Truths Must Be Recognized About the Perpetrator

The perpetrator

- was not teaching you (the victim) about sex or preparing either of you for womanhood or manhood
- didn't need you or your body (It wasn't his or her right.)
- wasn't making sure you were developing properly
- wasn't too sick to know what he or she was doing
- wasn't making sure you wouldn't be cold like your mother
- was using you for selfish needs
- was not considering your feelings or the effects on you
- violated you and robbed you of innocence
- betrayed your trust, and in turn you can't trust
- "made you feel weird, perverted, and different"[10]

Furthermore, the victim needs to face the truth about those who did not protect him or her from the abuse. Especially in cases of incest, many victims fantasize about their mother not knowing that the abuse took place. However, that is highly unlikely. The truth that their mother or other caregiver did know that the abuse was taking place can cause them to feel abandoned and depressed. Anger is a normal part of this process.

A child never wants to have sex with an adult. The child may mistake sex for love, affection, and attention but does not want to have sex with an adult.

3. Let Go of the Hurt and Anger

Anger can be a great motivator to find the truth about what happened and even face those who contributed to the abuse—even if it was a failure to protect the abused from the perpetrator. Sometimes a person tries to ignore the anger or simply repress it. Anger that is not expressed in some manner turns inward and brings depression. It makes a person feel guilty, inadequate, and worthless.

Often victims feel their parents must have been "good" and therefore blame themselves for everything and feel that the sexual experience must have been their fault.[11]

Releasing Anger Can Do the Following
- Alleviate guilt, shame, and self-hatred
- Improve your self-esteem
- Give you hope by taking a burden off of your shoulders
- Release physical tension
- Improve your relationships (you will be less likely to take your anger out on your friends, children, and so on)
- Affirm your innocence
- Help you to be more assertive[12]

(See this chapter's Homework for the Helpee.)

4. Confronting (This Step May Not Help)

Confronting is having the victim stand up to the ones who have brought pain. It is to tell them how they have brought pain and to let them know exactly what they did. It is important for the victim to let go of anger, as in Step 3, in order to be able to confront without losing control. Confrontation can be a very exhilarating experience. It can bring freedom and comfort. Confrontation can also bring regret and more hurt.

Before the confrontation takes place, the helpee will need to be prepared with friends he or she can count on. The helpee may need to practice and know exactly what he or she wants to say. The helpee needs to also realize that this step may not work. Prior to the confrontation the helpee needs to decide if it will be safe to confront in person, if it needs to be done in a letter, or if it does not need to be done at all.

In the confrontation it is important to realize that the perpetrator may not admit to the abuse, and in cases of incest, the mother might actually blame the victim, her child.

See this chapter's Homework for the Helpee for specific actions that should be taken in the confrontation process. Please note this is not always recommended. It can make the process of healing more difficult. Also, if the helpee is having difficulty forgiving the abuser, have him or her pray to *want* to forgive.

5. Healing Relationships by Staying Away or Resolving, with Forgiveness Required in Either Case

Either the helpee can stay away from the perpetrator or resolve the situation. The most important factor for true healing is that the abused must forgive. Developing the course of action can be included in homework. (See Homework for the Helpee for more information on guidelines.) It is also necessary for the victim to first work through a forgiveness process. See the forgiveness steps in chapter 3, "Root of Unforgiveness."

6. Know Yourself and Set Boundaries

It is important for the victim to discover who he or she really is, to know his or her values, beliefs, priorities, and feelings. Those who have been sexually abused seldom have a strong sense of who they are. It is important for the victim to find his or her own self-identity. It is important for the abused to discover who God has made them to be, reviewing their strengths, gifts, and abilities (see Homework for the Helpee).

Victims of sexual abuse often become caretakers of others. Often they think that they do not need care and tend to choose jobs and professions in which they are the caregivers. They have learned to give *all* to another and in that have lost their childhood. They have been set up to become a caretaking codependent—someone who only knows how to care for someone else.

Adjustments may need to be made by the victim and emphasized through the homework in the following areas:

- Putting personal needs first
- Valuing and respecting the self
- Praising the self
- Asking for what he or she wants and saying no to what he or she doesn't want
- Recognizing that he or she has rights and choices
- Having privacy and time alone
- Expressing feelings, opinions, and needs
- Making his or her own decisions
- Trusting himself or herself

One sign of healing is that the victim will start taking care of himself or herself by getting the proper food, rest, exercise, and vitamins. Self-care involves caring not only about the emotions and inner self but for the outer self as well. It is a process and takes time to change patterns of abuse to self-care.

Victims of childhood abuse often feel guilt and/or shame for the abuse itself, for things they did as a child as a result of the abuse, and for the things they have done since as a result of the abuse. This can make it hard to forgive themselves (even though they didn't cause the abuse).

Unconscious guilt can cause a person to be self-destructive—which includes abusing his or her body with food, alcohol, drugs, self-mutilation, being accident-prone, or sabotaging his or her success.

A victim cannot be held responsible for not telling anyone about the abuse, for being submissive in the involvement, or for his or her body's response. According to Beverly Engel in *The Right to Innocence*, a victim cannot be held responsible for choices made concerning the sexual abuse because it was not a free choice.

It may be necessary for the victim to make amends for the mistakes of the past. These are often behaviors developed from the hurt of the abuse. Recognizing the need for self-forgiveness is essential for recovery.[13]

Summary

Recovery for the abused is a process. A big part of the process is their desire to heal and a desire to make a major change in their lives. Because the process involves recognizing the truth and then facing the pain, it is sometimes easier to leave things the way they are. Recognizing just where they are in this process will be vital. Helping them through the small changes will be a big part of the road to recovery.

In the methods described here, there is a need for confrontational methods, role playing, homework, inner evaluation, and "remembering" techniques. These methods are helpful and essential for recovery. However, genuinely caring for the abused and providing a warm, safe, and secure environment will be of utmost importance. A safe environment is the most essential ingredient for healing, along with a real desire on the part of the abused to be open and to change.

Questions to Ask the Helpee

- How old were you when the abuse occurred?
- How often do you think about the abuse?
- Would you describe your abuse encounters?
- Have you been able to forgive the abuser?
- Describe how the abuse affects your daily life. Do you have nightmares?
- Describe your relationship with your spouse? Your parents?

- When did your parents find out about the abuse? Were they supportive of you?
- Do you feel that you live in guilt? Shame?
- On a scale of 1 to 10 (10 being high), how high would you rate yourself? (Note: most people who are not hurt are at an 8 or 9 in how they feel about themselves.)
- Given a list of characteristics (see sexual abuse information), which ones do you have? How do you feel toward God when you pray?
- See questions from chapters covering the roots rejection, unforgiveness, pride, rebellion, and dysfunction when they apply.
- See questions from chapters covering the fruits depression, anxiety, low self-esteem, anger, and shame/guilt when they apply.

Homework for the Helpee

1. If you are having a hard time releasing your anger, please finish the following sentence: "I don't want to release anger because . . ."
2. To get the anger out, have a rigorous exercise routine or do some other type of physical activity, but don't do anything that will cause harm to yourself or others.
3. Write letters to the following people: the perpetrator, your parents, and yourself. Don't send the letters, but put them aside for a day and then see how you feel. Be ready to start praying that you will want to forgive this person.
4. This format can be used to help prepare for a confrontation with the abuser:
    a. List what the abuser has done to make you feel angry, hurt, damaged, guilty, or afraid.
    b. List how you felt as a result of the abuser's behavior.
    c. List what effect your abuser's or your family's actions (or inaction) had on you and how your life has been affected.
    d. Tell the abuser how you feel about him or her and why.
    e. List what you want from the abuser, your family, and anyone else involved. Write out how you feel about the abuser.[14]
5. Whether or not you choose to reconcile, you need to work toward forgiveness. This may take a long time. Read over the Steps to Assist the Helpee and Homework for the Helpee sections in chapter 3, "Root of Unforgiveness."
6. Make a list of all the negative comments that your parents or abuser have spoken over you during your lifetime. Now, make a list of all

your positive characteristics, abilities, talents, and strengths. This list needs to be longer than the previous one. Dwell on who God has made you to be and give thanks to God for all the personal gifts He has given you.

As you learn to value and respect yourself, make your own decisions, and so on (see list in Steps to Assist the Helpee earlier in this chapter), make a note of it in your journal and reflect upon how it feels.

Books for the Helpee

Allender, Dan B. *Wounded Heart: Hope for Adult Victims of Childhood Sexual Abuse.* Colorado Springs: NavPress, 1990.

Barshinger, Clark E., Ph.D., Lojan E. LaRowe, Ph.D., and Andres T. Tapia. *Haunted Marriage.* Downers Grove, Ill.: InterVarsity Press, 1995.

Engel, Beverly. *The Right to Innocence.* New York: Ivy Books, 1998.

Fraser, Sylvia. *My Father's House.* New York: Ticknor and Fields, 1988.

Heitritter, Lynn, and Jeanette Vought. *Helping Victims of Sexual Abuse.* Minneapolis: Bethany House Publishers, 1989.

Jakes, T. D. *Woman, Thou Art Loosed: Healing the Wounds of the Past.* Shippensburg, Pa.: Destiny Image, 1993.

Langberg, Diane. *On the Threshold of Hope: Opening the Door to Healing for Survivors of Sexual Abuse.* Carol Stream, Ill.: Tyndale House, 1999.

Meyer, Joyce. *Beauty for Ashes.* Boston: Harrison House, 1994.

Meyer, Rick. *Through the Fire: Spiritual Restoration for Adult Victims of Childhood Sexual Abuse.* Minneapolis: Augsburg/Fortress, 2005.

Morrison, Jan. *A Safe Place: Beyond Sexual Abuse.* Colorado Springs: Shaw Books, 1990.

Sands, Christa. *Learning to Trust Again: A Young Woman's Journey of Healing from Sexual Abuse.* Grand Rapids: Discovery House Publishers, 1999.

Scriptures for the Helpee

2 Chronicles 20:17
You will not have to fight this battle. Take up your positions; stand firm and see the deliverance the LORD will give you, O Judah and Jerusalem. Do not be afraid; do not be discouraged. Go out to face them tomorrow, and the LORD will be with you.

2 Corinthians 4:8-9
We are hard pressed on every side, but not crushed; perplexed, but not in despair; persecuted, but not abandoned; struck down, but not destroyed.

Isaiah 43:18-21
Forget the former things; do not dwell on the past. See, I am doing a new thing! Now it springs up; do you not perceive it? I am making a way in the desert and streams in the wasteland. The wild animals honor me, the jackals and the owls, because I provide water in the desert and streams in the wasteland, to give drink to my people, my chosen, the people I formed for myself that they may proclaim my praise.

Deuteronomy 32:10-12
In a desert land he found him, in a barren and howling waste. He shielded him and cared for him; he guarded him as the apple of his eye, like an eagle that stirs up its nest and hovers over its young, that spreads its wings to catch them and carries them on its pinions. The LORD alone led him; no foreign god was with him.

Proverbs 3:5-6
Trust in the LORD with all your heart and lean not on your own understanding; in all your ways acknowledge him, and he will make your paths straight.

Psalm 138:7-8
Though I walk in the midst of trouble, you preserve my life; you stretch out your hand against the anger of my foes, with your right hand you save me. The LORD will fulfill his purpose for me; your love, O LORD, endures forever—do not abandon the works of your hands.

Joel 2:25-26
I will repay you for the years the locusts have eaten—the great locust and the young locust, the other locusts and the locust swarm—my great army that I sent among you. You will have plenty to eat, until you are full, and you will praise the name of the LORD your God, who has worked wonders for you; never again will my people be shamed.

Psalm 37:28-29
For the LORD loves the just and will not forsake his faithful ones. They will be protected forever, but the offspring of the wicked will be cut off; the righteous will inherit the land and dwell in it forever.

Psalm 91

He who dwells in the shelter of the Most High will rest in the shadow of the Almighty. I will say of the LORD, "He is my refuge and my fortress, my God, in whom I trust." Surely he will save you from the fowler's snare and from the deadly pestilence. He will cover you with his feathers, and under his wings you will find refuge; his faithfulness will be your shield and rampart. You will not fear the terror of night, nor the arrow that flies by day, nor the pestilence that stalks in the darkness, nor the plague that destroys at midday. A thousand may fall at your side, ten thousand at your right hand, but it will not come near you. You will only observe with your eyes and see the punishment of the wicked. If you make the Most High your dwelling—even the LORD, who is my refuge—then no harm will befall you, no disaster will come near your tent. For he will command his angels concerning you to guard you in all your ways; they will lift you up in their hands, so that you will not strike your foot against a stone. You will tread upon the lion and the cobra; you will trample the great lion and the serpent. "Because he loves me," says the LORD, "I will rescue him; I will protect him, for he acknowledges my name. He will call upon me, and I will answer him; I will be with him in trouble, I will deliver him and honor him. With long life will I satisfy him and show him my salvation."

Psalm 64:6-10

They plot injustice and say, "We have devised a perfect plan!" Surely the mind and heart of man are cunning. But God will shoot them with arrows; suddenly they will be struck down. He will turn their own tongues against them and bring them to ruin; all who see them will shake their heads in scorn. All mankind will fear; they will proclaim the works of God and ponder what he has done. Let the righteous rejoice in the LORD and take refuge in him; let all the upright in heart praise him!

Romans 8:18

I consider that our present sufferings are not worth comparing with the glory that will be revealed in us.

1 Peter 3:9

Do not repay evil with evil or insult with insult, but with blessing, because to this you were called so that you may inherit a blessing.

Psalm 12:6-8

And the words of the LORD are flawless, like silver refined in a furnace of clay, purified seven times. O LORD, you will keep us safe and protect us from such people forever. The wicked freely strut about when what is vile is honored among men.

Psalm 20:1-2

May the LORD answer you when you are in distress; may the name of the God of Jacob protect you. May he send you help from the sanctuary and grant you support from Zion.

Notes

1. Beverly Engel, MFCC, *The Right to Innocence: Healing the Trauma of Childhood Sexual Abuse* (New York: Ivy Books, 1989), 55-56.
2. Suzanne M. Sgroi, *Handbook of Clinical Intervention in Child Sexual Abuse* (New York: Simon and Schuster, Inc., 1982), 11.
3. Susan Forward with Craig Buck, *Toxic Parents: Overcoming Their Hurtful Legacy and Reclaiming Your Life* (New York: Bantam Books, 1989), 143.
4. Engel, *Right to Innocence*, 31.
5. Ibid., 50.
6. Forward, *Toxic Parents*, 149.
7. Engel, *Right to Innocence*, 106-7.
8. Forward, *Toxic Parents*, 150.
9. Engel, *Right to Innocence*, 90-91.
10. Ibid., 101.
11. Ibid., 115.
12. Ibid., 117.
13. Ibid., 216.
14. Adele Mayer, *Incest: A Treatment Manual for Therapy with Victims, Spouses, and Offenders* (Holmes Beach, Fla.: Learning Publications, Inc., 1983), 250.

8 – ROOT OF DYSFUNCTION

(Living with possible emotional abuse or neglect of needs such as love, security, approval, appreciation, and identity)

Many people feel that they have come from a healthy, functional home. If you ask them if their family was healthy, they almost always say, "Yes, my home was healthy. I have great parents." Then after you ask them a few specific questions about their home life you find that isn't true at all. It is best to ask pointed questions. These are questions that are specific to how the person grew up. For example, when you came home from school, how did your mother or father greet you? Did you discuss your day and what you did at school? Did they note when you seemed different and ask you how you were feeling? Did they talk to you about what was going on in your life? Did they value your opinions? You are trying to help the person see that there is no perfect family and that most parents want the best for their children but may be repeating a pattern their own parents made. All parents make mistakes.

Only when a person recognizes past issues and forgives his or her parents can he or she make choices to change the dysfunctional pattern. Trying to change past patterns out of anger will not work. Recognition of all the issues is vital. You can't change what you don't acknowledge.

Context: Symptoms of the Dysfunctional Home

Dysfunction is often thought of in terms of hurtful behavior as abuse. This can be part of a dysfunctional home, but there are other symptoms. Dysfunction can be what isn't said and done to show commitment, value, and love to family members. Emotional hurts can be from the lack of affirmation (covert) given to a person or the effect of criticism, anger, berating, and yelling (overt). Verbal abuse causes emotional abuse. Verbal abuse is the action, and emotional hurt is what follows. Verbal abuse is always done by a person for the purpose of controlling. It is a learned behavior. Any of these can constitute dysfunction in a home.

> Emotional abuse is a pattern of behavior that attacks a child's emotional development and sense of self-worth. Emotional abuse includes excessive, aggressive, or unreasonable demands that place expectations on a child beyond his or her capacity. Constant criticizing, belittling, insulting, rejecting and teasing are some of the forms these verbal attacks can take. Emotional abuse also includes a child's psychological growth and development—providing his love, support or guidance.[1]

Codependency is a type of a dysfunctional home. *Codependency* was a term given to the spouses of people who went to Alcoholics Anonymous. When alcoholics started getting better, it was assumed that the family would get better. That didn't happen. The spouse of the alcoholic had a role: help the alcoholic get to work, call in sick for him or her, keep the children from being around when things were bad, and so on. Without a role, spouses were leaving. Thus, the term *codependency* came to be. The spouse had become dependent on helping the alcoholic, even enabling him or her to stay as he or she was. Usually the children also took roles, such as:

- the hero—often the firstborn child who tries to help the enabler or codependent
- the clown—often the middle or last child who learns to live through the home issues by being funny
- the lost one—the child that pulls back and detaches from the family, finding it easier to survive without involvement
- the scapegoat—the child who is often blamed for upheaval in the home

Codependency now applies to those who are always wanting to help take care of others and most often at the expense of their own needs.

Most parents desire to be loving and caring to their children. If parents have low self-esteem, have never received approval from their own parents, lived in a dysfunctional home and/or never dealt with their issues, it is very likely they will repeat the same pattern with their children as their parents did with them. Emotional abuse always has elements of interfering with one's emotional development and self-esteem.

Neglect of words of praise, love, hugs, and other physical touch, giving value and trust can be just as destructive as negative words. Again, sometimes it is what didn't happen in one's childhood that brings so much hurt.

The three basic premises of dysfunction are as follows: (1) *Can't talk*, meaning people can't talk about personal feelings or issues within the family or outside of the family. (2) *Can't feel*, meaning family members can't feel because feelings haven't been allowed. When feelings aren't discussed or allowed, no one knows what he or she feels. (3) *Can't trust*, meaning the family members learn not to trust others and also learn (often without realizing it) that they do not trust one another. Stifling the emotions and the inability to trust are characteristics that begin in the home and extend to relationships outside. A home does not have to have all of these traits to be dysfunctional.

1. Can't Talk

a. Denial is used to avoid difficult topics, particularly as they relate to the family's weaknesses or failures. For example, no one is allowed to admit he or she has a problem, because it shows weakness. Talking about problems in the house or to others is not OK. A child learns surface talk. When a problem isn't mentioned, it almost seems as if it didn't happen.

b. Fear and guilt encompass the home. An example of this is when a child picks up the message, "When you disturb Dad, he may become very upset with you, and he will say it is your fault." A child learns to take most or all responsibility and blame in present and future relationships. Shame becomes a part of this pattern.

2. Can't Feel

a. Most emotions are not allowed. Emotions are repressed. Anger may cause emotional outbursts. This may not be allowed. Sometimes hurt is so much a part of life that a person learns to shut off emotion and feels nothing—no pain, no joy—what we call a flat affect. "I don't know how I feel."

b. The child must be there for the parents. The child feels he or she must be responsible for either one or both parents emotionally. Often it is the opposite-sex parent—the father wants emotional support from the daughter, or the mother wants emotional support from the son. A child loses his or her childhood in this environment. This is sometimes termed "emotional incest." It is role-taking inappropriate for the child's age. An example would be a nine-year-old girl who is an emotional support for her mother or who parents her brothers and sisters. She may have the burden of keeping the family together or keeping the parents from fighting. Most often she will attract people who need to be cared for the rest of her life.

This can also fall under premise three, "Can't Trust."

c. "Emotional abuse" is a term used to denote the effects of verbal slander, criticism, constant put-downs, neglect, disinterest, and any kind of hurtful words. This can also be under the premise "Can't Trust."

3. Can't Trust

a. Most areas of family life are controlled, including the use of money, personal styles, sports, food, and activities. Personal thoughts, ideas, and opinions are not encouraged or valued. A child grows up not knowing what he or she really likes or dislikes—it is all about what the parents want.

b. Weak boundaries result in overinvolvement and overprotection, or rigid boundaries—the other extreme—leave children without the support needed to develop independence. Children may learn that others' needs are more important than their own.

c. Anxiety becomes a part of daily life. Anxiety grows without the freedom to be oneself, talk through issues, and feel safe.

Basic Types of Dysfunctional Homes

Emotionally Needy Parents

The child parents the mom and/or dad. If the parent confides emotionally in the child at a young age, it is called emotional incest. It isn't sexual but does call on the child to give at a level that causes resentment and anger later. The child loses his or her childhood and is called upon to be an adult.

Having a Perfectionist Family

Every member must make the family look great on the outside by having positive feelings and learns value from doing things "perfect." Sometimes the child becomes a trophy for the parent. The trophy may be beauty for a girl and being an athlete for a boy. The child learns that his or her worth comes from outside approval—how he or she looks. Perfectionist families are enmeshed in unhappiness and often in depression. The problem with being "perfect" is that no one can be perfect. Frustration and guilt are common. Often the family is devoid of emotion.

Family of Strict Rules

In this home there is little or no hugging, saying "I love you," or kissing. Guidelines are strict in the family. Emotions are not allowed. A child often takes on a flat affect—the ability to look and feel the same no matter how wonderful or how tragic something is, and that is how he or she survives. This family could have other characteristics, such as workaholism, perfectionism, and/or control. Most emotional subjects are not addressed. A child often grows up with a hole in his or her personality (see chapter 2, "Root of Rejection") or a need that can't seem to be filled.

Angry Parent

The child feels responsible for the parent's anger. Children are not allowed to be angry. Often there is physical and emotional abuse. Anger is used to control all members of the family. Often it is the gap between what we expect and what we actually experience that produces anger.[2] When anger is not resolved, it will continue to hurt the family unit. Depression among family members is common.

Parents Who Overcontrol Through Guilt and Shame

The child learns that what he or she thinks and feels is wrong. One or both parents may act superior and can never see their child as grown up—able to feel his or her own personhood and identity. Control doesn't allow for differences or independence. A child of a controlling parent may say "I'm sorry" all the time, afraid of being different or causing conflict. A child may also have difficulty saying no. Through the parent the child may also learn to manipulate through anger, guilt, and/or withdrawal of love.[3] Parents use manipulation by guilt, shame, or anger to control their children.[4]

Possible Fruits

A person doesn't need to have all of these to come from a dysfunctional home.

1. **Rejection.** Feeling used or not as important as the parents.
2. **Unforgiveness.** Finding it hard to forgive parents who may not be consistent.
3. **Pride.** Having false pride to cover insecurities
4. **Perfectionism.** Since this can be a type of family, it is consuming and can bring anxiety, depression, and many such fruits.

5. **Rebellion.** Out of the hurt from the family members.
6. **Depression.** This is common and may be a way of coping through the difficulty of life.
7. **Anxiety.** Feeling apprehension because of never doing things right. This can be fear and worry.
8. **Low self-esteem.** When a child is treated less than others, put down, can never please, doesn't hear enough words of affirmation, low self-esteem will develop.
9. **Anger.** This is an outward sign of the pain.
10. **Guilt/shame.** Sometimes parents manipulate through guilt. Shame may come through abuse or other degrading acts or words said at home.
11. **Grieving over lost childhood.** As the child grows and realizes what has been lost, there is definitely a feeling of loss.

Gary Smalley, in the *Gift of the Blessing*, discusses what a truly healthy family is by describing it through a biblical blessing and dividing it into five different areas. This book is a must for those suffering from their past home life. The needed areas for health include:*

1. **Meaningful touch.** The need we all have to be touched, hugged, kissed, and loved. It brings health to our bodies emotionally and physically. I have met people who have never been hugged by their parents. That is a travesty. "Touch played a part in biblical examples of blessing. In Genesis 48, Jacob blessed Ephraim and Manasseh by putting his hands on their heads. The act of touch communicates warmth, affirmation—even physical health."[5]
2. **Speaking words of blessing.** "Touch, however important, can't carry the whole load. A verbal message of acceptance, appreciation, or encouragement is the next step in giving the blessing. When Jacob blessed Manasseh and Ephraim, he not only laid his hands on their heads, he also said, 'In your name will Israel pronounce this blessing: "May God make you like Ephraim and Manasseh"' (Gen. 48:20)."[6]
3. **Expressing high value.** "To be effective, our words and actions must express our esteem for the one we're blessing and affirm that this person is valuable. In the Scriptures, recognition is based on who a person is, not on his or her performance."[7]

---

*For text referenced by superscript Nos. 5 to 9: Reprinted by permission. *The Gift of the Blessing Workbook*, Gary Smalley and John Trent, Ph.D., 1993, Thomas Nelson Inc., Nashville, Tennessee. All rights reserved.

4. **Picturing a special future.** "We can give those we bless a sense of security and confidence by conveying that the gifts and character traits they have right now are attributes that God can bless and use in the future."[8]
5. **An active commitment.** "This element is a 'kicker.' It requires sticking with the program even when your child misbehaves or the person you're blessing disappoints you—and you're ready to toss up your hands in despair. It's committing time and energy to involvement in that person's life to see that the words of blessing you speak come to pass."[9]

If you miss receiving the needed love, acceptance, and security from the areas of blessing, you may fit in one of the following groups:**

1. **Seekers.** "People who are always searching for intimacy, but are seldom able to tolerate it. These are the people who feel tremendous fulfillment in the thrill of courtship. But after marriage, their lack of acceptance from their parents leaves them uncomfortable in receiving it from a spouse."[10]
2. **The Shattered.** "These are the people whose lives are deeply troubled over the loss of their parents' love and acceptance. Fear, anxiety, depression, and emotional withdrawal many times can be traced to a person's missing out on his or her family's blessing."[11]
3. **The Angry.** "As long as people are angry at each other, they are chained to each other. Many adults are still emotionally chained to their parents because they are angry over missing the blessing."[12]
4. **The Smotherers.** "They are left so emotionally empty from the past that they smother other persons with unmet needs and, like a parasite, drain these others of their desire to listen or help."[13]
5. **The Detached.** "After losing the blessing from an important person in their lives once, they spend a lifetime protecting themselves from its ever happening again."[14]
6. **The Driven.** "In this category line up extreme perfectionists, workaholics, notoriously and picky housecleaners and generally demanding people who go after getting their blessing the old-fashioned way: they try to earrrrrrn it."[15]
7. **The Seduced.** "Many people who have missed out on their parents' blessing look for that love lost in all the wrong places. As we men-

---

**For text referenced by superscript Nos. 10 to 16: Reprinted by permission. *The Gift of the Blessing*, Gary Smalley and John Trent, Ph.D., 1995, Thomas Nelson Inc., Nashville, Tennessee. All rights reserved.

tioned in an earlier chapter, unmet needs for love and acceptance can tempt a person toward sexual immorality—all in an attempt to try to meet legitimate needs in an illegitimate way. Also, in this category fall substance abusers."[16]

Signs of a Healthy Family

Many people have difficulty recognizing that they did come from a dysfunctional home. The reason is because that is all they know. Understanding what a healthy family is like along with key questions to ask the helpee will aid in discovering if dysfunction was a part of the family.

1. Each family member blesses and contributes to the others' well-being. Value is displayed by frequent hugs and by interest in each other's activities. Parents encourage one another and their children. Frequent, meaningful praise is given.[17]
2. All feel safe to think for themselves, disagree respectfully, and talk without fear.
3. Each member feels connected to the family. Members look forward to seeing one another and sharing part of their day. A close bond to family members is important.[18]
4. Parents promote an atmosphere of security and trust in one another and their children. Love is shown equally to everyone in the family. Security is promoted also by family members encouraging each other with faith that what God has promised in His Word He will do.

Changing the Family Cycle—Can It Be Done?

Recognition of what has happened in the family is the first step to changing it. The helpee must also forgive those who have hurt him or her. The choice to change things in his or her own family has to be thought out without anger. The helpee needs a clear plan of what he or she want to do differently in his or her own family. He or she may need ideas since a person generally knows only what he or she has lived. Without thinking through the past, a person will tend to revert back to exactly what his or her parents did. Continually being aware of the plan will bring the needed change in families.

Steps to Assist the Helpee Heal from Dysfunction

There could be additional roots involved here, such as rejection, unforgiveness, rebellion, pride, or perfectionism. Help the helpee discover what other roots are involved. See other chapters.

Have the helpee recognize his or her own behavior and change negative cycles.

1. How does the helpee feel about God? What is his or her time with Him like? Help the helpee establish a relationship with God.
2. Ask the helpee: What did you dislike growing up? Then help him or her make an effort to change that behavior. If the helpee denies there was ever a problem, the cycle won't change for his or her own children. It is time for denial to stop.
3. Have the helpee forgive those who have hurt him or her in the past. Discover if the root of rejection or unforgiveness is a part of the helpee's life. If so, see that chapter for help.
4. It is very likely that rebellion, pride, or perfectionism could be a part of the helpee's life. It would be very easy to set up a false pride out of hurt. It would also be easy for a helpee to have some rebellion toward authority, parents, or whoever represents the hurt. Pride or perfectionism could appear as a way to cope. It would temporarily assist the helpee to feel better about who he or she is until he or she failed (which inevitably would happen and recycle).
5. Help the helpee recognize family issues. One of the most common problems is a child never being able to express emotions or talk about hurtful things.
6. Help the helpee see the need to "grieve" the loss of childhood or the hurts involved in his or her family. Show the traits of the healthy family. Have him or her read *The Gift of the Blessing* by Gary Smalley.
7. Help the helpee recognize his or her self-talk and the situations he or she remembers vividly from the past. Go over each hurt.
8. Be sure to have the helpee deal with anger or unforgiveness toward others.
9. Have the helpee set goals for healing in every area of his or her life.

Questions to Ask the Helpee

- Describe the type of people who are most attracted to you on a friendship level.
- How do you feel and react when you are told that something is your fault?
- What things do you do for yourself on a daily basis?
- What were your mom and dad's expectations of you?
- What type of care did you give to your family members?
- As a child, what were your expectations as a part of the family?

- Did you feel as a child that you had responsibilities? If so, what were they?
- What are your responsibilities now? Who do you take care of?
- Who relies on you?
- Describe your relationship with your spouse. Is there a parent-child relationship?
- How do you view your relationship with your children?
- What is the definition of a healthy family?
- What were things that you think you had to do as a child that weren't fair or appropriate for your age?
- Did anything happen in your family as a child that was embarrassing to you or that you knew wasn't happening in your friends' homes?

Homework for the Helpee

1. Work on your devotional life. Do a study on a biblical character. Which one is most like your parent? Which characteristics do you like and why? Dislike and why?
2. Write letters to those who have offended you. Express all your feelings. Don't send it. See if your feelings are less intense in a few days.
3. Write down self-talk. Then refute it with the truth.
4. See supplemental material for the grieving cycle. What applies to you?
5. Do something good for yourself at least once a week.
6. Do something nice for a family member once a week.
7. Talk openly about situations with your family. Encourage family members to express all feelings, especially hurt ones.
8. Ask each family member to list needs that will help them feel valuable and loved. Then be sure to meet those needs. Reading about and knowing your love language can also be a powerful tool. See Gary Chapman's *The Five Love Languages*.
9. Don't become impatient with your progress. Never give up!
10. Make a list of the activities that you complete in one day. Total up the numbers that were things you did for others, and compare that number with the total number of things you did for yourself. Do this for three days. (NOTE: If the number of things you do for others far exceeds the number you do for yourself, reprioritize your goals.) Decide what balance is for you.

11. Every time you feel as though you are inadequate or that you need to "fix" something, stop. Write down the triggers and write down the reasons why you believe your "fixing" will be so important.
12. Reading *Boundaries* by Cloud and Townsend is a must.

Books for the Helpee

Backus, William. *Telling Yourself the Truth.* Minneapolis: Bethany House Publishers, 1980.

Chapman, Gary. *The Five Love Languages.* Chicago: Moody Publishers, 2004.

Cloud, Henry, and John Townsend. *Boundaries.* Grand Rapids: Zondervan, 1992.

_____. *Boundaries in Marriage.* Grand Rapids: Zondervan, 1999.

Groom, Nancy. *From Bondage to Bonding: Escaping Codependency, Embracing Biblical Love.* Colorado Springs: NavPress, 1991.

Hemfelt, Dr. Robert, and Thomas Nelson. *Love Is a Choice: The Definitive Book on Letting Go of Unhealthy Relationships.* Nashville: Thomas Nelson Inc., 2003.

Smalley, Gary, and John Trent, Ph.D., *The Gift of the Blessing.* Nashville: Thomas Nelson, Inc., 1993.

Smedes, Lewis B. *The Art of Forgiveness.* Nashville: Moorings, 1996.

_____. *Forgive and Forget.* New York: HarperCollins Publishing, 2000.

Scriptures for the Helpee

Ephesians 6:4
Fathers, do not exasperate your children; instead, bring them up in the training and instruction of the Lord.

Colossians 3:20
Children, obey your parents in everything, for this pleases the Lord.

Isaiah 49:15
Can a mother forget the baby at her breast and have no compassion on the child she has borne? Though she may forget, I will not forget you!

Isaiah 61:1-3
The Spirit of the Sovereign LORD is on me, because the LORD has anointed me to preach good news to the poor. He has sent me to bind up the brokenhearted, to proclaim freedom for the captives and release from darkness for the prisoners, to proclaim the year of the LORD's favor and the day of vengeance of our God, to comfort all who mourn, and provide for those who grieve in Zion—to bestow on them a crown of beauty instead of ashes, the oil of gladness instead of mourning, and a garment of praise instead of a spirit of despair. They will be called oaks of righteousness, a planting of the LORD for the display of his splendor.

Psalm 34:18
The LORD is close to the brokenhearted and saves those who are crushed in spirit.

Psalm 43:5
Why are you downcast, O my soul? Why so disturbed within me? Put your hope in God, for I will yet praise him, my Savior and my God.

Psalm 112:7
He will have no fear of bad news; his heart is steadfast, trusting in the LORD.

Psalm 138:7-8
Though I walk in the midst of trouble, you preserve my life; you stretch out your hand against the anger of my foes, with your right hand you save me. The LORD will fulfill his purpose for me; your love, O LORD, endures forever—do not abandon the works of your hands.

Joel 2:25-26
I will repay you for the years the locusts have eaten—the great locust and the young locust, the other locusts and the locust swarm—my great army that I sent among you. You will have plenty to eat, until you are full, and you will praise the name of the LORD your God, who has worked wonders for you; never again will my people be shamed.

Psalm 37:28-29

For the LORD loves the just and will not forsake his faithful ones. They will be protected forever, but the offspring of the wicked will be cut off; the righteous will inherit the land and dwell in it forever.

Isaiah 43:18-21

Forget the former things; do not dwell on the past. See, I am doing a new thing! Now it springs up; do you not perceive it? I am making a way in the desert and streams in the wasteland. The wild animals honor me, the jackals and the owls, because I provide water in the desert and streams in the wasteland, to give drink to my people, my chosen, the people I formed for myself that they may proclaim my praise.

Notes

1. National Committee for the Prevention of Child Abuse, 1987; http://www.safechild.org/childabuse3.htm

2. Gary Smalley, *Making Love Last Forever* (Dallas: Word Publishing, 1996), 44.

3. Dr. Henry Cloud and Dr. John Townsend, *The Mom Factor* (Grand Rapids: Zondervan, 1996), 100.

4. John Bradshaw, *The Family* (Deerfield Beach, Fla.: Health Communications, Inc., 1996), 44.

5. Gary Smalley and John Trent, Ph.D., *The Gift of the Blessing Workbook* (Nashville: Thomas Nelson Publishers, 1993), 24. Reprinted with permission.

6. Ibid., 26.

7. Ibid., 28.

8. Ibid., 31.

9. Ibid., 33-34.

10. Gary Smalley and John Trent, Ph.D., *The Gift of the Blessing* (Nashville: Thomas Nelson Publishers, 1995), 147. Reprinted with permission.

11. Ibid., 148.

12. Ibid.

13. Ibid.

14. Ibid., 149.

15. Ibid.

16. Ibid.

17. Gary Smalley and John Trent, *The Language of Love* (Pomona, Calif.: Focus on the Family Publishing, 1988), 136-37.

18. Ibid.

PART III
MOST COMMON (NEGATIVE) FRUITS

DEPRESSION
ANXIETY (WORRY AND FEAR)
LOW SELF-ESTEEM
ANGER
SHAME AND GUILT

Depression, anxiety, low self-esteem, anger, and shame and guilt appear to be the most common fruits or symptoms people have. We will explore each of these fruits in a similar fashion as the roots. It is important to find the root of each fruit. These roots have something in common in that all of them can come from any and all of the roots.

CONTEXT
Each fruit chapter first explains the context of the fruit.

STEPS TO ASSIST HELPEE
Steps are given to help you progress through ways to guide the helpee to healing.

HOMEWORK FOR HELPEE
Homework is strongly suggested for each helpee. Use all the ideas listed or tailor the ideas for the helpee's need.

BOOKS FOR HELPEE
Suggested books for the helpee to read.

SCRIPTURES FOR HELPEE
Scriptures are suggested for the helpee.

9 — FRUIT OF DEPRESSION

Depression affects millions of people in the United States each year, young and old, men and women, rich and poor, Christian and non-Christian. Depression affects a person's body, thinking patterns, and mood. People can't always just pull themselves together. The depression may be temporary from a situation or continual from a constant dysfunctional situation. The cause may not be clear. Hurt and disappointment can come so often that a person becomes numb to survive. The longer the person has had depression, the more difficult it will be to get over it. Also, the longer a person has had depression, the less able he or she is to recognize it. Many people deny that they are depressed even when faced with evidence. It is *often depressing* to think that you are depressed.

One of the biggest problems with depression is that sometimes the church sweeps it aside and says, "You need to read your Bible and pray more—and then you would be OK." This just adds to the depression—with feelings of failing God and elusive happiness. We need to visit many men in the Bible and see their bouts with depression and how they handled them (e.g., David and Jonah).

As with any issue, if the person speaks of suicide and has thought out a plan, he or she needs to have professional help immediately. The police have to be called and made aware of this. There may be procedures you will have to go through. Call your suicide hotline number and get advice from the phone attendant of your state's law. You need to have this information ready whenever it is needed.

Context of the Fruit of Depression

Depression is a state of being that has been recognized for thousands of years. This state of being plagues over 12 million women in America each year, which is almost twice as many as men.[1] Depression is not foreign to the Bible either. Job, Moses, Jonah, Elijah, David, and Peter are just some of the people who had periods of depression.

In the past, some people have been quick to condemn those who have depression as not being spiritual enough or a person who does not pray enough. There are so many causes for depression that judging a person's reason for having it only causes more anger and in turn depression. Only those who have experienced depression and have been judged can understand the depth of hurt by other Christians.

The Ways Depression May Develop

1. Physical Reasons

"We know that lack of sleep, insufficient exercise, the side effects of drugs, physical illnesses, or improper diet can all create depression. Thousands of women experience depression as part of a monthly premenstrual syndrome (PMS) and, as we have seen, some develop postpartum depression following childbirth."*

Depression can also have genetic tendencies. Depression has been connected to imbalances in the brain with regard to the neurotransmitters serotonin, norepinephrine, and dopamine. This can be caused through stress, and one can also have genetic tendencies from the home. This is difficult to assess since the environment plays such a big part in depression.

- **Vitamin deficiency.** A lack of vitamin B complex can show some nutritional issues. Our food or lack thereof can cause depression.
- **Exhaustion.** This can give a feeling of being overwhelmed or even hopeless.
- **Hormones.** Very common in women and can be caused also in men by too much testosterone.
- **Chemical imbalance.** Such as lack of enough serotonin.

2. Our Thinking

Basically, our thinking tells us life is bad, we have no control in life, we are a failure, we are worth nothing, and it sends many other negative messages.

---

*Reprinted by permission. *Christian Counseling*, Gary R. Collins, 2007, Thomas Nelson Inc. Nashville, Tennessee. All rights reserved. p. 123.

a. Guilt from the past whether true guilt (needing to ask forgiveness) or false guilt.
   b. Unfulfilled expectations can cause a person to be so let down that he or she goes into a period of depression.

3. *Our Past*
   a. Passed down intergenerational anger (learned anger).
   b. Genetics—some families have tendencies in their personality to become depressed.
   c. Unforgiveness can perpetuate depression.
   d. Hopelessness also has a form of depression.
   e. Low self-esteem and depression usually go together.
   f. Failure often brings depression.
   g. Unresolved hurt, abuse, or neglect brings depression.

4. *Stress*

   Burn-out—too much work for too long or working toward a goal that doesn't produce the expected reward.

5. *Grief and Loss*

   See chapter 14, "Grief and Loss." The process of loss brings a cycle that includes depression. It is very normal and part of the healing process.

6. *Anger*

   Anger turned inward or not dealt with—instead a person thinks about the situation and becomes depressed especially if there is nothing he or she can do about the issue.

7. *Other Causes*

   It is always important to find the cause of depression and when it started. If the person has had depression since childhood, refer him or her to a physician (who may prescribe medication to help the person get started on his or her healing). Medication can help heal the brain as the person works on daily behavioral and physical changes.

Symptoms of Depression

A person doesn't need to have all of these traits to have depression. Even three or four symptoms could be a concern.

1. *Physical*

   Trouble sleeping or sleeping too much
   Loss of appetite
   Loss of weight or gaining weight

Loss of interest in sex
Lack of energy

2. *Thinking Patterns*
   Problem with concentration
   Can't make decisions
   Self-criticism
   Thoughts of death or suicide
   Negative self-talk

3. *Emotions*
   Hopeless feeling
   Guilt/shame
   Irritable
   Excessive sadness

4. *Activity*
   Slowing of most activity
   Withdrawal from social contacts
   Deterioration of work and personal appearance
   Risk of suicide is real
   Irresponsible behavior and attitudes

All of the roots can have depression as a fruit. Depression is the most common fruit and affects all ages. Nearly everyone is affected by depression or by someone who has depression. It is up to us with how we view it and deal with it.

If the person speaks of suicide, talk to your pastor or overseer. Call the police and contact any relatives necessary. See chapter 21.

Steps to Assist the Helpee Out of Depression

1. Develop an understanding of the helpee's background. Ask questions about family history, illness, and/or drug history. This will help set up a guideline for helping the individual.
2. Remember that there are two kinds of depression. It is important to recognize that the depression may have a physical basis. A helper may need to ask the helpee to see a physician and possibly be put on antidepressant medication.
3. Help the helpee become aware of his or her self-talk. Negative self-talk can be very destroying to our self-concept. One example is picking out a single negative detail and dwelling on it when the rest of the information is positive. Another is making weaknesses worse

than they are and then minimizing strengths. Negative self-talk can also be blaming self for things that can't be done.
4. Encourage the helpee's goals and help him or her structure the accomplishment of the goals.
5. The person may have to work on self-esteem issues, guilt, unresolved anger, a feeling of rejection, and even unforgiveness. Help him or her explore each of those areas.

Depression can come from every root. Keep this in your mind as you ask the helpee questions.

Questions for the Helper to Ask the Helpee

- Do you feel you can speak openly with those you love about your feelings?
- What kinds of things make you feel down?
- Do you exercise regularly?
- Can you give an example of what you would eat in a day?
- What is your social life like?
- What makes you happy?
- Has anything in particular triggered your depression?
- What five words best describe you?
- What kinds of goals do you have for yourself?
- When did your depression begin?
- Describe your relationship with your parents. How were you viewed in the family?
- Tell me how you view yourself.
- Describe your daily self-talk.

Homework for the Helpee

If you have discovered the root of the depression, you may have other homework to do. If you haven't, this would be a good time for self-assessment.

1. What is your devotional life like? (Help him or her start a daily time with God.)

    Keep a prayer journal of things you want God to heal. As you begin to see those things, start the healing process, praise God for them and take joy in what God is doing. Read some of the psalms. David was often depressed and wrote psalms of praise as a way to encourage himself. Read through the psalms finding the ones that show David praising God through his down times.

2. Encourage the helpee to begin a regular exercise routine if he or she does not already have one. Exercise reduces muscle tension, helps vent pent-up frustration, reduces insomnia, and has many other benefits.[2]
3. Get out of bed. Do not sleep for more than eight hours a day.
4. Change lifestyle by creating an exercise plan and spend time outside. If using drugs or drinking, stop! Change your diet if necessary. It may be essential to increase the Omega 3 fatty acids in your diet as well as vitamin B-12.
5. Take time for a hobby or put energy into creating, building, or writing something that you enjoy or something that helps you remember the good times with a person (if it is a loss through death).
6. Think about a goal that you have never been able to accomplish. Instead of giving up on that goal, think of baby-step goals to get you to your ultimate goal. Review these goals in your helping session.

Books for the Helpee

Carter, Les, Ph.D., and Frank Minirth, M.D. *The Freedom from Depression Workbook.* Nashville: Thomas Nelson Publishers, 1995.

Eldredge, John. *Waking the Dead: The Glory of a Heart Fully Alive.* Nashville: Thomas Nelson, 2003.

Hart, Archibald. *Unmasking Male Depression.* Nashville: Thomas Nelson, 2001.

_____. *Unveiling Depression in Women.* Grand Rapids: Baker, 2001.

LaHaye, Tim. *How to Win over Depression.* Grand Rapids: Zondervan, 1996.

Meyer, Joyce. *Straight Talk on Depression.* New York: AOL Time Warner Book Group, 2003.

Scriptures for the Helpee

Isaiah 61:1-3
The Spirit of the Sovereign LORD is on me, because the LORD has anointed me to preach good news to the poor. He has sent me to bind up the brokenhearted, to proclaim freedom for the captives and release from darkness for the prisoners, to proclaim the year of the LORD's favor and the day of vengeance of our God, to comfort all who mourn, and provide for those who grieve in Zion—to bestow on them a crown of beauty instead of ashes, the oil of gladness instead of mourning, and a garment of praise instead of a spirit of despair. They will be called oaks of righteousness, a planting of the LORD for the display of his splendor.

Psalm 34:18
The LORD is close to the brokenhearted and saves those who are crushed in spirit.

Isaiah 25:8
The Sovereign LORD will wipe away the tears from all faces.

Psalm 147:3
He heals the brokenhearted and binds up their wounds.

Isaiah 53:4
Surely he took up our infirmities and carried our sorrows.

Psalm 119:28
My soul is weary with sorrow; strengthen me according to your word.

Psalm 43:5
Why are you downcast, O my soul? Why so disturbed within me? Put your hope in God, for I will yet praise him, my Savior and my God.

Psalm 112:7
He will have no fear of bad news; his heart is steadfast, trusting in the LORD.

Ecclesiastes 3:1-2, 4
There is a time for everything, and a season for every activity under heaven: a time to be born and a time to die . . . , a time to weep and a time to laugh, a time to mourn and a time to dance.

Psalm 30:11-12
You turned my wailing into dancing; you removed my sackcloth and clothed me with joy, that my heart may sing to you and not be silent.

Psalm 18:16-24 (TM)
But me he caught—reached all the way from sky to sea; he pulled me out of that ocean of hate, that enemy chaos, the void in which I was drowning. They hit me when I was down, but GOD stuck by me. He stood me up on a wide open field; I stood there saved—surprised to be loved!

GOD made my life complete when I placed all the pieces before him. When I got my act together, he gave me a fresh start. Now I'm alert to GOD's ways; I don't take God for granted. Every day I review the ways he works; I try not to miss a trick. I feel put back together, and I'm watching my step. GOD rewrote the text of my life when I opened the book of my heart to his eyes.

Psalm 33:18-22 (TM)
Watch this: God's eye is on those who respect him, the ones who are looking for his love. He's ready to come to their rescue in bad times; in lean times he keeps body and soul together. We're depending on GOD; he's everything we need. What's more, our hearts brim with joy since we've taken for our own his holy name. Love us, GOD, with all you've got—that's what we're depending on.

Psalm 146:7-8
He upholds the cause of the oppressed and gives food to the hungry. The LORD sets prisoners free, the LORD gives sight to the blind, the LORD lifts up those who are bowed down, the LORD loves the righteous.

Notes

1. Mental Health America, "Factsheet: Depression in Women," http://www.mentalhealthamerica.net/index.cfm?objectid=C7DF952E-1372-4D20-C8A3DDCD5459D07B (accessed August 3, 2009).

2. Frank B. Minirth, M.D., and Paul D. Meier, M.D., *Happiness Is a Choice: A Manual on the Symptoms, Causes, and Cures of Depression* (Grand Rapids: Baker Book House, 2007), 167, 184.

10 – FRUIT OF ANXIETY (WORRY AND FEAR)

When I said, "My foot is slipping," your love, O LORD, supported me. When anxiety was great within me, your consolation brought joy to my soul (Ps. 94:18-19).

Anxiety is something that affects many people in our culture. Although God built us with the capacity to be anxious, that was meant primarily for human survival. This "fight or flight" response was designed in us to be used on a limited basis for a small amount of time. When we begin to be frequently anxious for extended periods of time, our bodies begin to move into a state of unhealthiness. This excessive worry can be regarding one or many issues in a person's life, and it is important that you as a helper guide the helpee through the root or roots that may be causing this.

Context of the Fruit of Anxiety

We often worry about our fears and become physically anxious about that fear. Fear and worry become anxiety.

Over the past few decades, anxiety has become an increasingly pervasive part of our society. For most people, they or someone they know are trying to deal with being constantly worried. Because anxiety is affecting so many people, it is important to understand exactly what it is.

Anxiety is an inner feeling of apprehension, uneasiness, worry, and/or dread that is accompanied by a heightened physical arousal. . . . The heart beats faster, blood pressure and muscle tensions increase, neurological and chemical changes occur within, and the person may feel faint, jumpy, and unable to relax or sleep. Anxiety can arise in response to some specific danger (many writers would call this "fear" rather than anxiety), or it may come in reaction to an imaginary or unknown threat. The anxious person senses that something terrible is going to happen, but he or she does not know what it is or why.*

Anxiety, although common for all to experience, has become a part of everyday life. The news media gives us national and state concerns; stressors such as money, relationships, and workplace issues pressure us; and the hurried pace of everyday life brings undue stress. Anxiety can affect all agegroups, from children to the elderly and adults in between. In fact, a study by the National Institute of Mental Health determined that anxiety has become our "national emotional pastime."[1]

There are several types of anxiety. "Neurotic anxiety involves intense exaggerated feelings of helplessness and dread even when the danger is mild or nonexistent." Anxiety, in certain situations, is a good thing and can motivate us to take care of a situation. "Intense anxiety, in contrast, is more stressful. It can shorten one's attention span, make concentration difficult, cause forgetting, hinder performance, interfere with problem solving, block effective communication, arouse panic, and sometimes cause unpleasant physical symptoms such as paralysis, rapid heartbeat, or intense headaches."**

In this chapter we will only talk about and deal with more common anxiety, not more extreme forms such as neurotic anxiety or posttraumatic stress disorder.

Causes of Anxiety

1. **Conflict** with others almost always causes some type of anxiety.
2. **Rejection** from others brings anxiety from the hurt involved.
3. **Loneliness** causes anxiety mainly from what we tell ourselves about why we are lonely.
4. **Fear of the future** is quite normal if it doesn't run your life. Anyone can temporarily worry about money, situations, people, and health.

---

*Reprinted by permission. *Christian Counseling*, Gary R. Collins, 2007, Thomas Nelson Inc. Nashville, Tennessee. All rights reserved. p. 141.

**Ibid.

5. **Loss.** This could be anything from the death of someone close to losing a friend, a job, or an important paper.
6. **Circumstantial.** This could be weather situations, a car accident, a situation that occurs at work, or other.
7. **Guilt.** This can bring anxiety. It is sometimes helpful to see which came first and what is more influential.
8. **Trying to be perfect.** Anytime someone is trying to do the impossible.
9. **Living in a dysfunctional home.** There are varying degrees of dysfunction/emotional/verbal/physical abuse.
10. **Great hurt.** There are many reactions to hurt, but anxiety is common.
11. **Health issues** that sometimes arise bring anxiety, fear, and anger.

Effects of Anxiety

We all have some sort of physical reaction to stress depending on the extent of the anxiety, our beliefs, and personality.
1. Shortness of breath
2. Insomnia
3. Emotional withdrawing
4. Overeating (this is a very common reaction)

Possible Root Sources

All of the roots can have the fruit of anxiety. Anxiety often goes along with depression. It's not always apparent which comes first, and often they come together.

There are solutions, though, to combat this fruit and restore order to one's mind. An important factor in this process will be including God in the process. God is the source of peace (Phil. 4:6-7), and He must be a part of the healing and the reordering of one's mind in order to find true peace from this fruit.

God's Word says, "Do not be anxious about anything, but in everything, by prayer and petition, with thanksgiving, present your requests to God" (Phil. 4:6). Simply put, trust in God is an antidote to anxiety.

Steps to Assist the Helpee Out of Anxiety

Identify the root or roots of this fruit before proceeding with assisting the helpee. Remember, anxiety can come from every root.
1. What is the helpee's devotional life like? Help him or her establish a time with God and do a scripture study on worry or anxiety.

2. Use relaxation techniques like breathing deeply, sitting quietly, listening to music, or reading scriptures.
3. Go to the list of causes in the previous section and ask questions that would help locate the source or root. Then, listen to the effects of anxiety the helpee has and decipher if it is in the normal range or becoming out of control. Does he or she need to see a specialist?
4. What possible roots could be in the helpee's life? Does the anxiety appear learned, genetic, or circumstantial? Ask questions by referring to other root sources for help. Ask yourself what exactly you are dealing with. Is this occasional or chronic anxiety? Does this seem like a normal response to stress or an overreacting to the situation? It may be a way of life. Regardless, these patterns need to be unlearned and replaced with positive behavior.
5. Look at and have the helpee work on his or her self-talk.
6. Help the helpee change some of the things that bring anxiety. See what can be worked on a day at a time. Look at time management if that will help.

If the person has excess anxiety, panic attacks, or is dealing with posttraumatic stress disorder, refer him or her to a professional.

Anxiety can come from every root, so keep that in mind as you note the questions.

Questions to Ask the Helpee

- When are you typically most anxious?
- When are you most calm?
- When was the last time you were anxious? What was going on just before you became anxious?
- How do you feel when you are anxious?
- Describe your self-talk.
- How do you view life? Are you excited about living it or do you dread it?
- How much is worry a part of your life?
- Is life like a pyramid with the most fearful or worrisome problem at the top?
- If that problem is resolved, do you find another one right underneath it to worry about? Is this a pattern in your family?

Homework for the Helpee

If you have discovered the root of the anxiety, you may have other homework to do. If you haven't, this would be a good time for self-assessment.

1. Do a study in the Bible on anxiety, worry, and fear. See what God says about this and how He feels our minds should be trained.

   Make a point to renew your mind with Scripture. As thoughts come to mind that make you anxious, immediately go to speaking Scripture instead of repeating the negative self-talk. Start a devotional life by reading a psalm, a proverb, and a chapter in the Gospel of John each day.
2. Make a list of the things that make you anxious. Determine which things you can take care of and solve. For those that are too big or that you have no control over, allow God to be bigger and be in control of those things. Give them to Him daily, or hourly if you need to, until you can really leave it in God's hands.
3. When you become anxious, try different methods to calm yourself down. Call up someone and have him or her pray with you. Go take a walk and pray. Listen to praise music.
4. Write down what happened just before you became anxious. Keep a list so that you can see what you are repeating and what methods help stop it.
5. Learn to trust in God through daily spending time with Him. Listen to praise music. Listen to encouraging teaching tapes.
6. Help others in need. Get involved in community service or in a helping group at church. This helps you get your mind off yourself.

Books for the Helpee

Eng, Elaine Leong. *"Martha, Martha": How Christians Worry*. Binghamton, N.Y.: Haworth Press, Inc., 2000.

Hull, Bill. *Anxious for Nothing: Guidelines to Help You Fill Your "Anxiety Space."* Old Tappan, N.J.: Fleming H. Revell Co., 1987.

McGee, Robert S. *The Search for Significance*, rev. ed. Nashville: Word Publishing, 1998.

Osborne, Cecil G. *Release from Fear and Anxiety*. Waco, Tex.: Word Books, 1976.

Steincrohn, Peter J. *Antidotes for Anxiety: How to Untie Your Bundle of Nerves*. Los Angeles: Nash Publishing, 1972.

Scriptures for the Helpee

Psalm 94:19
When anxiety was great within me, your consolation brought joy to my soul.

Ecclesiastes 11:10
So then, banish anxiety from your heart and cast off the troubles of your body, for youth and vigor are meaningless.

1 Peter 5:7
Cast all your anxiety on him because he cares for you.

Proverbs 12:25
An anxious heart weighs a man down, but a kind word cheers him up.

Ecclesiastes 2:21-23
For a man may do his work with wisdom, knowledge and skill, and then he must leave all he owns to someone who has not worked for it. This too is meaningless and a great misfortune. What does a man get for all the toil and anxious striving with which he labors under the sun? All his days his work is pain and grief; even at night his mind does not rest. This too is meaningless.

Matthew 8:23-27
Then he got into the boat and his disciples followed him. Without warning, a furious storm came up on the lake, so that the waves swept over the boat. But Jesus was sleeping. The disciples went and woke him, saying, "Lord, save us! We're going to drown!" He replied, "You of little faith, why are you so afraid?" Then he got up and rebuked the winds and the waves, and it was completely calm. The men were amazed and asked, "What kind of man is this? Even the winds and the waves obey him!"

Philippians 4:6-7
Do not be anxious about anything, but in everything, by prayer and petition, with thanksgiving, present your requests to God. And the peace of God, which transcends all understanding, will guard your hearts and your minds in Christ Jesus.

Jeremiah 29:11
"For I know the plans I have for you," declares the LORD, "plans to prosper you and not to harm you, plans to give you hope and a future."

Matthew 6:25-34
Therefore I tell you, do not worry about your life, what you will eat or drink; or about your body, what you will wear. Is not life more important than food, and the body more important than clothes? Look at the birds of the air; they do not sow or reap or store away in barns, and yet your heavenly Father feeds them. Are you not much more valuable than they? Who of you by worrying can add a single hour to his life? And why do you worry about clothes? See how the lilies of the field grow. They do not labor or spin. Yet I tell you that not even Solomon in all his splendor

was dressed like one of these. If that is how God clothes the grass of the field, which is here today and tomorrow is thrown into the fire, will he not much more clothe you, O you of little faith? So do not worry, saying, "What shall we eat?" or "What shall we drink?" or "What shall we wear?" For the pagans run after all these things, and your heavenly Father knows that you need them. But seek first his kingdom and his righteousness, and all these things will be given to you as well. Therefore do not worry about tomorrow, for tomorrow will worry about itself. Each day has enough trouble of its own.

Psalm 46:10
Be still, and know that I am God; I will be exalted among the nations, I will be exalted in the earth.

Luke 12:22-34
Then Jesus said to his disciples: "Therefore I tell you, do not worry about your life, what you will eat; or about your body, what you will wear. Life is more than food, and the body more than clothes. Consider the ravens: They do not sow or reap, they have no storeroom or barn; yet God feeds them. And how much more valuable you are than birds! Who of you by worrying can add a single hour to his life? Since you cannot do this very little thing, why do you worry about the rest? Consider how the lilies grow. They do not labor or spin. Yet I tell you, not even Solomon in all his splendor was dressed like one of these. If that is how God clothes the grass of the field, which is here today, and tomorrow is thrown into the fire, how much more will he clothe you, O you of little faith! And do not set your heart on what you will eat or drink; do not worry about it. For the pagan world runs after all such things, and your Father knows that you need them. But seek his kingdom, and these things will be given to you as well. Do not be afraid, little flock, for your Father has been pleased to give you the kingdom. Sell your possessions and give to the poor. Provide purses for yourselves that will not wear out, a treasure in heaven that will not be exhausted, where no thief comes near and no moth destroys. For where your treasure is, there your heart will be also."

Matthew 11:28-30
Come to me, all you who are weary and burdened, and I will give you rest. Take my yoke upon you and learn from me, for I am gentle and humble in heart, and you will find rest for your souls. For my yoke is easy and my burden is light.

Notes

1. Bill Hull, *Anxious for Nothing: Guidelines to Help You Fill Your "Anxiety Space"* (Old Tappan, N.J.: Fleming H. Revell Co., 1987), 16.

11 – FRUIT OF LOW SELF-ESTEEM

How could we live where we do with so much and yet feel bad about ourselves? We have more than we have ever had before. Why do so many children and adults struggle with low self-esteem—especially when they have had great parents?

We live in a society that says looks, weight, and possessions are everything. The media constantly shows us beautiful models who look perfect (male and female). Even older women and men are compared to the now older models and actors that look extremely young and beautiful. After seeing these kinds of things daily, a person can't help but be affected by the barrage of beauty.

There are many reasons for low self-esteem. A person can go too far either way with self-esteem—work on feeling better so much that you become self-centered and selfish or feeling so bad about yourself you can't accept compliments; you degrade yourself and even loathe yourself. Either way you become obsessed with you. There is a balance with how you need to feel about yourself in order to be the best you can be. Balance what you want to encourage in those who are hurting, have guilt and shame, and/or basically feel bad about who they are.

Context for the Fruit of Low Self-Esteem

Self-concept is the view individuals develop of themselves. Self-esteem is the rating system that individuals put on their view or concept of themselves. Self-esteem, therefore, is directly related to self-concept. When the self-esteem is low, usually the self-concept is false or incorrect. Low self-esteem grows slowly in the individual until his or her worth is totally diminished.

Development of Low Self-Esteem

When we do not understand the place of Christ in our life or what He has done for us, it is easy to perceive self inaccurately. People think they are humbling themselves by seeing themselves as worth nothing. We demean what God made by belittling ourselves.

Low self-esteem can develop when parents withhold love. Those who have had repeated rejection from a parental figure most likely will have low self-esteem. These people probably feel that they never lived up to their parents' standards for them. What the individual does not understand is that the parents' expectations were unrealistic and inappropriate. The child may feel a lack of security, significance, and lovability. Overprotective parents can also instill a low self-concept in a child by not letting him or her learn natural aspects of life through trial and error. Overprotective or sheltering parents can diminish the child's view of his or her abilities by trying to constantly shield the child's fall.[1]

Low self-esteem can take root when there is recurring sin in a person's life. When people are stuck in habitual sins, they will find it hard to have a positive view of themselves. They are caught in a self-destructive pattern that will not let up. Therefore, instead of seeing victory and feeling satisfaction, they feel constant dissatisfaction with themselves for not overcoming the sin. The sin must be confronted and dealt with to see healing occur.

Past experiences with others can negatively affect one's self-esteem. Not only does the child's relationship with his or her parents affect the health of self-esteem, but the child's surrounding relationships also promote or inhibit a healthy self-esteem. For instance, negative interaction with other children can destroy self-esteem.

Some people set personal goals too high and never reach them. Others set goals too low so that they can't fail. Both hinder a healthy self-esteem.

Some Characteristics of Those Dealing with Low Self-Esteem

- Fear of rejection, of others in general, of life
- Disapproving of others to protect self
- Defensive in protection of self

- Depression—from feeling less than others
- Disappointment in life itself, in others, and especially in self
- Worry and fear of the future, of what others think, of what they have done
- Self-talk very negative
- Anger about life; anger toward people who have hurt them
- Denial of the way life is, of their own issues, of others
- Refusal to work on issues
- Jealousy of others and what they have, what they are—a lot of comparison of others
- Insecurities in general
- Anxious and analytical—always going over things in the mind to figure out what went wrong
- Lonely—feeling unworthy to be with others

In Matt. 22:39, Jesus tells the crowds: "Love your neighbor as yourself." That is a command for godly self-love. However, this kind of self-love is not conceited, does not brag, and does not put self-admiration above others. When developing healthy self-love, it is important not to go the other direction into ungodly self-love, which can develop into self-centeredness, conceitedness, and a lack of concern for others, almost indifferent to the needs of others. Understanding what a healthy self-esteem is like is important.

A healthy self esteem includes the following:
1. Ability to love others as well as yourself.
2. Capacity to give unselfishly of yourself.
3. Ability to give yourself permission to fail.
4. Being able to set reasonable expectations.
5. Having positive self-talk.
6. Ability to be connected to your feelings—knowing how you feel each day.[2]
7. Ability to say "no" when needed.
8. Accepting yourself for who you are. Changing what you can; letting go of what you cannot change.
9. Realizing how much God loves and values you.
10. Knowing your self-worth comes from God—He is the One who made you.

Possible root sources: All of the roots can have the fruit of low self-esteem.

Steps to Assist the Helpee Out of Low Self-Esteem

If possible, ask questions to try and discover the root. Any of the roots could apply to this fruit.

1. Guide the helpee in a devotional life. Give scriptures that will help him or her understand God's love and acceptance.
2. Give genuine worth and acceptance. This may need to be developed over time as you get to know the helpee.
3. Help the helpee find the cause of his or her low self-esteem. Ask questions to get to the source of issues. Always check on self-talk. What does he or she say to self each day? Change unhealthy self-talk.
4. Have the helpee list good traits, strengths, and assets as well as weaknesses and then focus on strong points. Discuss these. Where did the negative thinking come from?
5. Help the helpee set goals. Show examples of short-term (one day or one week) and long-term (one year) goals. Help in setting physical, emotional, and social goals.[3] Help the helpee see that he or she has valid reasoning and can make choices on his or her own. Remind him or her to celebrate progress on the way toward the goals.
6. What are the factors in the helpee's life that have been detrimental? Are there hurtful people, places, or things he or she can avoid?
7. Deal with the sin in the helpee's life. It is vitally important in moving forward to help him or her deal with any indiscretions in his or her life.

Questions to Ask the Helpee
- Do you feel that your parents are proud of your accomplishments? Give an incident when they showed that they were proud of you.
- Do you feel that you had many good friends growing up? Can you describe a time when you did not get along with your friends?
- What are you good at? What are your gifts?
- What are some of your life goals?
- What kinds of things do people give you compliments for? What do you say when they compliment you?
- What is your self-talk like?
- Do you compare yourself to others frequently? Do you feel you come out lesser than others when you compare?
- On a scale of 1 to 10, how would you rate yourself? Why?
- How would you describe yourself to someone who has never seen you?
- How would others describe you?
- How do you view other people?

- On a scale of 1 to 10, rate your feelings about your spouse, children, friends, and so forth.
- When do you feel your self-esteem began to decline?
- What was your family like? How did your parents treat you? What was expected of you?
- What do you think of yourself?
- How do you feel God views you?

Homework for the Helpee

If you have discovered the root of your low self-esteem, see what other homework you may need to do.

1. Pray daily that the Lord will help you love yourself with a healthy, God-given acceptance. Give God praise for the way that He has created you. Spend time praying for others too. Read in Psalms and Proverbs every day.
2. Make a list of your lifelong goals. Check off the ones that you have fulfilled. Analyze your goals. Are the goals realistic? What are some attainable goals?
3. Keep a record of your self-talk during the day. Read over the list at the end of the day and determine whether you are building yourself up or tearing yourself down. Why do you feel that way?
4. Make two columns on a piece of paper. Write all the negative lies that you have let yourself believe. In the other column write all of your positive characteristics. This column must be longer than the other one. If you are having a hard time, start out with what you are good at to get the ball rolling. Another way is to have someone who loves you help you with the list.
5. Journal about how your self-concept is changing.
6. Find a way to get involved helping others, such as a ministry at church or a homeless shelter.
7. Make a list of things that you enjoy doing, such as taking a leisurely walk, working in the garden, or scrapbooking. The next time you are feeling as though you are worthless, stop, reject the negative self-talk, quote a scripture, then do one of the activities you listed.
8. Write down ten good qualities about yourself, as well as three scriptures that remind you of how God sees you. Post them on your mirror to remind yourself of them daily.

9. Ask others how they view you. Write those things down, and when you are feeling low, read it over.
10. Keep a list of verses that shows how God views you. Keep it by your bed and read it over before bed and when you wake up.

Books for the Helpee

Adams, Jay. *Biblical View of Self-Esteem*. Eugene, Oreg.: Harvest House, 1986.

Backus, William. *Telling Yourself the Truth*. Grand Rapids: Bethany House Publishers, 2000.

Burwick, Ray. *Self Esteem: You're Better than You Think*. Carol Stream, Ill.: Tyndale House, 1983.

Hicks, Roy. *Healing Your Insecurities*. Tulsa: Harrison House, 1982.

McDowell, Josh D. *See Yourself as God Sees You*. Carol Stream, Ill.: Tyndale House, 1999.

McGee, Robert S. *Search for Significance*. Nashville: Thomas Nelson, 2003.

Sullivan, James. *Journey to Freedom*. Wheaton, Ill.: Good News Publisher, 2000.

Wegscheider-Cruse, Sharon. *Learning to Love Yourself: Finding Your Self-Worth*. Deerfield Beach, Fla.: Health Communications Inc., 1987.

Scriptures for the Helpee

Jeremiah 17:19
This is what the LORD said to me: "Go and stand at the gate of the people, through which the kings of Judah go in and out; stand also at all the other gates of Jerusalem."

Ephesians 4:20-22
You, however, did not come to know Christ that way. Surely you heard of him and were taught in him in accordance with the truth that is in Jesus. You were taught, with regard to your former way of life, to put off your old self, which is being corrupted by its deceitful desires.

John 15:1-6
I am the true vine, and my Father is the gardener. He cuts off every branch in me that bears no fruit, while every branch that does bear fruit he prunes so that it will be even more fruitful. You are already clean because of the word I have spoken to you. Remain in me, and I will remain in you. No branch can bear fruit by itself; it must remain in the vine. Neither can you bear fruit unless you remain in me. I am the vine; you are the branches. If a man remains in me and I in him, he will bear much fruit; apart from me you can do nothing. If anyone does not remain in me, he is like a branch that is thrown away and withers; such branches are picked up, thrown into the fire and burned.

John 16:7
But I tell you the truth: It is for your good that I am going away. Unless I go away, the Counselor will not come to you; but if I go, I will send him to you.

Romans 8:16
The Spirit himself testifies with our spirit that we are God's children.

Galatians 6:14
May I never boast except in the cross of our Lord Jesus Christ, through which the world has been crucified to me, and I to the world.

Galatians 4:7
So you are no longer a slave, but a son; and since you are a son, God has made you also an heir.

Jeremiah 30:17
"But I will restore you to health and heal your wounds," declares the LORD, "because you are called an outcast, Zion for whom no one cares."

Isaiah 41:9-10
I took you from the ends of the earth, from its farthest corners I called you. I said, "You are my servant"; I have chosen you and have not rejected you. So do not fear, for I am with you; do not be dismayed, for I am your God. I will strengthen you and help you; I will uphold you with my righteous right hand.

Jeremiah 29:11-14

"For I know the plans I have for you," declares the LORD, "plans to prosper you and not to harm you, plans to give you hope and a future. Then you will call upon me and come and pray to me, and I will listen to you. You will seek me and find me when you seek me with all your heart. I will be found by you," declares the LORD, "and will bring you back from captivity. I will gather you from all the nations and places where I have banished you," declares the LORD, "and will bring you back to the place from which I carried you into exile."

Psalm 139:1-16

O LORD, you have searched me and you know me. You know when I sit and when I rise; you perceive my thoughts from afar. You discern my going out and my lying down; you are familiar with all my ways. Before a word is on my tongue you know it completely, O LORD. You hem me in—behind and before; you have laid your hand upon me. Such knowledge is too wonderful for me, too lofty for me to attain. Where can I go from your Spirit? Where can I flee from your presence? If I go up to the heavens, you are there; if I make my bed in the depths, you are there. If I rise on the wings of the dawn, if I settle on the far side of the sea, even there your hand will guide me, your right hand will hold me fast. If I say, "Surely the darkness will hide me and the light become night around me," even the darkness will not be dark to you; the night will shine like the day, for darkness is as light to you. For you created my inmost being; you knit me together in my mother's womb. I praise you because I am fearfully and wonderfully made; your works are wonderful, I know that full well. My frame was not hidden from you when I was made in the secret place. When I was woven together in the depths of the earth, your eyes saw my unformed body. All the days ordained for me were written in your book before one of them came to be.

Hebrews 13:5-6

Keep your lives free from the love of money and be content with what you have, because God has said, "Never will I leave you; never will I forsake you." So we say with confidence, "The Lord is my helper; I will not be afraid. What can man do to me?"

2 Corinthians 3:5

Not that we are competent in ourselves to claim anything for ourselves, but our competence comes from God.

Ephesians 2:10

For we are God's workmanship, created in Christ Jesus to do good works, which God prepared in advance for us to do.

2 Corinthians 4:7-9

But we have this treasure in jars of clay to show that this all-surpassing power is from God and not from us. We are hard pressed on every side, but not crushed; perplexed, but not in despair; persecuted, but not abandoned; struck down, but not destroyed.

1 Peter 2:4-5
As you come to him, the living Stone—rejected by men but chosen by God and precious to him—you also, like living stones, are being built into a spiritual house to be a holy priesthood, offering spiritual sacrifices acceptable to God through Jesus Christ.

Psalm 146:1-7
Praise the LORD. Praise the LORD, O my soul. I will praise the LORD all my life; I will sing praise to my God as long as I live. Do not put your trust in princes, in mortal men, who cannot save. When their spirit departs, they return to the ground; on that very day their plans come to nothing. Blessed is he whose help is the God of Jacob, whose hope is in the LORD his God, the Maker of heaven and earth, the sea, and everything in them—the LORD, who remains faithful forever. He upholds the cause of the oppressed and gives food to the hungry. The LORD sets prisoners free.

Isaiah 49:14-16
But Zion said, "The LORD has forsaken me, the LORD has forgotten me." "Can a mother forget the baby at her breast and have no compassion on the child she has borne? Though she may forget, I will not forget you! See, I have engraved you on the palms of my hands; your walls are ever before me."

2 Corinthians 5:17
Therefore, if anyone is in Christ, he is a new creation; the old has gone, the new has come!

Zephaniah 3:17
The LORD your God is with you, he is mighty to save. He will take great delight in you, he will quiet you with his love, he will rejoice over you with singing.

Notes

1. Frank B. Minirth and Paul D. Meier, *Happiness Is a Choice: A Manual on the Symptoms, Causes, and Cures of Depression* (Grand Rapids: Baker Publishing Group, 2007), 52.

2. Beverly Engel, *Healing Your Emotional Self: A Powerful Program to Help You Raise Your Self-Esteem, Quiet Your Inner Critic, and Overcome Your Shame* (Hoboken, N.J.: Wiley, 2006), 159.

3. Sharon Wegscheider-Cruse, *Learning to Love Yourself: Finding Your Self-Worth* (Deerfield Beach, Fla.: Health Communications Inc., 1987), 79, 80.

12 – FRUIT OF ANGER

Often people say to me, "I'm not angry—just frustrated." Whether it is frustration, fear, or hurt, these are all forms of anger. Anger does not have to be demonstrated by yelling or pounding fists. It can be in forms of tension in the neck or back, talking louder when you bring up something painful, or acting hostile toward another person. Anger does not have to be bad—it is what you do with it that matters. Often forgiveness is a part of the healing process.

Anger is a natural part of loss and hurt. It also can be a motivator to help us get something done. We need to see anger for what it is so people will have an easier time healing from their anger. It is what they do about the anger that may become a problem.

Context: What Is Anger?

"In your anger do not sin": Do not let the sun go down while you are still angry (Eph. 4:26).

It is the attitude and behavior following our anger that hurts us. We can choose what we will do with our anger and whether or not we will let it fester.

"Human anger is normal and not necessarily sinful. Human beings were created in the image of God and given emotions, including anger. This anger is a necessary and useful emotion. It was seen in Jesus and is not sinful in and of itself."*

---

*Reprinted by permission. *Christian Counseling*, Gary R. Collins, 2007, Thomas Nelson Inc. Nashville, Tennessee. All rights reserved. p. 160.

Anger can be defined as a feeling of extreme displeasure, hostility, or frustration toward someone, something, or even an experience. Anger can be felt even when others don't see it.

What Is the Purpose of Anger?

Anger can also be a natural response to situational hurt, frustration, and/or fear. If anger is dealt with in a proper way, it can help with resolving an issue. It can also be very detrimental to health and relationships and can control a person's life.

Myths of Anger

Sometimes it helps to understand a subject by understanding what is not true about it, or understanding and rebuffing the myths of the topic. Many people have carried false beliefs about anger for so long that they do not even realize it. Knowing the truth about anger in general as well as one's individual anger can really help someone struggling with this problem. It is also important for the helper to identify any myths about anger that the helpee might be holding on to. Here are some common myths about anger:

Myth No. 1: The Bible Does Not Have Much to Say About Anger

Anger is actually a key theme in the Bible. The term "anger" is used 390 times in the NIV. In addition, other related terms are used frequently, such as "wrath" (197 times), "provoke" (52 times), and "vengeance" (32 times). The Bible holds many accounts of God's anger, humans' anger at God, and humans' anger at each other.[1]

Myth No. 2: All Anger Is Sin

Many Christians struggle with the assumption that all anger is wrong and sinful and ought to be purged from our lives. This is understandable because of the fear that stems from the fact that anger is difficult to manage and control. It can also stem from bad experiences of being on the receiving end of anger. At the same time, it is important not to fall into the trap of thinking that because anger is natural, it is right and should not be harnessed or questioned.

In Ephesians 4:26-27, the apostle Paul writes, "'In your anger do not sin': Do not let the sun go down while you are still angry, and do not give the devil a foothold." These words help Christians see that anger and sin are separate, and it is possible to be angry without sinning. It is not the feeling of anger that is the problem; it is what the person does with it.[2]

What Causes Anger?

Anger is caused by a variety of factors.
1. **Feeling rejected, betrayed, used, or treated in a dishonoring way.** This could be just what the person perceives, not the truth. However, it hurts when we feel others see us in a negative way and is a contributing factor to our emotions.
2. **Feeling judged.** Sometimes we turn back and judge them out of anger.
3. **Feeling stressed.** Stress brings anxiety and often frustration, all of which can be a form of anger. When life seems out of control, anger can be a motivator to actually get something done.
4. **Feeling unloved or even insecure in a relationship.** Those needs can cause us to feel hurt, a form of anger. If a person has low self-worth, then hurt can easily surface as anger.
5. **Feeling frustrated.** Frustration is a negative emotion that occurs when someone cannot reach a desired goal. Personal frustration is distress caused by personal characteristics that stop the progress toward the goal. External frustration is distress caused by outside situations that hinder steps toward the goal.[3]
6. **Genetics and learned behavior.** These are a part of how a person perceives anger and develops it in his or her life. When anger is a normal part of growing up, it is easy to fall into the same pattern. Sometimes it is difficult to tell if it is more genetics or environmental. Men who have a large amount of testosterone can experience anger more easily. Testosterone is the hormone that produces aggression, sexual drive, and increased aggression.
7. **Dealing with loss.** Anger is a stage on the grieving cycle. It is natural and necessary to help a person deal with the loss. It can be a motivator to accept the change and move on. Sickness is an example of loss. Life is not the way it used to be. Life may become extremely difficult. That is definitely a loss and frustration.
8. **Failure.** When we fail we often get angry at ourselves. There are many reasons we become angry with self. Sometimes we misdirect our anger and fail to see what really happened.

All the roots mentioned can have anger. It is a natural expression for a person dealing with rejection, unforgiveness, pride, perfectionism, rebellion, dysfunction, and/or types of abuse to experience anger in varying degrees.

Anger and Health

Anger not only has damaging emotional and relational effects but also can damage one's health. Emotionally induced illness accounts for 60 to 85 percent of all sicknesses today. Dr. Henry Brandt claims, "Approximately 97% of all the cases of bleeding ulcers without organic origin that I have dealt with are caused by anger."[4] Many common illnesses today are triggered by excessive tension. Some illnesses that can be caused by tension produced by anger or fear are: "high blood pressure, heart attack, colitis, arthritis, kidney stones, and gall bladder troubles and many others."[5] Theodore I. Rubin, psychiatrist and author of *The Angry Book*, believes that eating disorders, including overeating and starvation, are linked to anger. He also contends that phobias, obsessions, and compulsions are sometimes caused by anger.[6]

Expressing Anger

Just as every person is different, so is every person's style of expressing anger. Anger style is influenced by many factors, but one of the most important variables is how the person's family expressed anger throughout childhood. We often learn from parents and others how to deal with anger. Understanding why a person reacts the way he or she does is a step in the right direction when it comes to handling anger.

There are several styles of anger expression and many variants. Every person handles anger differently. However, by encouraging the helpee to identify the basic ways he or she reacts to life, the helper can then assist the helpee to analyze the pros and cons of his or her current anger style and work on improving it.

The Words of Anger

An important step in dealing with anger is admitting that you are angry. Many people who grew up hearing that anger is a sin still feel angry and express anger, but they call it by different names. Listed below are a few of the words we use to express our feeling of anger when we do not want to own up to our anger.[7]

Hurt	Touchy	Offended	Grumpy
Fearful	Vicious	Dread	Violent
Frustrated	Discontent	Stressed	Envy
Irritated	Evil thoughts	Indignant	Malice
Critical	Detest	Judgmental	Hatred
Resentment	Malicious talk	Indignation	Gossip
Revenge	Sarcastic	Vengeance	Mock
Wounded	Offend	Bitter	Ridicule

Characteristic Ways of Expressing Anger

Anger can be managed in many different ways. The most common ways of handling anger are "open aggression, suppression, passive aggression, assertive."

1. **Yelling, waving arms wildly, saying negative and hurtful things.** Angry outbursts tend to only have negative consequences and can be very painful to the recipient. They can result in guilt, a need to apologize, and sometimes the loss of a job or friend.
2. **Suppression.** Suppression of anger can be just as damaging to a person as explosive anger. It can lead to a cycle of self-punishment: a person turns anger inward and demands improvement. Failure to be perfect leads to more anger, and the self-talk that accompanies it helps the person along to low self-esteem and depression. Somatization is another possible consequence of suppressing anger. When anger is ignored, it sometimes shows up as physical symptoms, such as headaches and ulcers. The most likely candidates for this are people whose parents or others have always told them that anger is wrong.[8] Suppression can also be a form of depression. If anger is not dealt with in some way—whether by exercise, journaling, writing letters to those who have offended, or talking it out, then depression will set in.
3. **Passive aggression.** Passive aggression is another unsuccessful way of managing anger. It attempts to get even with the source of anger in very subtle ways.[9] These kinds of people are experts at hurtful comments disguised as compliments, sarcasm, pouting, and interfering with the plans of others.

Possible Roots

Any of the roots could apply to this common fruit.

1. **Rejection** produces anger—a form of hurt. Rejection goes deep in the soul.
2. **Unforgiveness** almost always has a form of anger. Again, it is coming from hurt.
3. **Pride** rears its ugly head by anger. "How dare you say that about me."
4. **Perfectionism** always brings anger. Since perfection is not possible, the person cannot attain the goal. This is frustration at its worst.
5. **Rebellion** is anger at a source. "Since I am angry with you for hurting me, I will never do what you say."

6. **Dysfunctional home.** Adult children are often angry from past hurts but don't even realize it. Since they learned not to talk about things, the hurt remains embedded deep in their heart.
7. **Abuse** of any form causes anger. It may come out as depression and/or physical complaints, but the anger will come out.

Although it is difficult to change our method of expressing anger, it can be done. There has to be an open awareness of what is happening and why it is happening. It is hard to change something that isn't recognized or accepted as being in one's life. Anger can help us be aware that something else is going on in our lives.

Anger is a way of expressing emotion, and it is what is done about the negative way of expressing it that becomes a problem. On the other side of it, anger can hurt us and/or others. Anger in and of itself can be a useful emotion to motivate change, settle disputes, and accept what cannot be changed.

Steps to Assist the Helpee Out of Anger

Try to find the cause/root of the problem.

1. Help the helpee see who God really is, how much He loves him or her, how he or she was made in His image. Have the helpee start a devotional life. Ask God to take away the angry habit pattern. If we ask anything according to the will of God, he not only hears us but also answers our requests (1 John 5:14-15).
2. Have the helpee face his or her anger! The minute he or she tries to justify it, explain it, or pretend it is not anger, he or she will not succeed. The helpee may need to write a letter to a person that hurt him or her, expressing everything that has hurt him or her and why. It is generally best not to send it; however, reading it out loud to a safe person can be helpful. Sometimes just the hurt feelings need to be acknowledged and validated.
3. Listen to the helpee's story. Have him or her tell you the situations that have triggered the anger. What is the helpee wanting to change?
4. What is the root? This is a good time to ask questions to find when the helpee saw a difference in the amount and kind of anger. Any root could cause a reaction of anger.
5. Have the helpee forgive the person who has caused the anger. Paul instructed the Ephesians to forgive each other "just as in Christ God forgave you" (4:32).

6. Give thanks for anything that "bothers" the helpee. Thanksgiving is therapeutic and helpful, especially when it comes to getting a handle on your anger! God desires that we as Christians "give thanks in all circumstances" (1 Thess. 5:18). Is the helpee giving thanks to God?
7. Have the helpee look at incidents where he or she has lost control. Find out what went on before the incident. Did that affect him or her? Is there a pattern? Is it always the same person, same kind of incident, and so forth? When a person gets angry, reason often gives way to feelings and something is said or done that is regretted later. By learning to slow their reactions, avoiding an angry mind-set, and using "I" statements can help practice self-control with anger. Have the helpee practice that with you. "I chose to get angry when my brother said those words. I let it happen."

Questions to Ask the Helpee

- How often do you feel anger?
- Do you often say that you are "frustrated" or "hurt" rather than "angry"? If so, what is your view of anger? What is your view of people who are angry?
- Which would you say bring anger to you—people, ideas, or things?
- What happens just before you become angry? What happens after?
- Was control a major attribute of one or more members in your home? Describe them.
- When have you seen a change in the amount of anger you have?
- Has the way you express anger changed?
- Who do you hurt by your anger most often?
- Who has hurt you the most? How much is rejection a part of your life?

Homework for the Helpee

If you have discovered the root of your anger, you may have other homework to do. If you haven't, this would be a good time for self-assessment. See Unforgiveness Homework. There may be other roots involved that need to be explored as well.

1. Pray daily that the Lord will help you forgive yourself for your anger against yourself and others. Give God praise for what He has taught you. Spend time praying for others too. Read in Psalms and Proverbs every day.
2. Do a Bible study on anger. Who was angry in the Bible? How did they handle it? What were the results? How does the Lord want us to work on anger? Make a list of those you feel anger toward and pray over your list daily.
3. Keep a journal and list every person who brings you anger. List every situation. It might be necessary to write a letter (and not send it) to the person who has hurt you.
4. Spend at least twenty minutes in vigorous exercise daily, especially when full of anger.
5. What happens just before and after you become angry? Write it down in your journal. Do this for several days in a row. See if there is a pattern or cause.
6. Choose one of the items you listed in number 5. How could you change that behavior after you become angry? Example: If you start feeling a rush of emotion, choose to talk or leave the room. If you close off, give yourself time then talk about it.
7. Express your feelings to a safe person.

Books for the Helpee

Carter, Les, Ph.D., and Frank Minirth, M.D. *The Anger Workbook*. Nashville: Thomas Nelson, 1993.

LaHaye, Tim. *Understanding the Male Temperament*, 2nd ed. Grand Rapids: Fleming H. Revell, 1977, 1996.

LaHaye, Tim, and Bob Phillips. *Anger Is a Choice*. Grand Rapids: Zondervan, 1982.

Oliver, Gary Jackson, and H. Norman Wright. *When Anger Hits Home*. Chicago: Moody Press, 1992.

Scriptures for the Helpee

Psalm 37:8
Refrain from anger and turn from wrath; do not fret—it leads only to evil.

Ecclesiastes 7:9
Do not be quickly provoked in your spirit, for anger resides in the lap of fools.

Proverbs 15:17
Better a meal of vegetables where there is love than a fattened calf with hatred.

Proverbs 17:1
Better a dry crust with peace and quiet than a house full of feasting, with strife.

Proverbs 21:19
Better to live in a desert than with a quarrelsome and ill-tempered wife.

Proverbs 15:18
A hot-tempered man stirs up dissension, but a patient man calms a quarrel.

Proverbs 25:28
Like a city whose walls are broken down is a man who lacks self-control.

Proverbs 22:24-25
Do not make friends with a hot-tempered man, do not associate with one easily angered, or you may learn his ways and get yourself ensnared.

Proverbs 16:32
Better a patient man than a warrior, a man who controls his temper than one who takes a city.

Proverbs 10:18
He who conceals his hatred has lying lips, and whoever spreads slander is a fool.

Proverbs 10:12
Hatred stirs up dissension, but love covers over all wrongs.

Colossians 3:8
But now you must rid yourselves of all such things as these: anger, rage, malice, slander, and filthy language from your lips.

James 1:19-20
My dear brothers, take note of this: Everyone should be quick to listen, slow to speak and slow to become angry, for man's anger does not bring about the righteous life that God desires.

Ephesians 4:26
"In your anger do not sin": Do not let the sun go down while you are still angry.

Notes

1. Glenn Taylor and Rod Wilson, *Helping Angry People* (Grand Rapids: Baker Books, 1997), 32-33.
2. Ibid., 40.
3. Dennis Coon, *Essentials of Psychology*, ed. 9 (Belmont, Calif.: Thomson, Wadsworth, 2003), 420.
4. Tim LaHaye, *Understanding the Male Temperament*, 2nd ed. (Grand Rapids: Fleming H. Revell, 1977, 1996), 200.
5. Ibid.
6. Theodore I. Rubin, *The Angry Book* (Austin, Tex.: Touchtone, 1998), 47.
7. Tim LaHaye and Bob Phillips, *Anger Is a Choice* (Grand Rapids: Zondervan, 2002), 146.
8. Neil Clark Warren, *Making Anger Your Ally*, 3rd ed. (Colorado Springs: Focus on the Family Publishing, 1990), 36-37, 41-42.
9. Ibid.

13 – FRUIT OF SHAME AND GUILT

Do you or someone you know suffer from shame or guilt? Shame and guilt rip at the very being of who a person is. Shame is the way we feel about ourselves. It is developed through acts of others toward us or acts we carry out. Although a person feels shame from the past, God can and will forgive.

Guilt can be true or false. True guilt is sin in our lives that only God can forgive. False guilt is something we believe we did wrong, didn't do, or should have done that isn't a sin. What we believe about ourselves will determine whether or not we have low self-esteem, depression, anxiety, and anger. All of these fruits can work together and compound each other. Any of the roots could have the fruit of shame and/or guilt.

Context of the Fruit of Shame and Guilt

The Beginning of Shame and Guilt

Erik Erickson developed a theory of eight stages of human development. Each one focuses on a conflict that a person needs to solve in order to develop successfully into the next stage of life. His idea is that if we don't resolve each stage, it will be much more difficult to deal with the next stage. The two stages that deal with shame and guilt are the second and third stage. Therefore we will start with the second stage, eighteen months to three years.

Ages Eighteen Months to Three Years: Autonomy Versus Shame and Doubt

Erik Erikson's theory of how shame and guilt can develop in early life demonstrates the importance of understanding our past. The theory states that between the ages of eighteen months and three years children struggle with a need to be independent or autonomous. Overprotective parents can do damage at this point. Too much protection will damage the children's ability to trust that they have the ability to do things on their own and that their parents believe in them. Their self-doubt will grow into shame. If parents are too permissive or harsh in this stage, the children may try to feel some control in life by becoming obsessive compulsive. This is a way of trying to gain control in life—overdoing to please others.[1]

Ages Three to Six Years: Initiative Versus Guilt

Children need freedom to select meaningful activities. This helps them with their view of who they are. If they are not allowed to make some choices, they will develop guilt and lose their initiative to try.[2]

When children are punished for trying to do things on their own, they will develop guilt. If a child is never punished, he or she could become heartless, not caring who he or she hurts. A child needs to learn responsibility and limitations at the same time. He or she needs not only freedom to explore but also an understanding of how his or her actions affect others. Praise and acceptance are needed as the child grows—a balance of boundaries, love, acceptance, and freedom.

Shame

Shame involves negative feelings and thoughts about who a person is. Shame is thinking about past failures or experiences of rejection. Shame is a feeling that a person cannot change and that he or she feels inferior and worthless. It can be a feeling a person has of ruining his or her life or being immoral. Shame can also be a feeling of being hurtful to someone or of having something hurtful done to him or her.

Shame keeps a person feeling like God hasn't forgiven him or her. If a person has done something wrong to another person, he or she needs to go make amends. Restitution to the person offended may be necessary. The person needs to ask for God's forgiveness also.[3]

Shame can keep a person feeling like God hasn't forgiven him or her for something that was done to him or her. Example: A sexually abused person feels shame. He or she often feels that the abuse was his or her fault and feels "dirty" and shameful.

Shame could result from any of the roots. Shame can destroy a person's ability to reach out to the future because he or she is so enmeshed in the past. A person will need to forgive self for the past to go forward in life.

Effects of Shame
1. **Inferiority.** See the fruit of low self-esteem.
2. **Destructive behavior,** such as overeating, alcoholism, and becoming promiscuous.
3. **Physical reactions.** The effects of shaming self for a long period of time can be quite detrimental to the physical body. Sometimes people inflict pain, feeling they deserve it.
4. **Defeated attitude.**
5. **Feeling worthless.**
6. **Feeling that they can never do or be enough.**

Guilt

True Versus False Guilt

Minirth and Meier, from *Happiness Is a Choice*, say: "Guilt is anger toward yourself."[4] If a person sins and never acknowledges the sin to God, he or she will feel guilty.[5] True guilt can be one's conscience telling the person that what he or she did is wrong. David felt true guilt when he sinned and admitted his adultery to Nathan in 2 Sam. 12:13, "I have sinned against the LORD."[6] True guilt can help us recognize when we do something wrong. Every root could have the fruit of guilt.

False guilt usually occurs because someone desires to have power over another and uses guilt as a weapon.[7] If a guilt-ridden environment has been going on for years, it is difficult for the one receiving the guilt to recognize it. False guilt can also develop because a person feels he or she hasn't done enough, hasn't studied enough, and so forth. These are often unrealistic expectations.

> When parents are good models of what they want to teach, when the home is warm, predictable, and secure, and when there is more emphasis on approval and giving encouragement than on punishment and criticism, then the child knows what it means to experience acceptance and forgiveness. In contrast, when moral training is punitive, critical, fear ridden, and unrealistically demanding, then the child becomes angry, rigid, critical and burdened by a continuing sense of guilt.*

---

*Reprinted by permission. *Christian Counseling*, Gary R. Collins, 2007, Thomas Nelson Inc. Nashville, Tennessee. All rights reserved. p. 182.

Effects of Guilt
1. **Defensive thinking.** A way to avoid or reduce feelings of anxiety, frustration, and stress.
2. **Self-condemnation.** This includes feelings of being inferior, inadequate, weak, and insecure.
3. **Living in regret.**
4. **Not forgiving self for behavior.**
5. **Feels he or she never did enough.**
6. **Says "I should have . . ."**
7. **Always tries to compensate by doing good deeds.**
8. **May easily have the root of perfectionism and/or pride.**

Most people deal with shame and/or guilt at some time in their life. It is vital to recognize it, examine it, and either repent if it is true or not accept it if it is false.

All of the roots could be sources of guilt and/or shame.

Steps to Assist the Helpee with Shame and Guilt

1. First help the helpee recognize what is true guilt and what is false guilt. Help him or her see if shame is part of his or her life. Does he or she need to repent from sin? Does he or she need to ask the Lord for forgiveness for something that happened in childhood?
2. Have the helpee recognize the truth about feelings. Feelings can be a poor judge of reality. Help him or her recognize that we can't always count on our feelings. Show that God's Word helps us see if we are wrong and need to repent. If we feel we never do enough, and so forth, what is really the truth?[8] "This then is how we know that we belong to the truth, and how we set our hearts at rest in his presence whenever our hearts condemn us. For God is greater than our hearts, and he knows everything" (1 John 3:19-20).
3. Have the helpee make two lists—one of all the things that represent his or her true guilt and the other list of what he or she feels could be false guilt or shame. Discuss each item. Have the helpee ask God's forgiveness for what is truly sin.[9]
4. Help the helpee learn closure. Have him or her read Eccles. 9:7-10: "Go, eat your food with gladness, and drink your wine with a joyful heart, for it is now that *God favors what you do.* Always be clothed in white, and always anoint your head with oil. Enjoy life with your wife, whom you love, all the days of this meaningless life that God has given you under the sun—all your meaningless days. For this is

your lot in life and in your toilsome labor under the sun. Whatever your hand finds to do, do it with all your might, for in the grave, where you are going, there is neither working nor planning nor knowledge nor wisdom" (emphasis added).

Study of this passage shows that Solomon is saying when we have met our spiritual, moral, and vocational duties we need to enjoy life. In all he is saying enjoy life and have your work "approved by God." The above translation says, *God favors what you do*. He calls the concept closure, something your helpee will need to learn. This passage can help.[10]

What *The Message* paraphrase says of the same passage may bring more clarity: "Seize life! Eat bread with gusto, drink wine with a robust heart. Oh yes—God takes pleasure in your pleasure! Dress festively every morning. Don't skimp on colors and scarves. Relish life with the spouse you love each and every day of your precarious life. Each day is God's gift. It's all you get in exchange for the hard work of staying alive. Make the most of each one! Whatever turns up, grab it and do it. And heartily! This is your last and only chance at it, for there's neither work to do nor thoughts to think in the company of the dead, where you're most certainly headed."

Have them read about the creation in Gen. 1:1-3, noting how God rested.

Questions to Ask the Helpee (Shame)

- What do you think has caused shame in your life?
- How do you see yourself compared to others?
- Explain the experiences that have been the most hurtful?
- What are your thoughts toward yourself during the day?

Questions to Ask the Helpee (Guilt)

- How have you dealt in the past with guilt feelings?
- What are the things right now that are making you feel guilty?
- What were your parental expectations about right and wrong?
- What happened when you failed?
- How often were you blamed or told you didn't do enough?
- What are things that you feel guilty about that don't bother other people?

Homework for the Helpee

1. Start each day with a time of praying about your guilt and/or shame. Ask the Lord to help you forgive yourself if you have sinned and to help you recognize what you haven't done wrong but keep blaming yourself for. Read the Word each day.
2. Find passages in the Bible where a biblical character finished his or her work. What happened after he or she finished? In other words, why do you think you must stay busy to be OK? Read from the Word daily. Study 1 John and study the scripture's view of knowing who you are in Christ.
3. List feelings you have had each day. Distinguish if your feeling(s) of guilt are accurate or misguided.
4. List each time you feel guilt. Write it down. What was it about? Try to assess whether it was true or false guilt. What was your thinking like?
5. Ask for God's forgiveness when you know you have been wrong in your actions or thoughts.
6. List all the things that you like about yourself. If you have difficulty, ask a good friend to help you.
7. Recognize how the thoughts of false guilt and shame are hurting you. Consciously choose to think better thoughts. Keep the Word before you.
8. Forgive yourself for what you "feel" you have done. Pray that you will forgive yourself. Pray about this every day. One of the "Prayers for Helpees" in chapter 22 may help.

Books for the Helpee

Arterburn, Stephen. *Toxic Faith: Experiencing Healing Over Painful Spiritual Abuse.* New York: Random House, 1991.

Barnhill, Julie Ann. *Motherhood: The Guilt That Keeps on Giving.* Eugene, Oreg.: Harvest House Publishers, 2006.

Beam, Joe. *Getting Past Guilt.* West Monroe, La.: Howard Books, 2003.

Bradshaw, John. *Healing the Shame That Binds You.* Deerfield Beach, Fla.: Health Communications, 2005.

Fehlauer, Mike. *Finding Freedom from the Shame of the Past.* Lake Mary, Fla.: Strang Communications, 1991.

Harris, Patricia. *Imprisoned Secrets of the Heart.* New Kensington, Pa.: Whitaker House Publishers, 2000.

Hawkins, David. *Living Beyond Guilt.* Eugene, Oreg.: Harvest House Publishers, 2006.

Matthews, David. *Crashing Without Burning After Failure.* Macon, Ga.: Smyth and Helwya Publishing Inc., 1997.

McGee, Robert. *The Search for Significance.* Nashville: W Publishing Group, 1998.

Parrott, Les. *Shoulda, Coulda, Woulda,* Audiobook on cassette. Grand Rapids: Zondervan Corp., 2004.

Smucker, Lori. *Shattered by Shame, Crowned in Glory.* Lake Mary, Fla.: Strang Communications, 2002.

Scriptures for the Helpee

Acts 13:14-15, 38-41 (NLT)
On the Sabbath [Paul and Barnabas] went to the synagogue for the services. After the usual readings from the books of Moses and from the prophets, those in charge of the service sent them this message: "Brothers, if you have any word of encouragement for us, come and give it." . . . [After recounting God's plan from Moses to Jesus, Paul said,] "Brothers, listen! We are here to proclaim that through this man Jesus there is forgiveness for your sins. *Everyone who believes in him is [freed from all guilt and] declared right with God*—something the law of Moses could never do. Be careful! Don't let the prophets' words apply to you. For they said, 'Look, you mockers, be amazed and die! For I am doing something in your own day, something you wouldn't believe even if someone told you about it.'"

1 John 3:16-24
This is how we know what love is: Jesus Christ laid down his life for us. And we ought to lay down our lives for our brothers. If anyone has material possessions and sees his brother in need but has no pity on him, how can the love of God be in him? Dear children, let us not love with words or tongue but with actions and in truth. This then is how we know that we belong to the truth, and how we set our hearts at rest in his presence whenever our hearts condemn us. For God is greater than our hearts, and he knows everything. Dear friends, if our hearts do not condemn us, we have confidence before God and receive from him anything we ask, because we obey his commands and do what pleases him. And this is his command: to believe in the name of his Son, Jesus Christ, and to love one another as he commanded us. Those who obey his commands live in him, and he in them. And this is how we know that he lives in us: We know it by the Spirit he gave us.

John 8:11
"No one, sir," she said. "Then neither do I condemn you," Jesus declared. "Go now and leave your life of sin."

Romans 5:16
Again, the gift of God is not like the result of the one man's sin: The judgment followed one sin and brought condemnation, but the gift followed many trespasses and brought justification.

Romans 5:18
Consequently, just as the result of one trespass was condemnation for all men, so also the result of one act of righteousness was justification that brings life for all men.

Romans 8:1
Therefore, there is now no condemnation for those who are in Christ Jesus.

Romans 14:22
So whatever you believe about these things keep between yourself and God. Blessed is the man who does not condemn himself by what he approves.

1 John 3:19-20
This then is how we know that we belong to the truth, and how we set our hearts at rest in his presence whenever our hearts condemn us. For God is greater than our hearts, and he knows everything.

1 John 3:21
Dear friends, if our hearts do not condemn us, we have confidence before God.

Isaiah 53:10
Yet it was the Lord's will to crush him and cause him to suffer, and though the Lord makes his life a guilt offering, he will see his offspring and prolong his days, and the will of the Lord will prosper in his hand.

Hebrews 10:22
Let us draw near to God with a sincere heart in full assurance of faith, having our hearts sprinkled to cleanse us from a guilty conscience and having our bodies washed with pure water.

Psalm 31:1
In you, O Lord, I have taken refuge; let me never be put to shame; deliver me in your righteousness.

Proverbs 13:18
He who ignores discipline comes to poverty and shame, but whoever heeds correction is honored.

Isaiah 45:17
But Israel will be saved by the Lord with an everlasting salvation; you will never be put to shame or disgraced, to ages everlasting.

Isaiah 50:7
Because the Sovereign Lord helps me, I will not be disgraced. Therefore have I set my face like flint, and I know I will not be put to shame.

Isaiah 54:4
Do not be afraid; you will not suffer shame. Do not fear disgrace; you will not be humiliated. You will forget the shame of your youth and remember no more the reproach of your widowhood.

Isaiah 61:7
Instead of their shame my people will receive a double portion, and instead of disgrace they will rejoice in their inheritance; and so they will inherit a double portion in their land, and everlasting joy will be theirs.

Romans 9:33
As it is written: "See, I lay in Zion a stone that causes men to stumble and a rock that makes them fall, and the one who trusts in him will never be put to shame."

Romans 10:11
As the Scripture says, "Anyone who trusts in him will never be put to shame."

Matthew 26:28
This is my blood of the covenant, which is poured out for many for the forgiveness of sins.

Acts 10:43
All the prophets testify about him that everyone who believes in him receives forgiveness of sins through his name.

Acts 13:38
Therefore, my brothers, I want you to know that through Jesus the forgiveness of sins is proclaimed to you.

Acts 26:17-18
I am sending you to them to open their eyes and turn them from darkness to light, and from the power of Satan to God, so that they may receive forgiveness of sins and a place among those who are sanctified by faith in me.

Ephesians 1:7
In him we have redemption through his blood, the forgiveness of sins, in accordance with the riches of God's grace.

John 16:8-11
When he comes, he will convict the world of guilt in regard to sin and righteousness and judgment: in regard to sin, because men do not believe in me; in regard to righteousness, because I am going to the Father, where you can see me no longer; and in regard to judgment, because the prince of this world now stands condemned.

Notes

1. Richard Niolon, Ph.D., *Resources for Students and Professionals*, www.psychpage.com

2. Gerald Corey, *Theory and Practice of Counseling and Psychotherapy* (Pacific Grove, Calif.: Brooks/Cole Publishing Co., 1986).

3. Norman Bales, ed., *All About Families Newsletter*, "Coping with Shame and Guilt," E-mail newsletter to author.

4. Frank Minirth and Paul Meier, *Happiness Is a Choice* (Grand Rapids: Baker Publishing Group, 2007), 69.

5. Bales, *All About Families Newsletter*.

6. Ibid.

7. Ibid.

8. Larry K. Weeden, *Feeling Guilty, Finding Grace* (Ann Arbor, Mich.: Servant Publications, 1993), 36-37.

9. Charles Swindoll, *Insight for Living*. Radio and audio Bible teaching ministry.

10. Robert Jeffress, *Guilt Free Living* (Carol Stream, Ill.: Tyndale House Publishers, Inc., 1995), 56, 89.

PART IV
COMMON PROBLEMS

GRIEF AND LOSS
DIVORCE
AFFAIRS
STEPPARENTING
SEXUAL ADDICTION

Grief and loss, as a common problem, does not have a root. There might only be a root if someone does not choose to get past the grief in a reasonable time.

Divorce doesn't have to come from a root either. Often there are roots, however, that need to be addressed. Generally, at least one of the spouses has a root(s).

Affairs occur for many reasons. Spouses who have affairs could be sexually addicted; they could be selfish and self-centered; they may be angry or they may be just unwilling to give to their own marriage. It may be a pattern they have seen growing up. To really help the situation, both the one who had the affair and the spouse need help. It can be a complicated process. Most often, the one who had the affair has root(s).

Stepparenting is a result of remarriage. There are so many complicating factors in this situation that to simply say *look at the root* will not suffice.

Sexual addiction can be caused through a dysfunctional family, through rejection, through rebellion, and through sexual abuse. It can also come about through looking at pornography early in life. There are many factors to sexual problems. It is important to have a good understanding of human sexuality.

CONTEXT
Each problem chapter explains (first) the context of the problem.

STEPS TO ASSIST HELPEE
Steps are then given to help you, the helper, progress through ways to guide the helpee to healing.

HOMEWORK FOR HELPEE
Homework is strongly suggested for each helpee. Use all the ideas listed or tailor the ideas for the helpee's need.

BOOKS FOR HELPEE
Books to read. These are suggestions for the helpee.

SCRIPTURES FOR HELPEE
Scriptures are also suggestions for the helpee.

14 — GRIEF AND LOSS

Webster's dictionary defines "grief" as: "intense emotional suffering caused by loss, disaster, misfortune, etc., also described as acute sorrow; deep sadness."

It is a very normal and natural experience to grieve over the loss of someone or something. In the Old Testament people would sit in ashes, tear their clothes, and wail. Often there were mourners that were with them. Throughout history we can see rituals people used to cope with loss. Grieving varies by culture. As late as 1950 people in America would wear black for a year as a sign of grieving. By the 1980s people wore black to the funeral but that was only for one or two days. Today, a black garment is not expected as part of the funeral attire. After the day of the funeral no one would be reminded of the death by a person wearing black. We often expect the person experiencing loss to get over their grief right away. We sometimes get frustrated if the griever shows sadness for too long a period. It isn't healthy for the grieving person to pretend everything is all right. If the grief is ignored now, he or she will just experience it later in life.

People who experience loss go through stages of grieving. There is not a set pattern for every person's grieving process. What is important is that the person experiences most of the stages. It is also important for the griever to talk about what he or she is going through with a friend or a professional. If a person doesn't want to get better, he or she might remain in the stages of grief forever. A good guideline for grieving is one year of grieving for every five years spent with a significant person (example: spouse, mother, father, child). This loss can occur just as easily through divorce and take just as long or even longer than death to heal. Time doesn't heal. Only if a person makes a choice to get better can time help heal.

Context of Grief and Loss

I have found that during loss (sometimes a crisis) people either withdraw to cope or they talk incessantly. When someone is grieving, it is important for the helper to listen intently, show compassion, and be nonjudgmental. We cannot say one loss is greater than another one. The degree of grief and ability to cope depends upon the person and the circumstance.

Possible examples of loss:
- Death of a loved one
- Moving to a new area (loss of environment, friends, family, etc.)
- End of a relationship (not through death), such as divorce, even an engagement or dating breakup
- Losing a pet, family heirloom, or other treasured things
- Loss of a childhood (can occur when a parent expects a child to take on adult responsibilities for him or her; the child feels abandoned by the parent)
- Losing one's virginity (before marriage)
- Loss of a job
- Terminal illness
- Natural disaster
- Life with a depressed person[1]

It is vital that in loss (crisis) situations that the helper says what is helpful and knows when to be quiet and listen. You can give a person a choice, but ultimately he or she must make the decision. A few things to remember:

1. Encourage the helpee not to make any big decisions for a year after the pain (depending on how big the loss).
2. Do not be shocked by what the helpee says. If the person mentions wanting to end his or her life, of course take the proper steps. Talk to your supervisor. Call your local suicide hotline and do as they say. Call the police and do as they say. Document all that you do. Do not show shock. It just intensifies the issue in the helpee's mind. Realize that the helpee may not be rational at this time. It isn't worth it to argue about what is said. Just care.
3. Do not say, "I know how you feel." You *do not* know how the person feels. Saying that you do can hurt him or her further.
4. Do not say, "Don't worry, it will all work out." That can minimize the situation.
5. Do not say, "Let me tell you what happened to me." He or she does not want to hear about your past with grief.

6. Realize the helpee may talk about the pain over and over. Just listen.
7. Be sure to validate the pain. "I can see you are going through a lot of pain."

When a significant loss occurs, everyone goes through the stages of grief in some manner. I have seen some people who are blocked off to emotion due to a dysfunctional childhood and have never grieved. This does not occur that often. Sometimes people deny grief or try to block it off, feeling that they are OK only to find that they go through it later in life. They may feel that only weak people go through a grief process. It is very biblical to mourn and is needed for the body to heal emotionally.

> The Spirit of the Sovereign LORD is on me, because the LORD has anointed me to preach good news to the poor. He has sent me to bind up the brokenhearted, to proclaim freedom for the captives and release from darkness for the prisoners, to proclaim the year of the LORD's favor and the day of vengeance of our God, to comfort all who mourn, and provide for those who grieve in Zion—to bestow on them a crown of beauty instead of ashes, the oil of gladness instead of mourning, and a garment of praise instead of a spirit of despair. They will be called oaks of righteousness, a planting of the LORD for the display of his splendor. (Isa. 61:1-3)

(See pages 188-90 for this passage explained.)

Stages of Grief

Through life there are happy experiences and sorrowful ones. When sorrowful experiences take place, people begin to funnel through the stages of grief. They may or may not go through them in the following order. It is important that they don't get stuck too long in one stage. It is important that the helpee know that it is more normal to grieve than not to grieve.

- **Shock/surprise.** Finding out that a traumatic thing has occurred will produce shock and surprise. This may be evident through a complete loss of control and feelings of desperation.[2]
- **Denial.** Denial creates a cushion of time so that the impact of grief is delayed. It temporarily shelters the person from the suffocating pain. This stage is essential because it gives the person time to allow his or her strength to come back. This is also a time for the grieving person to draw helpful information and assistance from others, especially those who have dealt with similar situations.
- **Anger/bitterness.** Not only is anger a stage of grief, but it is also an expression of grief. It is important for the grieving to express their

sorrow through the expression of anger. It is healthy when it is focused on the pain and actions that have taken place.³
- **Withdrawal.** During this time the grieving person begins to withdraw from others, because of a drive to prevent further pain. The grieving person may also begin to deal with a rejection, feeling blame, and withdrawing from others.
- **Shame/guilt.** Self-condemnation can develop feelings of guilt. The individual might feel that he or she is at fault for the loss.
- **Depression.** As a necessary part of the grieving process, depression can help a person pull back emotionally in order to think through a situation. Depression can help a person cry out to God. As God heals the person and pulls him or her up from this difficult time, a feeling of acceptance and new hope comes.
- **Grief.** This stage involves the time of mourning. Every person grieves in a different way, but everyone who goes through pain has to mourn in one way or another. Some people do not feel comfortable openly grieving, while others rely on their friends and family to support them during their time of mourning. All the questions brought up through the depression stage need to be addressed before the person can move forward.
- **Acceptance.** There are only two resolutions that come out of grief: guilt, blame, and/or shame or letting go and accepting what has happened. The goal of the process is that the loss would be accepted and that the individual might be able to move on.

People who experience loss almost always go through these stages. They may not go through isolation or guilt, but they will go through the others. The pattern fluctuates also. A person may go in and out of the stages and not straight through them. They may delay in one stage and then come back to it again later.

Monthly and yearly cycles have affect on the intensity of grieving. Usually, since the person is in shock, the grief is mild to moderate. Within a week to a month grief is much more intense. At about six months the grief usually dissipates somewhat. By one year the grief may intensify to the amount of grief experienced in the first month of loss. The anniversary of the loss is very significant to the person's pain.

How Long Is Too Long to Grieve?

There comes a time that a person has to choose to accept the loss and move on. That time will be different for everyone. There is more concern, however, in stopping a person too soon from his or her grief than if he or she has been grieving too long. Sometimes those around us try to speed up the process by telling the hurting, "You should be over it by now." And the hurting sometimes feels there is something wrong with him or her because he or she can't seem to get through the loss. As a society, we are often not patient enough with those who have experienced loss.

Some people do carry this hurt too long and refuse to go on with life. It doesn't mean they can't love and still remember their loss but that they need to accept life as it is. "The LORD said to Samuel, 'How long will you mourn for Saul, since I have rejected him as king over Israel? Fill your horn with oil and be on your way; I am sending you to Jesse of Bethlehem. I have chosen one of his sons to be king'" (1 Sam. 16:1). In other words, it is time to stop and get on with life.

Encourage those who have lost loved ones to:
1. In time accept the loss
2. Not to make major decisions for a year
3. Not to date for at least a year
4. To talk about their loss
5. To recognize the highs and lows in loss, including the feelings that may come at holidays, anniversaries, and other important times
6. To find a hobby or something new in life

(See Steps to Assist the Helpee Out of Grief, page 182.)

Although grief is from an event or events, all of the common fruits can be a part of the process. The roots of rejection and unforgiveness can be a part as a fruit and not a root.

The chart on page 182 shows the patterns of the intensity of grief. The grieving cycle is not the same for everyone, however most people have intensity of grief similar to this chart. At the time of the event, intensity is not high because denial is protecting the person. As denial wears off, grief goes higher and then generally goes up and down by weeks or months until about four months. Usually about this time, life is becoming a little more stable and some things are getting back to normal. The intensity continues to go down through about six months.

After that the intensity of the pain starts going up until it reaches the anniversary of the event at one year. This is almost always the most painful time. The events of that time of year, the weather, the sounds, all bring remembrances that can be difficult to deal with. This all affects the intensity of grief. After the anniversary time, the intensity of the grief starts declining once again going much lower by eighteen months.

It is important to remember that people are diverse and grieve differently from loss. Some people always feel pain around the anniversary time of the loss. If it is a loss of a person that was very close to the grieving, they will most likely go through the grieving cycle to some extent one year for every five years they knew the person (approximate time).

Things that affect the grieving cycle for an individual:
- Cultural—what is accepted and expected
- Personal characteristics
- Home values
- How close the person was to the death, loss, and so forth
- Male/female
- What else was going on in the person's life

There are many things that can affect how long and to what extent a person grieves.

Understanding Mourning

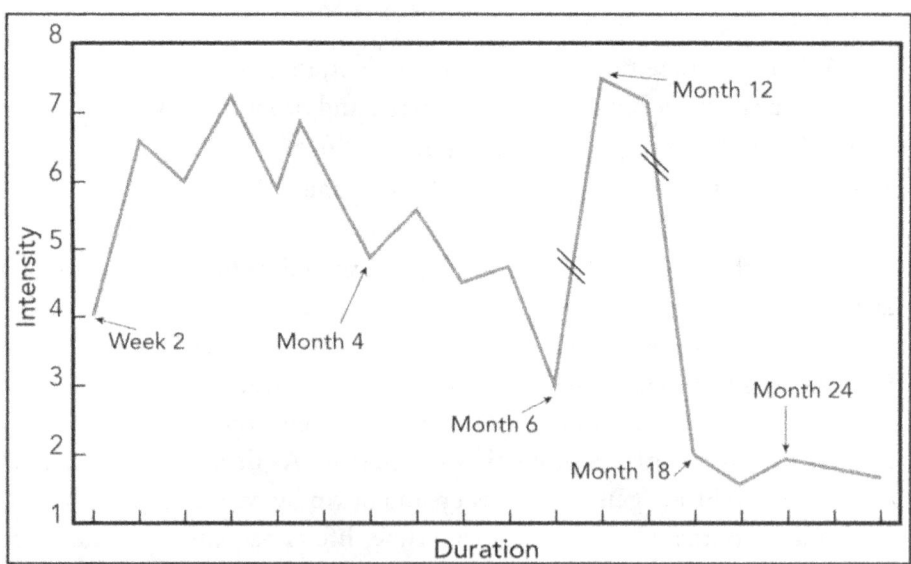

Adapted and reprinted from *Understanding Mourning* by Glen W. Davidson, copyright 1984 Augsburg Publishing House. Used by permission of Augsburg Fortress.

Steps to Assist the Helpee Out of Grief

1. Encourage the helpee to set small goals, such as reading their Bible each day, praying, and writing in a journal. Encourage him or her to take small steps in every area of life. If he or she is angry at God, have him or her read the relevant sections in chapter 3 and work on

choosing to want to forgive God (not for what He did but for what he or she feels He did). This may take time.
2. Help the helpee know that there is hope in Christ. Let him or her know that grief is a normal part of life. Share the phases of grief and encourage the helpee to identify where he or she is in the process. Let the helpee express loss in detail. This is very important.
3. Help the helpee in setting a new routine. They need to realize that grief can go away in time. He or she needs to understand the impact of the time of year, holidays, and special days. Help the helpee in assessing what he or she is doing and how to establish normalcy as much as possible.
4. Discuss the helpee's fears. If possible, help the person find a new group to spend time with. Encourage him or her to talk about the lost loved one and to remember the happy times.
5. Give the helpee hope through the Scriptures. It is imperative that the helper understand the various emotions that can go into grieving and how individuals grieve differently.
6. The helpee may have to work on self-esteem issues, guilt, unresolved anger, a feeling of rejection and even unforgiveness. Help him or her to explore each of those areas. See those chapters for help.

Questions to Ask the Helpee

- How are you dealing with your grief?
- How has this loss affected your everyday life?
- Are you taking time to share your feelings? With whom? How often?
- What seems the most difficult to deal with?
- What feelings are you experiencing?
- Where are you in the grief cycle?
- Do you have unforgiveness toward anyone in this process?
- Is guilt a part of your life? If so, explain.

Homework for the Helpee

1. Keep in prayer and in the Word regardless of whether you feel like it. If you are dealing with anger toward God, pray every day that you will want to forgive God (even though He didn't do this).
2. Keep track of your feelings by referring to the grieving cycle.
3. Make a memory book of pictures, memories, and personal items about the person lost. This gives the chance for the helpee to re-

member the person lost in a good way and gives him or her something to remember the person by.
4. Write a letter to the one you love, telling what he or she meant to you and say good-bye.
5. Often people don't take time to grieve, and they tell others that "everything is OK" when it isn't. Find at least one person you are willing to share your feelings with.
6. Take time out of your day to do something that makes you feel happy and good about yourself.
7. Journal the good times you had with the deceased person, and thank God for allowing you to have the time that you did to spend with him or her.
8. Have a regular exercise routine. Exercise reduces muscle tension, helps vent pent-up frustration, reduces insomnia, and has many other benefits.[4]
9. Do a Bible study on grief. How was it handled long ago? How to you think God looks at death?

Books for the Helpee

Black, Claudia, Ph.D. *Changing Course, Healing from Loss, Abandonment and Fear.* Center City, Minn.: Stanton Publication Services, Inc., 1999.

Detrich, Richard. *How to Recover from Grief.* Valley Forge, Pa.: Judson Press, May 1996.

Dobson, James. *When God Doesn't Make Sense.* Carol Stream, Ill.: Tyndale, 1997.

Freeman, Joel. *When Life Isn't Fair: Making Sense Out of Suffering.* Green Forest, Ark.: New Leaf Press. 2002.

Jacobs, Joy. *When God Seems Far Away.* Washington, D.C.: Daybreak Ministries, 1996.

Lewis, C. S. *The Problem of Pain.* New York: Harper Collins, 1996.

Rando, Therese. *How to Go on Living When Someone You Love Dies.* New York: Bantam Doubleday Dell Publishing, 1991.

Sissom, Ruth. *Moving Beyond Grief: Lessons from Those Who Have Lived Through Sorrow.* Grand Rapids: Discovery House Publishers, 1994.

Scriptures for the Helpee

Isaiah 61:1-3
The Spirit of the Sovereign LORD is on me, because the LORD has anointed me to preach good news to the poor. He has sent me to bind up the brokenhearted, to proclaim freedom for the captives and release from darkness for the prisoners, to proclaim the year of the LORD's favor and the day of vengeance of our God, to comfort all who mourn, and provide for those who grieve in Zion—to bestow on them a crown of beauty instead of ashes, the oil of gladness instead of mourning, and a garment of praise instead of a spirit of despair. They will be called oaks of righteousness, a planting of the LORD for the display of his splendor.

Psalm 34:18
The LORD is close to the brokenhearted and saves those who are crushed in spirit.

Isaiah 25:8
The Sovereign LORD will wipe away the tears from all faces.

Psalm 147:3
He heals the brokenhearted and binds up their wounds.

Isaiah 53:4
Surely he took up our infirmities and carried our sorrows.

Psalm 119:28
My soul is weary with sorrow; strengthen me according to your word.

Psalm 43:5
Why are you downcast, O my soul? Why so disturbed within me? Put your hope in God, for I will yet praise him, my Savior and my God.

Psalm 112:7
He will have no fear of bad news; his heart is steadfast, trusting in the LORD.

Ecclesiastes 3:1-2, 4
There is a time for everything, and a season for every activity under heaven: a time to be born and a time to die . . . a time to weep and a time to laugh, a time to mourn and a time to dance.

Psalm 30:11-12
You turned my wailing into dancing; you removed my sackcloth and clothed me with joy, that my heart may sing to you and not be silent.

Notes

1. H. Norman Wright, *Crisis Care: Hope for the Hurting* (Richardson, Tex.: Grace Products Corporation, 2002), 5.

2. Claudia Black, *Changing Course, Healing from Loss, Abandonment, and Fear* (Center City, Minn.: Hazelden Foundation, 2002), 115.

3. Ken Moses, "The Feeling Stages of Grief" (Carbondale, Ill.: Department of Education, Southern Illinois University).

4. Frank B. Minirth, M.D., and Paul D. Meier, M.D., *Happiness Is a Choice: A Manual on the Symptoms, Causes, and Cures of Depression* (Grand Rapids: Baker Book House, 2007), 167, 184.

15 – DIVORCE

Divorce is one of the most devastating, demoralizing, overwhelming, distressing, and destructive experiences one can have, especially accompanied by a partner having an affair. Divorce changes a person—he or she is never the same. The person can become hardened and closed off. If the person wasn't independent, he or she has to learn fast. Some who have difficulty with their own needs end up in a relationship right away. God is the miracle worker however, and what was meant for harm will be used for good. Genesis 50:20 is true. The victim must learn to praise and trust God through this very difficult time.

Sometimes the church doesn't know quite what to do with those in this situation. We as the church need to love these people as ones who lost a loved one through death. We need to be there without judgment. We need to be there to help them heal.

Context: Understanding the Divorced

Three Things Each Divorced Person Will Deal With
1. Experiencing loneliness—from guilt, anger, depression, withdrawal, and failed relationships. The inner world of the divorced includes feelings of devastation and hopelessness.
2. Feeling that they have failed God (failed relationship with God).
3. Receiving judgment from Christians.

Divorce Produces Three Immediate Results

1. **An everlasting scar.** This can be healed but as with a physical scar, there is always a reminder. Life is never the same. It can be better in time but doesn't feel that way in the beginning.
2. **A stigma.** Divorce definitely carries a feeling of dishonor, a feeling of being different. Some people feel they are second rate.
3. **A changed state in relationships.** Usually one's couple friends tend to "fall off" and new relationships with single people will begin. This is a very difficult and confusing time.

To help the divorced we need to see what Isa. 61:1-3 says and put it into action:

> The Spirit of the Sovereign LORD is on me, because the LORD has anointed me to preach good news to the poor. He has sent me to bind up the brokenhearted, to proclaim freedom for the captives and release from darkness for the prisoners, to proclaim the year of the LORD's favor and the day of vengeance of our God, to comfort all who mourn, and provide for those who grieve in Zion—to bestow on them a crown of beauty instead of ashes, the oil of gladness instead of mourning, and a garment of praise instead of a spirit of despair. They will be called oaks of righteousness, a planting of the LORD for the display of his splendor.

"Preach the good news." The good news is that with the issue of divorce there is hope for healing and a way to get through the trauma. But before we can share the good news with the divorced, we need to examine our own hearts. Before we can help we must be free of preconditioned ideas that the divorced person did something to make his or her spouse leave. There are many reasons why a person leaves. People are less willing to tolerate an unsatisfactory marriage than ever before. The ideology of marriage has become increasingly hedonistic, focusing on what brings pleasure rather than faithfulness and commitment. With the increasing availability of pornographic material, there are more and more people who are looking for another high and are finding it outside their own marriage. We must not pronounce judgment on those who are experiencing divorce.

"Bind up the brokenhearted." "Bind" denotes a commitment to defend or oversee a broken heart, not put a bandage on it. A bandage simply says to the hurting, "Oh, I hope things get better. I will pray for you." What we need to give the divorced is a safeguard: "I may not understand, but I support you. You can trust me to help you through this. I will not abandon you."

It means more than words. It means phone calls, visits, and listening to the same story time and time again. It may mean helping with household repairs or helping with a financial need.

"Proclaim freedom for the captives." "Freedom" does not necessarily mean freedom from an ex-spouse or freedom to love again. It means freedom from the bondage that failure brings. Those in the church who have spouses leave them not only feel they have failed in the relationship but feel they have failed God and the church. They feel they will never again be a whole person—one who is free from the past. God forgives. We cannot keep reminding the divorced of their past. We must extend loving acceptance as a person.

"Comfort all who mourn." There is no grief quite like the grief of those who go through divorce. Their grief is not only for the loss of a person and the death of dreams for the future but the loss of trust, loss of belief in marriage, and often a loss of friends. "Comfort" indicates a strengthening and uplifting of the spirit.

Those who have lost a spouse need a time to mourn. It takes about one year (for every five years with the person) to go through the grieving process before going on with life. We must be patient with the person as he or she goes through emotional ups and downs.

Dealing with anger and unforgiveness are all part of this process. Forgiveness may take nine to twelve months, even with daily prayer for those who have caused hurt. Time does not always bring healing. Choosing to forgive and bless those who hurt us will bring change. Our job is to pray, guide, and be patient with the hurting.

"Bestow on them a crown of beauty instead of ashes." "Ashes" signify being covered with grief. Yet this verse says we are to bestow "a crown of beauty" to the hurting.

Wearing a crown of beauty depicts giving value and honor to someone, especially after all feelings of worth have been ripped away. We need not be afraid that this step endorses divorce.

"Bestow on them a garment of praise instead of a spirit of despair." "Despair" pictures a depth of suffering that many of us will never encounter. The remorse and regret of things not done seem to bring a pervasive spirit of depression. What a complete opposite we see when someone is clothed in praise. We must guide hurting people to praise and worship God, regardless of their feelings. Praising God wins the battle and moves us out of despair (2 Chron. 20:17-22).

We must encourage the divorced to make choices that will move them step-by-step to complete healing. Encouraging includes modeling optimism in what God can and will do. It means never giving up on them.

"They will be called oaks of righteousness." If people truly heal from life-changing traumas, they can be a source of strength to the church. No one can provide hope to the divorced more than one who has already been through the suffering and has not only survived but learned to live full of the joy of the Lord.

If we will stop expecting less from those who have experienced pain and instead encourage them to reach for their potential, the hurting will find their potential; they will find the untapped inner strength that will minister to others. "The LORD is close to the brokenhearted and saves those who are crushed in spirit" (Ps. 34:18).

Characteristics of a Person Going Through Divorce

1. Feels like life and everything believed in has been ripped out from underneath him or her.
2. Feel abandoned not just from the former spouse but from others.
3. Has grief over the loss of a marriage and will experience the grieving process. (See Grief and Loss.)
4. Has a loss of self-esteem, feeling like a failure in life.
5. Experiences increasing loneliness.
6. Feels overloaded with all the tasks to run a home and raise children.
7. Feels frustration with the prospect of possibly dating again.
8. Experiences a lot of anger toward the ex-spouse. Often the anger becomes depression.
9. Finds life in general difficult, often overwhelming to deal with. Many changes take place making it difficult to adjust to life.
10. Has a need to tell and retell his or her story over and over again.
11. Needs a lot of validation for the pain.
12. Experiences a multitude of feelings from hate to great loss of the love that he or she once had.
13. May feel guilt over what he or she could have done during the marriage.
14. May feel the desire to take revenge on the ex-spouse.

When Parents of the Divorced (Adult Child) Get Involved with the Ex-Spouse

Sometimes the parent of a divorced person has a need to stay friends with the ex-spouse. The parent's need to maintain friendship with the ex-spouse will often alienate his or her own adult child. When a parent takes interest in the ex-spouse, it is often seen as a betrayal by the adult child. It may even feel like abandonment because the ex-spouse is being valued and shown respect. The hurt of the adult child will seem minimized by the parents.

It is difficult for someone going through divorce, in the midst of great pain, to see how their parent values them and cares about their hurt when that same parent is seeking friendship with the source of the adult child's pain.

Whether or not the parents agree with the divorce and/or how it came about, this is the time to totally support the adult child or the parents will end up pushing him or her away, sometimes forever.

Questions to Ask Yourself in Ministry and Helping Positions

1. Have I done everything I can to help marriages by having extensive engagement helping in the church?
2. Have I done everything within my power to save this marriage?
3. Are both parties willing to work at the marriage?
4. If one party is having an affair, is he or she truly repentant and willing to break it off?
5. If physical and or verbal abuse is involved, is the party willing to have extensive helping?
6. If one or both parties insist on the divorce, have I made them fully aware of the possible consequences and long-lasting effects to their lives?
7. Regardless of their choice, as a helper, have I given them unconditional positive regard, unconditional acceptance, and am I willing to help them as they progress through some difficult stages toward recovery?

What About the Children?

Children definitely suffer through their parents' divorce. Their entire life and what they believe in has been ripped out from underneath them. Life will never be the same. It doesn't have to remain difficult though. In time, children can heal. Most of the healing process will depend on the parents.

1. Parents should not talk badly about each other in front of the children. Children shouldn't be asked to spy on the other parent or told secrets that they must keep from the other parent.
2. Parents need to give their children freedom to talk about how they feel about what is going on. The children's feelings need to be validated. Answer questions as well as possible yet protect them from hurt. Children usually figure out what happened, so being truthful and open is most often the best mode. How much you can tell depends on maturity and age. Asking them what questions they have is better than just telling everything. Use wisdom for your situation. Listen to your child talk.
3. Parents need to make sure that their children know the children did not have anything to do with the breakup.
4. Parents need to keep their financial issues (child support) between each other and not discuss money issues with the children.
5. Parents should not lean on one of their children to support them emotionally. Children should not have to hear about a parent's hurt in the divorce. Children are not there to support the parent. It is the other way around.
6. Parents need to keep discipline the same at each of the homes. Children should not be indulged materially or given their way because of the divorce. Life needs to be the same as it was as much as possible. Parents should have a united front to benefit the children.
7. Love is given daily, reassuring that things will get better. A feeling of security and safety must be given in order for the children to heal. They need to hear words of comfort and hope. They need to know that their parents will always be there for them and that they will get through this hard time.
8. Parents need to be extremely careful if they start to date. This is disruptive to the children's lives. There needs to be at least a year or two of healing before dating. Then as the parent dates the child's needs, feelings, and concerns need to be attended to with respect.
9. Parents need to recognize that they are the parents, not the children. If their children reject them through hurt, the parents need to be mature enough to keep loving unconditionally.
10. If a parent says, "Oh, my children are fine. They are doing OK," they are either totally unaware of the real issues or are in denial. Denial will prevent the children from healing.

Children need time to grieve the loss of a family as they knew it. They need to be able to voice their fears and frustrations (respectfully). Children need to recognize that they weren't to blame for the breakup. They also need to recognize their anger, however the anger expresses itself, and find ways to deal with it. If a child is having great anxiety, he or she may need to see a counselor with experience working with children. Insecurity is common among children of divorce. Unless the child can talk it through with someone and be aware of these issues, he or she will take it into future relationships.

Characteristics of Children Going Through Their Parents' Divorce
1. Abandonment
2. Anxiety and insecurity (fear) over the future
3. Anger toward the situation and often anger toward one parent
4. Depression
5. Grief over the loss of their parents living together
6. Self-blame
7. Rejection from the parent that left the home
8. Embarrassment that their parents divorced
9. Insecurity
10. Feelings of inadequacy
11. Low self-esteem
12. Can leave a hole in their personality where no matter what a parent, future spouse, and so forth, do for them, it is never enough (like a hole that cannot be filled)

All of the common fruits are possible in the event of divorce. Rejection, unforgiveness, pride, perfectionism, rebellion, and sometimes a dysfunctional home can develop more as a fruit.

Help parents realize that if they will always do what is in their children's best interest they can help the child heal. They should not cater to or discipline too little or too much but always show love, respect, and value to the child. They need to allow their children to talk about the divorce and answer questions in wisdom. Reading *The Gift of the Blessing* by Gary Smalley and John Trent would be one of the best things a parent could do for their children.

Steps to Assist the Helpee Out of the Hurt of Divorce

First, suggest to the person to read *Growing Through Divorce* by Jim Smoke. He or she may also need to work through the steps in the Forgiveness/Rejection section. Also guide him or her in the stages of grief. The person will most likely experience all of the stages.

1. Help divorced helpee learn to take time to heal. Help him or her know that time is a healer only if he or she wants it to be. The choice is up to the helpee. It will take time to heal, but there does come a time when he or she needs to *move on and let go of the past.*

   This is not the time to make decisions. The helpee needs to wait a minimum of one year before making *major* decisions. Emotional decisions made before one year are often disastrous.

   Let the helpee see the information in chapter 14 on the stages of grief so that he or she can understand what he or she is going through. Help the helpee understand the grieving process. Let him or her chart where he or she is from week to week.

2. Tell the helpee to let go of the past. The usual time for healing is one year for every five years the helpee was close to the person. However, there does have to be a conscious choice to let go and move on. Help him or her recognize attitude, anger, guilt, loss of control, stress, loneliness, and depression. All these areas are important and may need to be worked on periodically. Depression is very normal at this time. There are behavioral things that a person can do that will help as he or she continues through the process. See homework on depression.

3. Accept life as it is. This is probably the most difficult step. Help the helpee to accept that God will use all things for our good if we let Him (see Rom. 8:28). "Give thanks in all circumstances, for this is God's will for you in Christ Jesus" (1 Thess. 5:18).

4. Help the helpee to formulate short-term goals. If he or she has difficulty, help him or her to visualize where he or she wants to be in one year. If the helpee doesn't progress with goals, he or she will be in the very same place—miserable. Part of this is taking responsibility for self. From this the helpee needs to learn as much as possible about self and where he or she wants to go.

5. In time, guide the helpee toward forgiving all of those who caused the hurt. The helpee may have to start with praying that he or she will want to forgive and may also need to forgive himself or herself. Anger with God will also need to be addressed.

6. Guide the helpee in growth—spiritual, physical, emotional, and social. He or she needs to see this as a new beginning, a possibility of growth and some good changes.[1]

7. Healing can take place in time. Guide the helpee toward praising God for how he or she is now. Encourage him or her to pray for those who have caused the hurt.

This is a good time for the helpee to work on practical issues, such as other relationships, how he or she is dealing with the children, other rejection issues, and any issues that existed before marriage. *Growing Through Divorce* by Jim Smoke is a must for people going through divorce.

Questions to Ask the Helpee

- When I say the name of your spouse, what emotions come to mind?
- How often do you think of your spouse? What do you think?
- What makes you really angry now? How often do you feel this way?
- What are things that give you comfort at this time?
- How are you taking care of yourself in this situation?
- What are you doing for yourself for fun?
- What do you want to change in your life now?
- What is your self-talk like?
- How often do you tell someone your story about divorce?

Look at the root of rejection and unforgiveness.

Homework for the Helpee

1. Work on having daily devotions. Start in Psalms and Proverbs (preferably one chapter a day). Also, read a chapter in one of the Gospels.
2. Read *Growing Through Divorce* by Jim Smoke.
3. Write in a journal—writing can be helpful at this time.
4. Start on an exercise program. Start with twenty minutes every other day.
5. Find a hobby or sign up for a class that you would enjoy.
6. Do one good or fun thing for yourself a day (within reason). Reward yourself when you reach a goal.
7. Write a letter to your spouse (that you don't send), telling all of your feelings.
8. Plan personal time once a week to go to a movie or lunch with a friend.

9. Work on establishing your own identity apart from your former spouse. Change your names on credit cards, checks, and bank accounts.
10. Evaluate what your children are going through and things you can do to help them.
11. Look at forgiveness, God's forgiveness of you and your forgiveness of those who hurt you.
12. Set goals for the future. Set goals to get you through the next week. Set emotional, spiritual, and physical goals.
13. Look at the stages of grief and how you are working through the loss. Keep track of where you are on a grief chart.

Books for the Helpee

Anderson, Neil T. *The Bondage Breaker.* Eugene, Oreg.: Harvest House Publishers, 1993.

Backus, William. *Telling Yourself the Truth.* Minneapolis: Bethany House Publishers, 1980.

Caruthers, Merlin. *Power in Praise.* Wheaton, Ill.: Tyndale House, 1971.

Cloud, Henry, and John Townsend. *Safe People.* Grand Rapids: Zondervan Publishing House, 1995.

Dobson, James. *Love Must Be Tough: New Hope for Marriages in Crisis.* Colorado Springs: Multnomah Publishers Inc., 2003.

Smoke, Jim. *Growing Through Divorce.* Eugene, Oreg.: Harvest House Publishers, 1986.

_____. *Suddenly Single.* Westwood, N.J.: Fleming Revell Company, 1973.

Smedes, Lewis B. *The Art of Forgiving.* Nashville: Ballantine Publishing Group, Random House, Inc., 1996.

Scriptures for the Helpee

Psalm 34:18
The LORD is close to the brokenhearted and saves those who are crushed in spirit.

Isaiah 54:4-8
"Do not be afraid; you will not suffer shame. Do not fear disgrace; you will not be humiliated. You will forget the shame of your youth and remember no more the reproach of your widowhood. For your Maker is your husband—the LORD Almighty is his name—the Holy One of Israel is your Redeemer; he is called the God of all the earth. The LORD will call you back as if you were a wife deserted and distressed in spirit—a wife who married young, only to be rejected," says your God. "For a brief moment I abandoned you, but with deep compassion I will bring you back. In a surge of anger I hid my face from you for a moment, but with everlasting kindness I will have compassion on you," says the LORD your Redeemer.

Isaiah 51:12-16
I, even I, am he who comforts you. Who are you that you fear mortal men, the sons of men, who are but grass, that you forget the LORD your Maker, who stretched out the heavens and laid the foundations of the earth, that you live in constant terror every day because of the wrath of the oppressor, who is bent on destruction? For where is the wrath of the oppressor? The cowering prisoners will soon be set free; they will not die in their dungeon, nor will they lack bread. For I am the LORD your God, who churns up the sea so that its waves roar—the LORD Almighty is his name. I have put my words in your mouth and covered you with the shadow of my hand—I who set the heavens in place, who laid the foundations of the earth, and who say to Zion, "You are my people."

Isaiah 49:15-21
"Can a mother forget the baby at her breast and have no compassion on the child she has borne? Though she may forget, I will not forget you! See, I have engraved you on the palms of my hands; your walls are ever before me. Your sons hasten back, and those who laid you waste depart from you. Lift up your eyes and look around; all your sons gather and come to you. As surely as I live," declares the LORD, "you will wear them all as ornaments; you will put them on, like a bride. Though you were ruined and made desolate and your land laid waste, now you will be too small for your people, and those who devoured you will be far away. The children born during your bereavement will yet say in your hearing, 'This place is too small for us; give us more space to live in.' Then you will say in your heart, 'Who bore me these? I was bereaved and barren; I was exiled and rejected. Who brought these up? I was left all alone, but these—where have they come from?'"

Isaiah 41:8-16
"But you, O Israel, my servant, Jacob, whom I have chosen, you descendants of Abraham my friend, I took you from the ends of the earth, from its farthest corners I called you. I said, 'You are my servant'; I have chosen you and have not rejected you. So do not fear, for I am with you; do not be dismayed, for I am your God. I will

strengthen you and help you; I will uphold you with my righteous right hand. All who rage against you will surely be ashamed and disgraced; those who oppose you will be as nothing and perish. Though you search for your enemies, you will not find them. Those who wage war against you will be as nothing at all. For I am the LORD, your God, who takes hold of your right hand and says to you, Do not fear; I will help you. Do not be afraid, O worm Jacob, O little Israel, for I myself will help you," declares the LORD, your Redeemer, the Holy One of Israel.

Isaiah 62:3-4
You will be a crown of splendor in the LORD's hand, a royal diadem in the hand of your God. No longer will they call you Deserted, or name your land Desolate. But you will be called Hephzibah, and your land Beulah; for the LORD will take delight in you, and your land will be married.

Jeremiah 30:17
"But I will restore you to health and heal your wounds," declares the LORD, "because you are called an outcast, Zion for whom no one cares."

Genesis 50:20
You intended to harm me, but God intended it for good to accomplish what is now being done, the saving of many lives.

Romans 8:28
And we know that in all things God works for the good of those who love him, who have been called according to his purpose.

Matthew 10:30-31
And even the very hairs of your head are all numbered. So don't be afraid; you are worth more than many sparrows.

1 John 1:9
If we confess our sins, he is faithful and just and will forgive us our sins and purify us from all unrighteousness.

Job 5:19
From six calamities he will rescue you; in seven no harm will befall you.

Joel 2:25
I will repay you for the years the locusts have eaten—the great locust and the young locust, the other locusts and the locust swarm.

Notes

1. Jim Smoke, *Growing Through Divorce* (Eugene, Oreg.: Harvest House Publishers, 1986), 85-86.

16 – AFFAIRS

No one can know the devastation from an affair unless he or she has experienced it. It is like having everything you once believed was true stripped away. A person's entire view of the world changes. Life is not the same. It is not secure. A person feels rejection, betrayal, and helplessness. Hope has disappeared. Restoration is vital. Trust needs to be restored. This process can take anywhere from one year to many years. The one betrayed is fragile. *What you say and don't say can make all the difference in the world. Don't blame the betrayed because of the affair. If you blame the betrayed, you are letting the betrayer go free.*

    Perhaps this illustration will help. Imagine you are on top of a hill and someone pushes you off the edge. You fall all the way down the hill, becoming bruised and wounded. You look for someone safe to help you but instead you hear, "Why did you fall down the hill? Don't you know how to be careful?" You are now confused, betrayed, and hurt. The one on the top of the hill who pushed you is confused too. The pusher knew what he or she was doing was wrong but didn't care enough to stop. He or she was just hoping not to be caught. Now the pusher has an excuse for the sin—those who finally come to help you think it is your fault.

    If you have ever been betrayed and were blamed instead of restored, you know this story well. We must be messengers of hope, health, and safety, not blame.

Gary Collins speaks of the reasons for affairs in his book *Family Shock*:

> When asked the reasons why they were involved in adultery, a large group of people who had been involved in affairs replied that they were unfaithful because of their sexual frustration, curiosity, desire for revenge, boredom, need for acceptance and recognition, depression, urges for sex without intimacy, and escape. Affairs also come because some people are addicted to compulsive sex, to romance, or even to relationships. In a detailed description of how even Christians get hooked on sex, psychologist Grant Martin shows how some people get so caught up in adulterous behavior that they become like drug addicts—powerless to stop without help.[1]

Context: Understanding the World of Affairs

While it is difficult to pinpoint the exact percentage of those Christians or non-Christians who become involved in affairs, some statistics are as follows:

- "Conservative estimates are that 60% of men and 40% of women will have an extramarital affair."[2]
- Sixty percent of men and as many as 40 percent of women will have an extramarital affair.[3]
- Ten percent of adultery victims claim to be Christians and the cheating spouse attends church or religious activities. One to 5 percent of adulterers are pastors or clergy.[4]

The number of affairs each year is *not* decreasing. The media continues to portray the excitement of having an affair. Also, morals are not being taught in many homes. Some understand the pain and devastation of an extramarital affair and can see the downward spiral the unfaithful take. How should we as leaders in the church guide the flock to keep these statistics from being a part of our own church?

Understanding the Descent of Adultery

Having an affair is not something a true Bible-believing Christian sets out to do. We must, however, be aware that none of us are above temptation or the possibility of having an affair.

1. **The first problem is thinking that we are above succumbing to temptation.** First Corinthians 10:12 admonishes us to take heed lest we fall into temptation.

2. **Daniel 7:25 says that Satan's strategy is to wear out the saints.** Satan does this by setting up the perfect circumstance to promote failure, and then adds stress, fatigue, and frustration, giving a person clouded judgment and a weakened will.
3. **The gradual descent toward an affair always includes the eye gate (seeing someone and being tempted) and goes to the mind.** For a person to actually consummate the affair, he or she has allowed the thought processes to become part of the spirit.
4. **There is a decline in one's spiritual life.** The desire has been entertained and has gone from the mind into the heart. What was wrong before is now excused. What was forbidden is now a possibility. With this change in thinking, statements will be made, "Well, that's not the worst sin" referring to almost anything that is clearly wrong, particularly the sin of adultery. It almost seems as if saying it out loud makes it true.
5. **In the descent of an affair there is always some blame placed on the adulterer's spouse.** The blame starts long before the actual affair. The adulterer has inner frustrations and begins seeing his or her spouse in a different light—a tainted light that focuses on what is wrong with the spouse, not what is right.

    Frustration is also apparent in spouses having affairs by the inner turmoil and guilt produced by going against what they know is right. This frustration grows into anger and soon irrational thoughts are used as leverage to prove that the marriage is failing. "You cause me so much anger, I have to leave." This type of irrational thinking can actually culminate to this scenario: One man who desired an affair actually told his wife that he would fast to see if it was God's will to leave her for another woman.
6. **When people get to the point of praying about leaving, they have been deceived and have rationalized any behavior to the point that they will actually believe there is a justification in adulterous actions.** That descent in thinking seems to mark a "point of no return," a point where the affair will be culminated.

Taking Action as a Pastor

1. Stay daily in the Word and prayer. Be alert to your own sexual issues and needs. Clarity in your own life will give you greater insight into the needs of others.
2. Know you are not beyond temptation. Be an example of sexual purity. One of the best ways to guide the flock is to demonstrate love

to your own wife in your actions and speech. People need hope that their marriage can be good.

3. Be alert to your congregation's needs. Tune into body language and the dynamics of relationships. Hear with your heart what people say. Do we miss what people are really saying and feeling because we are too busy?

4. Teach on the downward spiral and consequences of sexual sin. Speak gently but firmly in regards to the tug the world puts in our hearts to stray. Dr. Jack W. Hayford, president, International Foursquare Churches, says in his sermon on "Why Sex Sins Are Worse than Others" that sexual immorality by a believer prostitutes the Body of Jesus. He goes on to explain that the pain and devastation brought about through an adulterous act does not merely affect those immediately involved but affects the entire Body of Christ. It wounds us all.[5] Therefore an adulterer must be quickly confronted in order to bring healing to the entire church. Silence will not bring healing. When sin such as this is ignored, it can pollute the hearts and minds of those in the church.

5. We must provide a place of healing for the wounded, the brokenhearted, and the guilty to be effective in the church. Jesus cared for and ministered to the sick, the lame, and the brokenhearted. He spoke judgment to those who sat in judgment over others.

    a. Be ready to help bring healing to those marriages that have been wounded and to bring healing to those who have been the victim of betrayal without judgment. Patriarchal custom has often given his wife's deficiencies as a reason a man has an affair. Many people also believe that having an affair is a normal response to an imperfect marriage and is, by definition, the marriage partner's fault. Friends often encourage the unfaithful one to put the blame on the spouse.[6] However, we must not abuse the victim by placing the blame on him or her.

    b. Bring restoration to those who have fallen. Christ always spoke to sin and gave the opening for repentance and a time to experience forgiveness. Forgiveness can occur quickly if there is an immediate forsaking of the third party by the adulterer.

    Although there is also hurt on the part of the adulterer (which often started before marriage), the adulterer must be willing to repent and take full responsibility for his or her actions. He or she must recognize the progression of decisions that brought him or her to the adulterous act. The devastation from continual affair(s) may be so great, the wounds may be so deep, and the lack of trust so compounded that chances for healing the marriage may be almost nonexistent. We can, however, bring hope that life in Christ can begin anew.

All of the common fruits are normal to the event and process of divorce.

Steps to Assist the Helpee Through the Betrayal of an Affair

Most affairs are born out of a lack of commitment on the part of the betrayer. The betrayer turned outward to solve issues rather than inward. Out-of-control lust can also be a big part of affairs (see sexual addiction). Everyone contributes to the problems in a marriage in some way. There are issues that always need to be addressed. Make sure in that process that you do not blame the victim for *causing* the affair. You are bringing insult to injury.

Never ask: What did you do to make your spouse leave? People have affairs for many reasons, however there is no excuse. As Shirley Glass, Ph.D., put it in "Shattered Vows" "people think a person having an affair isn't getting enough at home. The truth is, the person isn't giving enough."[7]

Regardless of the reason, there has been moral compromise and deception. Life as the betrayed knew it has been violated. The betrayed has wounds that need to be healed.

First Session
1. Don't feel you have to walk on eggshells with the hurt person. Just make sure he or she feels comfortable with you, trusts you, and believes that you can empathize with the pain. Let the betrayed know that you see the pain and you know that his or her entire world has been ripped apart. (It is also a time that decisions shouldn't be made and absolute statements should not be said; i.e., "I never want to see you.")
2. First deal with just the pain, the details of survival at home. The unfaithful one is usually the one walking on eggshells. Help the couple find ways to survive day by day.
3. Next, deal with the one who had the affair. Help him or her see the other's destroyed world and the difficulty in regaining trust. See how willing he or she is to work on the relationship. Hopefully the unfaithful one will see the need to humbly ask for forgiveness. At this time do not deal with his or her frustrations with the marriage.

Help him or her understand the need to listen to the spouse and be there until the spouse heals.

4. Then, deal with the one who feels betrayed. Help the betrayed realize that in time he or she will need to forgive. It will be difficult, but in order for the relationship to survive, he or she needs to think toward that end. Also, see how willing the betrayed is to save the marriage and to work toward the healing process. Allow times to vent to the spouse but not all the time. That can be overwhelming to the betrayer.

5. Give them a set time to discuss these issues—possibly twice a week. Give them rules to help them in setting limits for talking about this painful subject. Help them know that a total healing can take one to three years (with work). Are they willing to work hard on this and never give up?

Second Session

1. Observe their progress. What is difficult for each? What do they need to survive? Help them especially in the little things day by day.

2. Deal with the forgiveness issue in small bites. Let the unfaithful party tell what led him or her down this road. In other words, is there anything that can be said to help the betrayed understand a little of the downward trend? Don't expect the betrayed to "just understand." The unfaithful spouse needs to take the responsibility and the blame. If the unfaithful tries to put the blame on the faithful spouse, the marriage *will not* heal.

   Be sure to validate the pain of the betrayed. Understand the need to vent and to express anger. Don't feed the anger, but let the betrayed know he or she certainly has a right to be angry but in time will have to let it go *if* they are going to heal—with or without the spouse. Healing can only take place by forgiving the betrayer.

3. The betrayed needs to have a time once or twice a week to vent or express hurt to the spouse. The unfaithful one needs to listen without becoming defensive. The unfaithful spouse needs to show love and support and let the spouse know that he or she will never be unfaithful again. (This needs to be said over and over as long as the betrayed spouse needs to hear it.)

4. In time, you will need to deal with what *both* of them need to do to improve the marriage. You have to gauge this by: (1) how long the betrayed has known about the affair; (2) how much the couple has

discussed this issue; (3) how much the betrayed has dealt with forgiving; and (4) the attitude and total repentance of the unfaithful. The issues in the marriage may have to wait until some forgiveness and adjustment have taken place related to the affair.

Dos and Don'ts of Guiding Helpee Through the Crisis of an Affair

1. Do not expect the helpee whose spouse has been unfaithful to forgive instantly. Be patient. It takes time to digest the shock and hurt. Understand the helpee's need to withdraw emotionally. As you give the helpee time, encourage him or her to (*choose to*) forgive the spouse.
2. Do not blame the affair on the faithful spouse, giving reasons why he or she may have caused this to happen. *Do not ask the helpee what he or she did to make the spouse leave!* This adds insult to injury. A person chooses to have an affair out of his or her own free will. Satan sets up the perfect circumstances.
3. Do not say right away, "This is the problem . . . causing the affair and you both need to work on these issues." Give it a little time before you start working toward reconciling the problems in the marriage before the affair. There needs to be time to grieve, to hurt, and to heal.
4. Make sure the unfaithful spouse is truly repentant and ready to do what it takes to help the marriage heal. Speak to the *sin*. Are they going to be patient and understanding of their hurt spouse or impatient wanting to forget it?
5. If the couple can decide to work through this hurtful act but the hurt continues to pop up, give safe ways to converse.
6. There is *no* slow process for letting the unfaithful one break off the adulterous relationship. Encourage a quick and final break off. Nothing else will work.
7. If a couple decides that they want a divorce, encourage them to try and work it out. If they can't work it out over time, can you truly support them and help them heal in their decision? (You may not agree with their decision, but you can help them heal.)

Questions to Ask the Helpee

- What other times have you been betrayed?
- How long has this been going on? (If it is as recent as a few weeks, the helpee is probably not ready to decide how committed he or she wants to be to the relationship or if he or she is ready to forgive.)

- How long have you known?
- What are your feelings right now?
- What do you need your spouse to do to help you through this?
- What are you most angry about?

Questions to Ask the One Who Had the Affair
- How committed are you to this relationship?
- Do you feel you have taken full responsibility for the pain you have caused?
- Explain how you think your spouse is feeling right now.
- What are the other times you have been unfaithful (even in dating)?
- Are you willing to let your spouse express the pain he or she is feeling once or twice a week until he or she can move onward?
- Do you feel you have fully repented?

Homework for the Helpee

The Betrayed

1. Write a letter telling about all your anger. Do not feel you need to hold back. You do not have to give this letter to your spouse.
2. Possibly set aside two times a week that the topic of the affair can be discussed. Set up guidelines with your helper as to specific times to converse in the right setting.
3. Write out what you want to be different in the marriage. Write out what you can't live with at this time—what things bother you too much.
4. Work on areas of your self-esteem by watching your self-talk. Also, see the list of books to read.
5. In time you will need to work on the homework in chapter 3 to set about forgiving your spouse.

The Unfaithful (If pornography is an issue, see chapter 18, "Sexual Addiction.")

1. Write a letter to your spouse telling of your feelings. This letter needs to be humble and repentant. This isn't the time for talking about your own hurt.
2. Pray each day that the Lord will help you to forgive yourself. Stay in the Word every day. A suggestion is to read a psalm, a proverb, and several chapters out of the Book of John each day. Be in prayer for your marriage.

3. Each day look for something good in your spouse and write him or her a note about it or just tell your spouse the things you love about him or her.
4. Give your spouse time to grieve and heal. Do not be demanding or pushy. Understand your spouse's need to "talk things out."
5. Decide what you want to change in the marriage and what changes you need to work on.

Books for the Helpee

For the Betrayed

Abrahms-Spring, Janis. *After the Affair: Healing the Pain and Rebuilding Trust When a Partner Has Been Unfaithful*. New York: Harper-Collins, 1996.

Backus, William. *Telling Yourself the Truth*. Minneapolis: Bethany House Publishers, 1980.

Carder, Dave. *Torn Asunder: Recovering from Extramarital Affairs*. Chicago: Moody, 1992.

Carnes, Patrick. *Facing the Shadow: Starting Sexual and Relationship Recovery*. Carefree, Ariz.: Gentle Path Press, 2001.

Caruthers, Merlin. *Power in Praise*. Wheaton, Ill.: Tyndale House, 1971.

Dobson, James. *Love Must Be Tough: New Hope for Marriages in Crisis*. Colorado Springs: Multnomah Publishers, Inc., 2003.

McGee, Robert S. *The Search for Significance*. Nashville: Thomas Nelson, 2003.

Shriver, Gary and Mona. *Unfaithful: Rebuilding Trust After Infidelity*. Colorado Springs: Life Journey, 2005.

Smedes, Lewis B. *The Art of Forgiving*. Nashville: Ballantine Publishing Co., Random House, Inc., 1996.

For the Betrayer

Anderson, Nancy C. *Avoiding the Greener Grass Syndrome*. Grand Rapids: Kregel, 2004.

McGee, Robert S. *The Search for Significance*. Nashville: Thomas Nelson, 2003.

Pearlman, Ann. *Infidelity: A Love Story*. New York: Broadway Books, 2000.

Roberts, Ted. *Pure Desire: Helping People Break Free from Sexual Struggles*. Ventura, Calif.: Regal Books, 1999.

Shriver, Gary and Mona. *Unfaithful: Rebuilding Trust After Infidelity*. Colorado Springs: Life Journey, 2005.

Weiss, Douglas. *Sex, Men and God*. Lake Mary, Fla.: Charisma House, 2002.

Scriptures for the Helpee

For the Betrayed

Isaiah 61:1-3
The Spirit of the Sovereign LORD is on me, because the LORD has anointed me to preach good news to the poor. He has sent me to bind up the brokenhearted, to proclaim freedom for the captives and release from darkness for the prisoners, to proclaim the year of the LORD's favor and the day of vengeance of our God, to comfort all who mourn, and provide for those who grieve in Zion—to bestow on them a crown of beauty instead of ashes, the oil of gladness instead of mourning, and a garment of praise instead of a spirit of despair. They will be called oaks of righteousness, a planting of the LORD for the display of his splendor.

Isaiah 54:4-6
"Do not be afraid; you will not suffer shame. Do not fear disgrace; you will not be humiliated. You will forget the shame of your youth and remember no more the reproach of your widowhood. For your Maker is your husband—the LORD Almighty is his name—the Holy One of Israel is your Redeemer; he is called the God of all the earth. The LORD will call you back as if you were a wife deserted and distressed in spirit—a wife who married young, only to be rejected," says your God.

Isaiah 49:14-18
But Zion said, "The LORD has forsaken me, the LORD has forgotten me." "Can a mother forget the baby at her breast and have no compassion on the child she has borne? Though she may forget, I will not forget you! See, I have engraved you on the palms of my hands; your walls are ever before me. Your sons hasten back, and those who laid you waste depart from you. Lift up your eyes and look around; all your sons gather and come to you. As surely as I live," declares the LORD, "you will wear them all as ornaments; you will put them on, like a bride."

Isaiah 51:12-14
I, even I, am he who comforts you. Who are you that you fear mortal men, the sons of men, who are but grass, that you forget the LORD your Maker, who stretched out the heavens and laid the foundations of the earth, that you live in constant terror every day because of the wrath of the oppressor, who is bent on destruction? For where is the wrath of the oppressor? The cowering prisoners will soon be set free; they will not die in their dungeon, nor will they lack bread.

Isaiah 62:2-4
The nations will see your righteousness, and all kings your glory; you will be called by a new name that the mouth of the LORD will bestow. You will be a crown of splendor in the LORD's hand, a royal diadem in the hand of your God. No longer will they call you Deserted, or name your land Desolate. But you will be called Hephzibah, and your land Beulah; for the LORD will take delight in you, and your land will be married.

Jeremiah 30:16-18
"But all who devour you will be devoured; all your enemies will go into exile. Those who plunder you will be plundered; all who make spoil of you I will despoil. But I will restore you to health and heal your wounds," declares the LORD, "because you are called an outcast, Zion for whom no one cares." This is what the LORD says: "I will restore the fortunes of Jacob's tents and have compassion on his dwellings; the city will be rebuilt on her ruins, and the palace will stand in its proper place."

Jeremiah 29:11-13
"For I know the plans I have for you," declares the LORD, "plans to prosper you and not to harm you, plans to give you hope and a future. Then you will call upon me and come and pray to me, and I will listen to you. You will seek me and find me when you seek me with all your heart."

Psalm 34:15-18
The eyes of the LORD are on the righteous and his ears are attentive to their cry; the face of the LORD is against those who do evil, to cut off the memory of them from the earth. The righteous cry out, and the LORD hears them; he delivers them from all their troubles. The LORD is close to the brokenhearted and saves those who are crushed in spirit.

For the Betrayer

Matthew 5:28
But I tell you that anyone who looks at a woman lustfully has already committed adultery with her in his heart.

Romans 13:12-13
The night is nearly over; the day is almost here. So let us put aside the deeds of darkness and put on the armor of light. Let us behave decently, as in the daytime, not in orgies and drunkenness, not in sexual immorality and debauchery, not in dissension and jealousy.

Acts 15:29
You are to abstain from . . . sexual immorality.

1 Corinthians 6:13
The body is not meant for sexual immorality, but for the Lord.

1 Corinthians 6:18
Flee from sexual immorality.

1 Corinthians 5:11
But now I am writing you that you must not associate with anyone who calls himself a brother but is sexually immoral or greedy, an idolater or a slanderer, a drunkard or a swindler. With such a man do not even eat.

Notes

1. Gary R. Collins, *Family Shock* (Wheaton, Ill.: Tyndale House Publishers, Inc., 1995), 129.

2. Peggy Vaughan, *The Monogamy Myth* (New York: Newmarket Press, 1998), 7, 26.

3. Robert Huizenga, "Extramarital Affairs: What Everyone Needs to Know and What You Can Do to Help," 2007. http://EzineArticles.com/?expert=Dr._Robert_Huizenga

4. Williams Mitchell Jr., President Mitchell Reports Investigations, 2002.

5. Jack Hayford, "Why Sex Sins Are Worse than Others" (audiotape) (Van Nuys, Calif.: Living Way Ministries, CO179 and 180).

6. Frank Pittman III, M.D., *Psychology Today*, "Beyond Betrayal: Life After Infidelity" (May/June 1993), 32-38.

7. Shirley Glass, Ph.D., *Psychology Today*, "Shattered Vows" (July/Aug. 1998).

17 – STEPPARENTING

Stepparenting is a very difficult process. Before I counseled those having stepchildren I felt that the standard for a family with only their own children should be the same for those with stepchildren. I have since changed my mind.

Children suffer through the process of divorce and then have to adapt to additional parents. Even if their parents were hurtful to them, they were still their parents. Few children respond well to someone new coming in and giving them orders. Even when the relationship seems fine before marriage, it often changes after marriage. It is difficult for children to accept a new parent. It can be done, however, but takes time and working hard on the relationship. I believe that it is the job of the biological parent of the children to do all or most all of the discipline. There need to be guidelines set up for behavior and consistent rules whether the children are with their biological parent or with the stepparent.

This process is also difficult for the new stepparent. Trying to love children who may be determined that they do not want this parent in their life is extremely difficult. The children never asked for a stepparent and never asked for a divorce. They never asked to go to two homes on a rotating schedule. This situation can make the stepparent feel like an outsider at times. The stepparent may have guilt that he or she has to parent children that are not his or her own, especially when his or her own children could be at another home.

The biological parent of the children in this stepparenting situation is also in a dilemma. If the spouse (stepparent) and children are at odds, what do they do? Often *blood becomes thicker than water* and the stepparent feels out of the loop. This causes problems in the marriage. A parent may feel, "No one talks to my child that way." The stepparent may feel, "Why do you side with your children?" The children feel, "Why should I have to do what this stepparent says? This person isn't my parent." Then there is also the problem of the stepparent having a child. It may be difficult to treat this child the same as one's own.

The biggest reason that stepparenting situations fail is because of the children—his, hers, and theirs. Most children do not even want this set-up. They may feel there is no safe place to be. A stepparenting marriage can work but generally it takes several years for all the factors to work together.

Context of Stepparenting

One out of three Americans is now a stepparent, stepchild, or some other member of a stepfamily. More than half of Americans today have been, are currently, or will eventually be in one or more step situations during their lives.[1] With these kinds of statistics, it is evident why material on stepfamilies is important.

The Marriage

The statistics for the success rate of all second marriages are staggering. Studies from the Stepfamily Foundation show that 60 percent of all second marriages end in divorce. Although the percentage seems bleak, there are many things that can be done to have a successful second marriage.[2]

Most Difficult Stepfamilies

Most all stepfamilies are difficult to some degree, however these may have added stressors.
- A never-married man or woman or formerly married person without children marrying a divorced person with children. Often this person has little realistic expectations for children and can have a tendency to be self-centered.
- A divorced person marrying a widowed person can bring difficulty in that one person is dealing with unpleasant memories and the other is dealing with good memories.
- One person has children and doesn't want any more. This person marries someone who has never had children and wants to have children.[3]

Successful Characteristics of a Second Marriage

- The couple is aware of the risk of unhealthy reliance and has come to acknowledge that a successful marriage demands that they care for their own individuality while giving freely to the partner.
- Rebellion is not the source of the second marriage in most cases. By the time men and women commit themselves to second marriages they have usually resolved many of these self-defeating influences.
- Remarried couples are usually older. The individuals have matured to a point that they probably will not change much more.
- Patterns of behavior and attitudes are more firmly established, for better or worse.
- The couple has a much more informed view of what marriage entails.
- The couple has invaluable insights carried into the second marriage from the first.
- It offers a new start, which might be just what the couple needs.
- They will enter the marriage willing for it to be successful and will be more willing to work to make it happen.[4]

It is very important for the family as a whole that the marriage is strong. It needs to be able to endure the pressures that will come from all of the different relationships within the family. It is important for the parents to work together for the well-being of each child, step or biological children.[5]

It is also important to realize that the stepparent coming into the marriage with a spouse who has children may feel like the outsider, like he or she isn't a part of the family. The parent with the children may feel torn between keeping peace and giving time to his or her children and the new spouse.

The Children and the Stepparent

Ron Deal, in *The Smart Stepfamily*, suggests that the stepparent, along with the parent, make a map for the path of the stepfamily. This will enable the stepparent to determine what makes or breaks his or her position in the home. It is very important that the stepparent allow the children to take the development of the relationship at their own stride. It will only produce resentment for the child to be pushed into a relationship.[6]

In the beginning the biological parent needs to be the head disciplinarian. Although the biological parent will initially distribute the discipline, both parents need to agree on the methods and strength of discipline, backing each other up in unity. Gradually the stepparent can work into a disciplinarian position, but it needs to be a slow transition for the children. It also depends on the age of the children. If the children are young, the stepparent can slide into that role easier. However, if the stepchild is an older teen, the stepparent may never develop a disciplinarian role in the teen's life.

Remember the Children's Pain

There is never an easy time for children to experience their parents' breakup. How the parents handle interaction with the ex-spouse and daily life will be very important.

It is important for all involved to realize the pain that the children have gone through. They might feel:

- Rejected. Children are very hurt from the loss of a parent. They feel everything in their life has been stripped out from underneath them.
- Identity confusion. Living with the same-sex parent is generally the most positive antidote toward establishing identity.
- Jealousy. Children sometimes feel they have to compete with their stepparent for time with their parent.
- Internal conflict over loyalty to biological parents. Most children want to be loyal to both parents.
- Powerless. Children feel there is nothing they can do to make their life better. They feel at the mercy of their parents/stepparents.
- Angry. Anger is very common and difficult to dissipate. Parents need to model a forgiving spirit to their children. Children need to be able to talk out their feelings in a safe atmosphere.
- Withdrawn/depressed. Boys often show more aggression out of frustration and girls show more depression.
- Humiliated/ashamed. It is embarrassing to children that their parents have divorced. Keep that in mind and let them talk it out.
- Unloved. This can be their real feeling regardless if it is true.
- Abandoned. Children feel this most often from the parent who physically left the home.
- Like they are a tool or a bargaining chip. This is particularly true if one parent gives them messages to give to the other parent, especially if it has to do with money or when to see the children.
- Guilty. If they have fun at one parent's house and the other parent doesn't want them to, they could feel guilty. Parents should never criticize their ex-spouse in front of their children.
- Worried about finances. As children enter their teens they often become aware of the finances of their parents and become worried. It is vital that a parent doesn't share the state of financial affairs with the children.

Not only do the children experience all of these feelings, but they have no authority or maturity to make decisions for themselves and are relying on their parents to make decisions for them. Because of this the children have to deal with the outcome of their parents' decisions, such as:
- The initial divorce
- Moving from home to home; custody
- Living with the new stepfamily
- Sharing a room with stepsiblings
- Going to a new school, meeting new friends, having a new teacher

Parents need to be aware and sensitive to those feelings of pain that their children or stepchildren experience. They need to understand that, although the remarriage for them is positive, that for the child it is another loss.[7]

Bringing Awareness to the Family

1. Time is everything in the development of the stepfamily. James Bray, stepfamily researcher, suggests that it takes two to three years for a stepfamily to function as a family.[8] On average, intimacy in the family is not experienced until after seven years of existence as a stepfamily.
2. Many issues in a stepparent family are the result of unresolved past relationships.
3. This union will always look different from a first-time union that starts with no children.
4. Education on the topic of stepfamilies is vital for every stepfamily.

Steps to Assist the Helpee as a Stepparent

Steps for the Couple in Their Marriage Relationship

1. Help the couple see the need to continue developing their relationship. The couple needs to learn to stand in unity. Engagement counseling is a must. Previous marriage experience helps, however two unique individuals getting married need unbiased guidance from a helper.
2. Determine whether or not there is bitterness building up between the couple. If so, lead the couple through the forgiveness steps in chapter 3 (pages 53-54). It is important for the unity of their relationship to forgive their spouse for inappropriate priorities or insensitive actions in the past.

Steps for the Couple as Parents

1. Are the parents aware of what they say in the presence of their children? Help the parents realize that they need to keep adult business solely to adult ears. This will help to build unity between the parents and to diminish stress for the children.
2. Evaluate the family dynamic. Is it hostile, friendly, unstable, and so forth? Help the family set a goal for their family dynamic. This can be done by instituting family meetings.
3. Identify unforgiveness and bitterness the stepparent might have toward the child. Lead him or her through the forgiveness steps in chapter 3 (pages 53-54), which will let go of grudges held against stepchildren. This will help to promote unity within the family.
4. Make clear distinctions between the roles of the parents, which will help tear down unrealistic expectations.[9]
5. Help the parents determine a united discipline and guidance system as a couple for when the parent is not at home. The stepparent should do more backing up of the rules already established.
6. Evaluate the consistency and security already present for the children. Help parents set goals to institute consistency and security for the children.
7. Break the lie that the stepfamily will someday function as a natural family.[10] It will not; it is a different entity.
8. Make sure that the parents know that the stepparent cannot take the place of a biological parent.[11]

Steps for the Children

1. Determine what areas of unforgiveness lie in the way of unity. Begin to work through the forgiveness steps in chapter 3 (pages 53-54).
2. Determine if there are areas of rejection. If so, focus on the rejection steps in chapter 2 (pages 39-41). Children almost always feel rejected by the parent that left the home.
3. Focus on the children's self-esteem and discover trouble areas that the children deal with. Take them through the steps to healthy self-esteem in chapter 11 (pages 145-47).
4. Evaluate the children's expectations. If they are unrealistic, help them tear down unhealthy expectations and build up new, realistic ones. It is completely appropriate for the children to have expectations, but it is important that those expectations are attainable. Talk with them.

5. Help the children learn to see the stepparent as an authority figure who does not take the place of a biological parent. Do not make them call their stepparent Mom or Dad.
6. Help the children accept life as it is—with a stepparent. This is a choice and will take time, effort, and validation of the children's hurt feelings.

Questions to Ask the Family
- What do you feel is the biggest issue that you are working on right now?
- What would need to happen to help you feel valued in this family?

Questions to Ask the Parents
- How much time do you spend with your biological children a week? Your stepchildren? Your spouse?
- Could you describe your discipline strategy? Who is the disciplinarian?
- How do your children react to discipline by their stepparent?
- What do you think you could do to make your children feel special? To make your spouse feel special?
- To the stepparent: Do you ever feel jealous of the time that your spouse spends with his or her children?

Questions to Ask the Children
- Do you feel that you have forgiven your parents for the divorce?
- Did your parents discuss the idea of remarriage with you? How did that make you feel?
- Do your mom and dad and your stepmom and stepdad get along? How do you feel about your stepparent?
- What place do you want your stepparent to have in your life?

Homework for the Helpee

Homework for Couples in Their Marriage
1. Go on dates once a week. Make sure that you have time alone.
2. If you are not doing devotions together, start setting aside time for devotions as a couple a few times a week.
3. Practice keeping stressful conversations out of earshot of the children.

4. Keep a journal of all of the reasons why you love your spouse and chose to marry him or her. When conflicts come up, review the list and remind yourself of all the positive reasons for this new family.

Homework for the Couple as Parents
1. Work on spending time with your husband or wife's children. Take them out for one-on-one time.
2. Try to create consistency between the houses of the children. Make a list of family rules that apply to all living within your household. In unity the parents need to follow through on these rules. This will help the children settle into their new lifestyles.
3. Brainstorm on activities that the family can do together.

Homework for Family as a Whole
1. Meet as a family and discuss things that are going to take place, schedules, rules, and so forth. Make sure everyone is on the same page.
2. Each person needs to pick one stepparent or stepsibling a day to find a positive truth. These truths need to be recorded in written form in a journal or notebook. If the child is too young to write, the biological parent can remind the child during the day and ask him or her in the evening before bed what positive trait he or she saw in the stepparent or stepsibling.

Books for the Helpee

Artlip, Mary. *The New American Family: Tools for Strengthening Step Families*. Twin Lake, Wis.: Lotus Press, 1993.

Block, Joel D., and Susan S. Bartell. *Stepliving for Teens: Getting Along with Stepparents and Siblings*. New York: Price Stern Sloan, 2001.

Bray, James. *Step-parenting: Love, Marriage, and Parenting in the First Decade*. New York: Broadway Books, 1999.

Deal, Ron. *The Smart Stepfamily: Seven Steps to a Healthy Family*. Grand Rapids: Bethany House Publishers, 2002.

Focus on the Family. *The Blended Marriage*. Springfield, Mo.: Gospel Light, 2004.

Papernow, Patricia. *Becoming a Stepfamily: Patterns in Development in Remarried Families*. New York: Analytic Press, 1993.

Webster, Joann. *Step Families Done Right*. Lake Mary, Fla.: Strang Communications, 2001.

Scriptures for the Helpee

Psalm 68:5-6
A father to the fatherless, a defender of widows, is God in his holy dwelling. God sets the lonely in families, he leads forth the prisoners with singing; but the rebellious live in a sun-scorched land.

John 1:12-13
Yet to all who received him, to those who believed in his name, he gave the right to become children of God—children born not of natural descent, nor of human decision or a husband's will, but born of God.

Romans 8:15
For you did not receive a spirit that makes you a slave again to fear, but you received the Spirit of sonship. And by him we cry, "Abba, Father."

2 Corinthians 6:18
I will be a Father to you, and you will be my sons and daughters, says the Lord Almighty.

Psalm 27:10
Though my father and mother forsake me, the LORD will receive me.

Psalm 23:1-6
The LORD is my shepherd, I shall not be in want. He makes me lie down in green pastures, he leads me beside quiet waters, he restores my soul. He guides me in paths of righteousness for his name's sake. Even though I walk through the valley of the shadow of death, I will fear no evil, for you are with me; your rod and your staff, they comfort me. You prepare a table before me in the presence of my enemies. You anoint my head with oil; my cup overflows. Surely goodness and love will follow me all the days of my life, and I will dwell in the house of the LORD forever.

Notes

1. The Stepfamily Foundation, President Jeannette Lofas, 1975. http://www.stepfamily.org.
2. Ibid.
3. www.crosswalk.com.
4. Frederic F. Flach, *A New Marriage, A New Life*, rev. ed. (New York: Hatherleigh Press, 1998), 98.
5. Ron Deal, *The Smart Stepfamily: Seven Steps to a Healthy Family* (Minneapolis: Bethany House Publishers, 2002), 141.
6. Ibid., 148.
7. Ibid., 166-69.
8. James Bray, *Stepfamilies: Love, Marriage, and Parenting in the First Decade* (New York: Broadway Books, 1998), 56.
9. The Stepfamily Foundation.
10. Ibid.
11. Ibid.

18 – SEXUAL ADDICTION

"Sexual addiction is not just a struggle over a mental perspective; it touches God's very image, as well as the depths of a man's soul."[1]

Chuck Swindoll posted on his Insight for Living Web site: "The most recent studies available suggest that one out of every two people—that's 50% of the people sitting in our pews, are looking at and/or could be addicted to Internet pornography.... Truth be told that statistic could be even higher."[2]

We know that between the Internet and the media the ability to view pornography and have sex without limits knows no bounds. This has affected women as well as men. Although women are still more likely to be obsessed with romance, love, and relationships, the numbers are rising as far as women viewing pornography and becoming involved in emotional affairs over the Internet. More women are also becoming compulsive with masturbation.

Context: Sexual Addiction—on the Rise

"Whenever a married man has a severe battle with sexual bondage, it's always preceded by deterioration in his marriage. A man always walks away from God long before he walks away from his wife."[3]

Could half of Christian men have a problem with porn, as so many of the statistics say? Porn is reported to be a 12 billion dollar industry in the U.S. . . . 50 percent of men viewed pornography within one week of attending a Promise Keepers stadium event . . . 54 percent of pastors said they viewed porn within the past year in a Pastors.com survey . . . in a 2003 Focus on the Family poll 47 percent of respondents said porn is a problem in their home.[4]

Most of the 600 men surveyed were men at church, in their late 30s to early 40s, married and with children. These numbers should get our attention to the effect of the Internet.

Patrick Carnes was one of the first authors to talk about sexual addiction in 1983 with his book *Out of the Shadows: Overcoming Sexual Addiction*. Now there are many books and resources, both Christian and secular on this topic that will help define sexual addiction.

The National Council on Sexual Addiction and Compulsivity defines sexual addiction as "persistent and escalating pattern of sexual behavior acted out despite increasing negative consequences to self and others."[5]

Sexual addiction is a pattern of out-of-control behavior. There becomes an inability to stop despite adverse consequences. There also becomes:

1. Ongoing desire to limit sexual behavior
2. Sexual obsessions as a primary coping strategy
3. Mood changes around sexual activity (does not have to be the Internet)
4. Great amounts of time spent in obtaining sex and being sexual
5. Neglect of important social, occupational ties because of sexual behavior[6]

Addictive sex is always done in isolation, meaning the person has sex for its own sake—almost mechanical in nature, not in a personal way. It is always done in a secret manner and it never involves intimacy.[7]

Additional Clues to Being Addicted to Internet Porn

(These are just a few Dr. Simpson gives in his seminar on Treating Compulsive Sexual Behaviors.)

1. Spending increased amounts of time online focused on sexual or romantic intrigue
2. Involvement in multiple romantic or sexual affairs on the Internet (e.g., in chat rooms)
3. Not considering online sexual or romantic "affairs" to be a possible violation of spousal/partnership commitments

4. Failed attempts to cut back on frequency of the involved time in sexual or romantic online relationships
5. Lying or minimizing to partner about online activities
6. Becoming angry when asked to stop time on Internet[8]

Creating the Insatiable Appetite for More

According to Carnes addicts have core beliefs about themselves that will affect how they perceive reality. He says that addicts do not perceive themselves as worthwhile persons. They often feel others would not care for them if they knew everything about them. They also believe that sex is their most important need.[9]

Schaumburg, in *False Intimacy: Understanding the Struggle of Sexual Addiction*, says that sexual addiction "is an avoidance of the pain often caused by real intimacy." The goal "of sexually addictive behavior is to avoid relationship pain—essentially, to control life."[10]

Premarital sex, pornography, sexual abuse, low self-esteem, and depression can all be factors in creating sexual addiction. Premarital sex, pornography, and abuse can change perceptions about what constitutes real, wholesome sex. Sex becomes a means to an end—self-pleasure and/or a need to escape without emotional commitment or involvement. These forms of sex diminish satisfaction with the physical appearance of the person's spouse. Sex becomes a drug that is needed in ever-increasing levels to maintain the mood-altering affects that were first experienced by the individual. The addict becomes desensitized, needing more stimulation to produce the same level of results. Sex is used in an attempt to deaden the pain of rejection, loneliness, fear, anxiety, and other hurts.[11]

The Part Shame Plays

Sexual shame poses an enormous obstacle to a man's sexual success and feeling about himself. This shame will keep him from being available in the bedroom and may perpetuate a man having sexual experiences away from his spouse. According to Weiss in *Sex, Men, and God*, a man can feel shame from his inability to have a gratifying experience with his spouse: (1) not being able to get or maintain an erection, (2) premature ejaculation, or (3) not bringing his spouse to orgasm. "Some men attach much of their identity to bringing their spouse to orgasm."[12] Some men take it personally and feel it is a sign of being inadequate. Generally as many as 30 to 50 percent of women may not have orgasm at all or on a regular basis. It is unrealistic to think that it is always the husband's fault if his wife doesn't have orgasm. Study of the female's sexual anatomy can help in this area.

Sexual history shame has to do with previous sexual experiences, involvement with pornography or other such fantasies. It could also be a sexual secret such as masturbation habits, impregnating a girlfriend who has an abortion, or getting an STD. The third type of shame is sexual deviant behavior in the past that is seldom experienced by the general population.[13]

Significance of the Brain to a Person's Sexuality

During sex, chemicals called endorphins and enkephalins rush to the preoptic neuron of a man's brain and give a "reward" or "high." Sex produces the greatest chemical release, making the brain and body feel their best. Whatever a man looks at while having an ejaculation is what he will sexually connect to or "glue" to. This conditioning will cause him to be primarily conditioned to prefer fantasy, pornography, objects, or the use of people as objects.[14] This can be a part of perpetuating sexual addiction. If a man has *glued* to beautiful women in pornography, he may not be able to be aroused with his wife without fantasizing thoughts of the beautiful women in pornography. Those pictures are imprinted on his mind by the strong release of endorphins.

Who Becomes Addicted to Internet Pornography?

The sex addict becomes mentally and emotionally detached from human relationship. He or she has generally experienced masturbation with pornography or some form of fantasy, has had some form of relationship pain, stress, or shame, and uses a form of sex to escape this pain.[15]

According to Simpson there are three types of people who get involved:

1. **Recreational users.** Those that do it for fun. There are people that might accidentally get on a site or just do it out of curiosity. The problem is that some become addicted. This group is growing in number. The allurement is being able to act out sexually in private.
2. **At-risk users.** These are people who have had difficulty in the past yet still get hooked. They don't always know that they are "at risk." Those at risk are mostly male and heterosexual; 38 percent are married and 15 percent are committed to their marriage.
3. **Sexual compulsive users.** Eight percent of those looking at porn are on sites eleven hours a day plus.[16]

How Many People Look at Porn Sites?

The following statistics are from Paul Simpson, Ed.D.
- Twenty to 30 percent of people that use the Internet use porn sites.

- Twenty million people visit sexual sites each month.
- Sex is the most frequent topic searched on the Internet.
- Nine million people need intervention.
- An additional 15 million people are showing significant sexual and relationship problems.[17]

Keep in mind that most sexual addicts are in denial. To them there are always reasons for their sexual behavior. A modified version of the 12-step program (originally used for alcoholics/drug users) is being used for healing. The difference, however, with drugs and sexual addiction is that you can give up drugs—you can't give up who you are or the desire to be sexual. Only when a person admits he or she has a problem can he or she then begin the work to heal. See steps for healing the sexually addicted beginning on page 228.

Women and Sexual Addiction

Now that we understand that the addictive process comes through a void, pain, or shame in one's life, it will be easier to understand the heart of a woman. Women turn to masturbation and fantasy, sexual relationships, romantic novels or videos, chat rooms, or pornography (approximately 17 percent) to fill emptiness, loneliness, pain, or shame.[18]

Women use romance whether fantasy or real relationships, whether codependent or dysfunctional, to fill their needs. If that requires sex with someone and/or sexual fantasies, then that, too, will play a part in their addiction.[19]

Dr. Kasl cites in *Women, Sex, and Addiction* that more men use sex to escape issues in their life. Men use relationships in order to have sex. Women, on the other hand, use sex to attract a partner so that they can have a relationship. The core beliefs are the same: "I have shame, I am unlovable, I am defective, and I am powerless."[20]

A woman hooked on romance is usually consumed by thoughts of romance. She may devise plans to find the romantic high. The thinking becomes obsessive until she finds what brings her the romantic high feeling.

A woman hooked on relationships finds the attachment to another person to be the feeling needed to take away pain. Sex may or may not be involved. Romance may or may not be involved. The relationship addict goes from relationship to relationship looking for identity and a filler for the void in his or her life.

Sex can also be used by women, whether masturbating with a fantasy or having a sexual relationship. Weiss in *She Has a Secret*, states that in her survey 68 percent of the women had been forced or pressured to have their first sexual encounter, over half was with age-inappropriate males and 12 percent with age-inappropriate females.[21] Sexual abuse has a significant role in creating and/or maintaining the sexual addiction. This is an example of women using sex to numb the pain from the abuse.[22]

For sexual abuse, see the Root of Sexual Abuse.

The roots of dysfunctional family, rejection, and/or unforgiveness are other roots that could be the origination of a woman becoming obsessed with sex.

Are We Helping People Heal?

Ted Roberts, a well-known Christian speaker and author in the area of sexual addiction, says that we as the church often hurt men and women more by shaming them for their sexual issues. We need to give people hope. Let them know God can heal.[23]

The Word of God says, "But he was pierced for our transgressions, he was crushed for our iniquities; the punishment that brought us peace was upon him, and by his wounds we are healed" (Isa. 53:5).

Steps to Assist the Helpee in Healing from Sexual Addiction

Steps to Help a Man

1. Encourage him to get involved in a Christian group that uses a 12-step plan for those who are having difficulty in the sexual area. This is vital. There are many churches that have these groups for men struggling with sexual temptation. Admitting that he has a problem is essential. A man can't change what he won't acknowledge. A helpful book to use with the 12 steps is *A Gentle Path Through the Twelve Steps* by Patrick Carnes, Ph.D. In this book men look at the consequences that they are facing as a result of their addiction. They also look at a family tree of addiction to see how it intertwines their family. Going through their own history with sexual problems will be an eye-opening experience.
2. Team him up with an accountability partner that is stable in this area, trustworthy, and can be a mentor.

Steps for a Man or a Woman

1. Admit powerlessness over our sexual issue. This is the beginning of the 12 steps. This will be a condensed and summarized version to guide you, the helper, with the one struggling with sexual sin.
2. Often it is good to have the spouse look at how he or she has contributed to helping his or her mate with the sexual sin stay in it

rather than forcing him or her to get out of it. Sometimes just by taking care of everything that goes wrong as a result of the problem (such as spending too much money), the spouse contributes. The mate is kept from facing the truth about his or her sexual sin.
3. A relationship with Jesus Christ is of utmost importance. Encourage the helpee in devotions each day. Help him or her see that without Jesus Christ, this addiction will not go away. It is a spiritual battle.
4. Steps 4 and 5 of the 12 steps deal with an inventory of wrongs—taking responsibility for all the hurts given to others. Encourage the helpee to make a list of all the people he or she has offended and how they were offended.
5. After working through the inventory of offenses that the helpee has done (could take several sessions), have him or her repent before God.
6. With the list, have him or her go to all who have been offended or hurt. If he or she has been offended by someone, the helpee also needs to make a list of those hurts—ones given to him or her.
7. Again, the helpee needs to choose to forgive all of those who have hurt him or her. If the hurt can be worked out with the person, that is good. It is difficult, however, to go to someone and tell him or her, "You have offended me."
8. This is a good time to see what kind of roots you are dealing with. A possibility would be hurts from Mom and/or Dad, which could be a dysfunctional family (emotional abuse). It could be a feeling of rejection from family and of course unforgiveness. Rebellion could have developed in order to cope. Check all of those chapters in this handbook.

As far as fruits: Depression, low-self esteem, anger, and guilt would be evident. Use as many ideas from those chapters as would be helpful. Shame is definitely a fruit of sexual sin.

It is always good for someone who is facing sexual temptation to see a medical doctor. Generally depression is a large part of this problem. Some medications can help both areas—obsessive sexual desire and depression. It can help temporarily while the person gets better through group and individual help.

Questions to Ask the Helpee (Male)

- When was the first occurrence of the sexual issue?
  - Was this done in secret?
  - How often?

- How much fantasy was involved?
- Explain the amount of porn in your life currently. Explain your sexual experiences with pornography (masturbation).
- How much time did you spend with your dad when growing up? What kinds of activities did you share?
- Explain your relationship with your mother.
- Answer this question quickly: When I think of women I think of _____.

Questions to Ask the Helpee (Female)
- How much a part does the idea of being "in love" play in your life?
- What is romance to you? How much of a role does romantic movies and novels play in your life?
- Tell me about the first sexual experience you had.
- Explain to me what your relationship with your dad is like. How much time did you spend with him on a daily basis? What are the kinds of things he said about women in general?
- How often is masturbation a part of your life? Is fantasy involved? What kind?

Homework for the Helpee

1. Do a Bible study on sexual sin and what God says about it.
2. Set aside time each day to have devotions. Start reading in the Book of Proverbs. Read over the first six chapters every couple of days. Read in the Book of John.
3. Every day choose to be grateful to God.
4. Watch your self-talk.
5. Be working on at least one of the 12 steps each week. Purchase *A Gentle Path to the 12 Steps*.
6. Keep a mood chart to see the times it is most difficult to stay away from the source of the problem. What happens just before you *fall*? What kind of behavior do you have afterward?

Paul Simpson, author of *Treating Compulsive Sexual Behaviors*, says you need ways to *prevent* the problem, ways to help you when you are *in the midst* (which he calls fire escapes) of the problem, and ways to help yourself if you fail so you can be *restored*.

Prevention
1. Block out all sexually related Internet sites.
2. Put the computer in the living room with the screen facing the door.

3. Have a card with a number of your mentor or accountability partner to call.
4. Keep a list of all the problems the addiction has cost you.
5. Keep a daily mood chart to see what comes before you start falling.[24]
6. Keep working on your 12 steps.

In the Midst

1. Write a letter to yourself, encouraging you at the opportune moment to resist what is tempting you.[25]
2. If you are a man, practice the three-second rule; that is, wait no more than three seconds before turning away from something bothersome in a journal, magazine, and so forth.
3. Have tapes available of worship music to play.
4. Keep scriptures available that encourage you.

Restore (If You Fall)

1. Look at past progress.
2. Call your accountability partner to get on the right track again.
3. Reestablish boundaries. In other words, assess what happened. What do you need to do differently?
4. Reestablish your devotions. Be determined.

Books for the Helpee

Male

Anderson, Nancy C. *Avoiding the Greener Grass Syndrome.* Grand Rapids: Kregel, 2004.

Arterburn, Stephen, and Fred Stoeker. *Every Man's Battle.* Colorado Springs: Waterbrook Press, 2000.

Carder, Dave. *Torn Asunder: Recovering from Extramarital Affairs.* Chicago: Moody, 1992.

Carnes, Patrick. *Clinical Management of Sex Addiction,* 2002.

_____. *Don't Call It Love: Recovery from Sexual Addiction.* New York: Bantam, 1992.

_____. *Facing the Shadow: Starting Sexual and Relationship Recovery.* Carefree, Ariz.: Gentle Path Press, 2001.

_____. *A Gentle Path Through the Twelve Steps: The Classic Guide for All People in the Process of Recovery.* Center City, Minn.: Hazelden, 1994.

_____. *In the Shadows of the Net.* Center City, Minn.: Hazelden, 2003.

_____. *Out of the Shadows: Understanding Sexual Addiction.* Center City, Minn.: Hazelden, 1992.

———. *Sexual Anorexia: Overcoming Sexual Self-Hatred*. Center City, Minn.: Hazelden, 1997.

Earle, R. H., and M. Laaser. *Pornography Trap: Setting Pastors and Laypersons Free from Sexual Addiction*. Kansas City: Beacon Hill Press of Kansas City, 2002.

Hall, Laurie. *An Affair of the Mind*. Wheaton, Ill.: Tyndale House Publishers, 1996.

Hart, Archibald D. *The Hart Report: The Sexual Man*. Dallas: Word Publishing, 1994.

———. *Unmasking Male Depression*. Nashville: W Publishing, 2001.

Irons, Richard. *The Wounded Healer: An Addiction-Sensitive Approach to the Sexually Exploitative Professional*. Northvale, N.J.: Jason Aronson Publishers, 1999.

Roberts, Ted. *Pure Desire: Helping People Break Free from Sexual Struggles*. Ventura, Calif.: Regal Books, 1999.

Schaumburg, Dr. Harry W. *False Intimacy: Understanding the Struggle of Sexual Addiction*. Colorado Springs: NavPress, 1997.

Vereen, Bob. *How Can a Man Control His Thoughts, Desires, and Passions?* Colorado Springs: Waterbrook, 2004.

Weiss, Douglas. *Sex, Men, and God: A Godly Man's Road Map to Sexual Success*. Lake Mary, Fla.: Charisma House, 2002.

Female

Anderson, Nancy C. *Avoiding the Greener Grass Syndrome*. Grand Rapids: Kregel, 2004.

Arterburn, Stephen. *Addicted to Love*. Ann Arbor, Mich.: Vine Books, 1991.

Carder, Dave. *Torn Asunder: Recovering from Extramarital Affairs*. Chicago: Moody, 1992.

Eldredge, John and Stasi. *Captivating*. Nashville: Thomas Nelson, 2005.

Ethridge, Shannon, and Stephen Arterburn. *Every Woman's Battle*. Colorado Springs: Waterbrook Press, Random House, 2005.

Hanes, Mari. *Dreams and Delusions: The Impact of Romantic Fantasy on Women*. New York: Bantam Books, 1991.

Schaef, Anne. *Escape from Intimacy: Untangling the "Love" Addictions: Sex, Romance, Relationships*. San Francisco: Harper-Collins, 1990.

Shriver, Gary and Mona. *Unfaithful: Rebuilding Trust After Infidelity*. Colorado Springs: Life Journey, 2005.

Weiss, D., Ph.D. *She Has a Secret: Understanding Female Sexual Addiction*. Fort Worth: Discovery Press, 2000.

Scriptures for the Helpee

Proverbs 5

My son, pay attention to my wisdom, listen well to my words of insight, that you may maintain discretion and your lips may preserve knowledge. For the lips of an adulteress drip honey, and her speech is smoother than oil; but in the end she is bitter as gall, sharp as a double-edged sword. Her feet go down to death; her steps lead straight to the grave. She gives no thought to the way of life; her paths are crooked, but she knows it not. Now then, my sons, listen to me; do not turn aside from what I say. Keep to a path far from her, do not go near the door of her house, lest you give your best strength to others and your years to one who is cruel, lest strangers feast on your wealth and your toil enrich another man's house. At the end of your life you will groan, when your flesh and body are spent. You will say, "How I hated discipline! How my heart spurned correction! I would not obey my teachers or listen to my instructors. I have come to the brink of utter ruin in the midst of the whole assembly." Drink water from your own cistern, running water from your own well. Should your springs overflow in the streets, your streams of water in the public squares? Let them be yours alone, never to be shared with strangers. May your fountain be blessed, and may you rejoice in the wife of your youth. A loving doe, a graceful deer—may her breasts satisfy you always, may you ever be captivated by her love. Why be captivated, my son, by an adulteress? Why embrace the bosom of another man's wife? For a man's ways are in full view of the LORD, and he examines all his paths. The evil deeds of a wicked man ensnare him; the cords of his sin hold him fast. He will die for lack of discipline, led astray by his own great folly.

Psalm 34:6 (TM)

When I was desperate, I called out, and GOD got me out of a tight spot.

Psalm 33:18-22 (TM)

Watch this: God's eye is on those who respect him, the ones who are looking for his love. He's ready to come to their rescue in bad times; in lean times he keeps body and soul together. We're depending on GOD; he's everything we need. What's more; our hearts brim with joy since we've taken for our own his holy name. Love us, GOD, with all you've got—that's what we're depending on.

Psalm 32:1-7 (tm)

Count yourself lucky, how happy you must be—you get a fresh start, your slate's wiped clean. Count yourself lucky—GOD holds nothing against you and you're holding nothing back from him. When I kept it all inside, my bones turned to powder, my words became daylong groans. The pressure never let up; all the juices of my life dried up. Then I let it all out; I said, "I'll make a clean breast of my failures to GOD." Suddenly the pressure was gone—my guilt dissolved, my sin disappeared. These things add up. Every one of us needs to pray; when all hell breaks loose and the dam bursts we'll be on high ground, untouched. GOD's my island hideaway, keeps danger far from the shore, throws garlands of hosannas around my neck.

Isaiah 53:5
But he was pierced for our transgressions, he was crushed for our iniquities; the punishment that brought us peace was upon him, and by his wounds we are healed.

Colossians 2:13-14
When you were dead in your sins and in the uncircumcision of your sinful nature, God made you alive with Christ. He forgave us all our sins, having canceled the written code, with its regulations, that was against us and that stood opposed to us; he took it away, nailing it to the cross.

Matthew 5:28
But I tell you that anyone who looks at a woman lustfully has already committed adultery with her in his heart.

Romans 13:12-13
The night is nearly over; the day is almost here. So let us put aside the deeds of darkness and put on the armor of light. Let us behave decently, as in the daytime, not in orgies and drunkenness, not in sexual immorality and debauchery, not in dissension and jealousy.

Acts 15:29
You are to abstain from . . . sexual immorality.

1 Corinthians 6:13
The body is not meant for sexual immorality, but for the Lord.

1 Corinthians 6:18
Flee from sexual immorality.

1 Corinthians 5:11
But now I am writing you that you must not associate with anyone who calls himself a brother but is sexually immoral or greedy, an idolater or a slanderer, a drunkard or a swindler. With such a man do not even eat.

Notes

1. Ted Roberts, *Pure Desire: Helping People Break Free from Sexual Struggles* (Ventura, Calif.: Regal Books, 1999), 32, 216.
2. Mike Genung, "How Many Porn Addicts Are in Your Church?" Crosswalk.com Director of blazinggrace.org.
3. Roberts, *Pure Desire*, 209.
4. Genung, "How Many Porn Addicts Are in Your Church?"
5. Paul Simpson, Ed.D., *Treating Sexual Compulsive Disorders: A Training Seminar for Mental Health Care Professionals* (NCSAC Web site, 2004), 1.
6. Ibid., 2.
7. Stephen Arterburn and Fred Stoeker, *Every Man's Battle* (Colorado Springs: Waterbrook Press, 2000), 28.
8. Simpson, *Treating Sexual Compulsive Disorders*, 6-7.
9. Patrick Carnes, *Facing the Shadow: Starting Sexual and Relationship Recovery* (Carefree, Ariz.: Gentle Path Press, 2001), 6.
10. Dr. Harry W. Schaumburg, *False Intimacy: Understanding the Struggle of Sexual Addiction* (Colorado Springs: NavPress, 1997), 20.
11. Stephen Arterburn, "Freeing the Sex Addict," *Leadership Journal* (Christian Today, Inc., 1995), 2.
12. Douglas Weiss, *Sex, Men, and God: A Godly Man's Road Map to Sexual Success* (Lake Mary, Fla.: Charisma House, 2002), 15, 21, 57, 67. Used by permission.
13. Ibid., 15, 21.
14. Ibid., 67.
15. Patrick Carnes, Ph.D. *Out of the Shadows: Understanding Sexual Addiction*, 3rd ed. (Center City, Minn.: Hazelden Publishing, 2001), 21.
16. Simpson, *Treating Sexual Compulsive Disorders*, 9.
17. Ibid., 6.
18. D. Weiss, Ph.D. *She Has a Secret: Understanding Female Sexual Addiction* (Fort Worth: Discovery Press, 2000), 51-53.
19. Ibid.
20. Dr. C. Kasl, *Women, Sex, and Addiction* (New York: Harper and Row, 1990), 45.
21. Weiss, *She Has a Secret*, 51-53.
22. Arterburn, *Addicted to Love* (Ann Arbor, Mich.: Vine Books, 1991), 52, 54
23. Roberts, *Pure Desire*, intro.
24. Simpson, *Treating Sexual Compulsive Disorders*, 15.
25. Ibid., 20.

PART V
SUPPLEMENTAL TOPICS

ENGAGEMENT
MARITAL HELPS
LEGAL AND ETHICAL ISSUES
SUPPLEMENTS

The engagement period offers an opportunity for a couple to learn more about each other and greatly improve the prospects of their marriage. Thorough pastoral guidance is vital for engaged couples. Chapter 19 includes seven individual sessions complete with topics, questions, and homework for helping a couple as they prepare for their life together.

The Marital Helps chapter contains ideas and insights into the basic issues that arise when helping a married couple. The bottom line is found in understanding two things: (1) when a man is not honored and admired as a man and provider, problems will arise, and (2) when a woman is not cherished and protected, she will be resentful, and other issues will emerge.

Knowledge of legal and ethical issues is essential for every pastor and layperson that chooses to help. Many of the guidelines for licensed counselors also apply to helpers in the church even if the helper is just listening, praying, and sharing the Word. We must know all the ways to protect ourselves and the church. Chapter 21 provides much assistance in these matters.

The Supplements chapter contains additional forms to assist you in the helping process, as well as written prayers for the helpee.

19 — ENGAGEMENT

This chapter is based on the experience gained from helping many engaged couples. Most research shows that the more intense help an engaged couple receives, the better the chance the couple has for a lifelong, fulfilling marriage. I believe the seven helping sessions described in this chapter are the minimum number of sessions required. The engaged couple should also be assigned a large amount homework, which they must do each week to be prepared for the next session.

It is your job as the helper to let the couple know when and if you see *red flags* (things that concern you). You are responsible to God for what you recognize in this process.

Along with the seven detailed helping sessions, this chapter includes the following sections:
- Discussions Before Marriage
- How Much Do You Know About Yourself and Your Future Spouse?
- What the Bible Has to Say

Premarital Tests and Helping Sessions

John and Susan* were one of the most strikingly attractive engaged couples that I had seen. They seemed to be passionately in love. They came for engagement counseling but didn't feel they needed it. On one pretest I gave them I found they both had a very unrealistically high view of each other. They hadn't been with each long enough to work past the infatuation to the working stage of a relationship. This is not the time to decide to get married. It takes nine months to one year to start seeing the person as he or she really is.

This couple decided after one session of intensive counseling that they didn't need counseling. They took a few Gary Smalley relationship tapes and left. One year later John came to me very distraught, almost begging me to counsel him and his wife. She had left him a few days earlier to live with her parents. As we talked it became clear to me that much of this could have been avoided with many sessions of intensive engagement counseling.

The most recent statistics from the 2002 census show 50 percent of marriages end in divorce, yet 75 percent of adult Americans believe that marriage is a lifelong commitment and should not be ended except under extreme circumstances.[1] This shows us that most Americans want a good marriage but for many reasons do not have one. I have no doubt that John and Susan felt the same way about marriage, yet they didn't have the necessary skills to work out their relationship.

In Modesto, California, the divorce rates have dropped by 30 percent in the past thirteen years. This occurred after ninety-five clergy signed a Marriage Savers Community Marriage Policy, an "agreement between clergy to their congregation, community and other area churches to proactively decrease divorce rates and raise the standard for marriage. The agreements in which the churches will support marriage, such as offering pre-marital counseling, marriage enrichment programs and increased resources for married couples." This agreement requires, among other things, four months of premarital education.[2]

It is clear that with commitment to extensive engagement counseling there can be a decrease in divorce and an increase in the quality of marriages. There is no other way than for us as ministers to see that those under our care receive ample counseling.

There are many useful tests for premarital help that clergy have access to as a pastor.

---

*Not their real names.

Premarital Tests

Taylor Johnson Temperament Analysis

This is a 180-item questionnaire designed to measure nine personality traits, including dominant-submissive, hostile-tolerant, and self-disciplined-impulsive. It is easy to administer and score. It allows couples to compare themselves with their prospective mates. This is available from the Psychological Publications, Inc. (phone: 800-345-8378; inquiries: 805-373-7360). Once you attend a training class you will be able to order your own materials, score, and interpret the tests.

Prepare-Enrich

A series of three highly regarded and widely used inventories, each one with 125 items. "Prepare" is for premarital couples, "Prepare MC" is for premarital couples with children, and "Enrich" is for married couples. Each gives useful information in categories such as personality issues, sexual relationship, realistic expectations, and conflict resolution. Phone: 1-800-331-1661. Training is also needed for this test. Each test is mailed in for scoring for a small fee.

There are many other tests available also. Gary Collins in his *Christian Counseling* gives the names of several tests as well as many helping tips for couples.

Sessions

I suggest a *minimum* of seven sessions (one hour each) to enable the couple the hope of a good marriage as outlined below. The following is a blueprint for basic minimal engagement counseling.

First Session

The first session should include the following questions and background.

Questions to Ask
- Why do you want to marry this person?
- How do you know you love him (her)?
- What do you have to stand on when troubles come to know that this is the will of God? What is your devotional life like?
- What are your expectations of your fiancé?
- What do you see as your fiancé's needs?
- How will you make your fiancé's life better?

- Do you feel you are equal in value to your fiancé?
- Do you both forgive easily?
- If your fiancé never changed, can you accept him (her) as he (she) is now? This is a key question.

Possible Red Flags
- Note their understanding of what denotes the will of God. I have found that some couples have not thought through as to why they know this marriage is of God. There has not been much prayer, if any, to seek God's direction.
- A feeling that they can bring happiness to their future spouse.
- They both have low self-esteem.
- There is defensiveness, emotional withdrawing, critical nature, and disrespect of the other. These are what John Gottman calls the four horsemen of marriage—the four things that can destroy a marriage.[3]

Assign for Homework
- Writing unspoken rules they see in their own home as well as their partner's. Example: "You can never talk about sex at home"; "The dishes must be done before we go to bed"; "Never wake Dad if he is sleeping."
- Write down things they are losing as a result of marrying (independence, making their own decisions, receiving money from mom and dad, etc.).
- Write out what they see as their own needs.
- List what they see as their spouse's needs.
- Have them take the Taylor Johnson tests.
- Have the couple start reading: for women—*For Better or Best* by Smalley; for men—*If Only He Knew* by Smalley. Another good book for the man to read is *Every Man's Marriage* by Arterburn. I suggest both read *Every Man's Battle* by Arterburn.

Second Session

Go over the Taylor Johnson tests. This takes at least an entire session. Explore the areas of possible depression, ability to transmit and receive deep emotional intimacy, ability to perceive the needs of others, hostility—whether suppressed or apparent, self-worth, and possibly perfectionism. This is a time to explore family backgrounds.

Discuss homework from the first session.

Possible Red Flags
- Low self-esteem (Recommend the *Search for Significance* by McGee or *Telling Yourself the Truth* by Maria Chapman.)
- High amount of depression
- Difficulty bonding
- Blocking off feelings from others
- Imperceptive of own issues
- Overly perfectionistic

If there is time, deal with their arguments—how many, how often, over what? Explore ways to communicate in the next session.

Assign for Homework
- Read *Communication: Key to Your Marriage* by Norman Wright.

Third Session

Go over communication and conflict fighting. Continue to discuss arguments, more in depth. The couple needs to recognize that arguing in itself is not a problem. Arguing is an issue when disrespect (name calling), one becoming silent, and high defensiveness are exhibited. If the couple has never argued, they will more likely have issues than those who argue. If a couple does not argue, one partner is not giving his or her opinion. As John Gottman (marriage research expert) says, "Fighting whether rare or frequent is sometimes the healthiest thing a couple can do for their relationship." He further says satisfied couples maintain a "five to one ratio of positive to negative moments" in their relationship.[4]

Questions to Ask
- How was conflict settled in their home?
- **Discuss communication.** How did their parents communicate? How did this affect them? Give ways to increase communication. Discuss the importance of validating feelings and using "I" rather that "you" statements. (Example: *"I feel* hurt when you talk to me that way"—not *"You made* me feel hurt"). Discuss ways to paraphrase each other's statement to aid understanding. Give them listening skills such as: reflecting each other's statement to check for understanding and validating each other by acknowledging the frustration or hurt the other is experiencing.

- **Discuss spiritual maturity.** Where are you in your relationship? Give ways to work on spiritual unity. Talk to them about their need for praying together.

Possible Red Flags
- Argue to win, not to resolve difficulties
- Inability or refusal to forgive
- Not able to take responsibility for his (her) part of arguments
- Unable to see the other one's view on an argument
- Fighting in a verbally abusive manner
- Incompatibility spiritually

Assign for Homework
- Work on conflicts and attitudes toward roles. Have them write separately what they see as the responsibility and tasks of a man and a woman. Have them list as many jobs as possible—everything from buying groceries to cleaning the sink—the real details of life.

Fourth Session

Discuss roles and responsibilities. Talk about parenting, children, discipline, and so forth. Always continue to go back to see how they are communicating.

Questions to Ask
- What is submission? Is your view realistic?
- Do you know each other's needs?
- How much do you understand male/female differences? What have you learned from the books you have been reading? Are you committed to learning about your fiancé?

Possible Red Flags
- Unable to realistically look at roles
- Rigid in thinking, no flexibility on roles or rules; have totally different roles in mind
- Controlling, skewed view of submission
- Feel his (her) gender is superior
- Having little understanding of the other one's needs

Assign for Homework
- Have them continue reading in the Smalley and Arterburn books as mentioned in the first session. Have them discuss their readings with each other.

- Ask them for their parents' phone numbers. Call their parents and ask the woman's parents to write and send a letter to their (to be) son-in-law. Have them relay their joy to have a new son-in-law in their family, giving him encouragement and acceptance. Have the man's parents do the same for their (to be) daughter-in-law. If in-laws are close, this can be done together as a group.

Fifth Session

Read letters from in-laws if this is appropriate for the couple.

Questions to Ask
- What are the attitudes of your parents and how do you feel about your fiancé's parents?
- Are your parents accepting of this relationship?
- How close will they live?
- Are you taking money from your parents?
- Have you discussed how you will spend holidays?
- Continue discussing how you are communicating and if any problems have arisen.
- Talk about in-laws, relationships, and guidelines for them in regard to their new in-laws. Gary Collins' book *Christian Counseling* has tips in this regard.

Possible Red Flags
- Parents are not accepting new daughter-in-law/son-in-law.
- The man (engaged) is not able to leave and cleave (seems to be too attached to parents).
- Parents that may be controlling or nonsupportive of the couple. If they are not supportive, is their reason legitimate?

Assign for Homework
- Do a real budget together.
- Have the woman start reading *The Act of Marriage* by LaHaye.

Sixth Session

Talk about the budget.

Questions to Ask
- Who is in charge of the checkbook?
- Is one of you a spender and one a saver?

- Do you have similar or different spending habits (example: one shops at a thrift store, the other at Saks Fifth Avenue)?
- How much will you save of your budget?
- What will be the highest amount that either one would spend before calling the other and talking about it?
- Have you gone shopping together? If so, any problems?
- Do you see any problems with how the other handles money?
- Talk about friendships with other people.
- Do you like his (her) friends?
- Do you have friends in common?

Possible Red Flags
- Great diversity in spending habits.
- One is used to a great deal of spending.
- One or both have not worked to any degree in the past few years (dependent on parents).
- Great diversity in friends (she has hers, he has his, and neither meet).
- The man has not exhibited stability in work-related environments.

Assign for Homework
- Have the man read *The Act of Marriage* by Tim LaHaye one or two weeks before the wedding.

Seventh Session

Wedding plans. Meet with each separately if need be in regard to sexual issues. Talk about birth control, sexual satisfaction, giving suggestions to keep their intimacy alive. There are many Christian sources on sexual intimacy.

Did anything give you concern as a helper from their Taylor Johnson test in regard to sexual issues? (The Taylor Johnson test can show a blocking off to closeness, inhibited in expression, and a negative feeling about his or her body.)

Questions to Ask
- Do you know what "making love" means to the other (opposite sex)? (They need to understand the vast differences in thinking and in needs.)
- Can you talk to the other about everything?
- Do either of you have concerns or fears in this regard?

Discuss the wedding plans and helper's part (if applicable) in the ceremony.

Possible Red Flags
- Not understanding the differences in gender. This can be improved by reading material.
- Previous sexual contact by either in the past. God provides healing.
- Either have continually dealt with a pornography habit. This can create insatiable appetites or the other extreme—a dulling, where after marriage there is a lack of interest in sex.
- Woman not feeling good about her body.
- Negative perception of sex.
- Current sexual involvement between the two. This creates guilt, a blocking off from God, and problems in communication. It can affect their sexual intimacy in marriage.

Assign for Homework
- Have them write love letters to each other, giving their intimate feelings of love. Have them read and discover their love languages in Gary Chapman's *Love Languages*.

There are many variations to engagement helping, but being thorough is key. In some cities where community marriage policies have been adopted, divorce rates have dropped as much as 48 to 79 percent.[5] It is easy to see the need for engagement helping, and with the right tools, such as the method given to work with the couple, a helper can make a great difference in the future of marriages in his or her community. Take on the challenge that our culture has presented. Make a difference in your community!

In Washington State a number of churches are now partnering with the Washington Family Council to strengthen marriages and reverse the trend of divorcing couples. Washington Family Council reports of 1998-99 that 80 percent of all the state's weddings were performed by a clergy member. However, only 35 percent of married Washingtonians have received premarital instruction. Of those who have received premarital education, 80 percent found it helpful.[6]

We can see that with ample premarital instruction and counseling, problems like the one John and Susan encountered can be avoided.

Discussions Before Marriage

These are some important topics for the engaged couple to discuss. It is not a requirement that you discuss all of these topics, however, I recommend as much discussion as possible before marriage.

1. How to spend your leisure time
2. Relationship to in-laws
3. How to discipline children
4. Expectations for children's achievements
5. How many children to have
6. How much time to spend with the children
7. What kind of care or education to give children (baby-sitting, nursery school, public/private school, college)
8. Whether or not to have a pet
9. Expectations for the level of involvement in each other's careers; attending business functions
10. How to express feelings
11. How to fight
12. How to show love for one another
13. Expectations for fidelity
14. How much we will be involved in outside organizations
15. Whether or not to move due to one spouse's job
16. Whether or not to live in a certain area (neighborhood, city, state, etc.)
17. How open our home is to others
18. Politics
19. How much television is too much
20. What kinds of movies to watch
21. Whether or not to sleep in often
22. Views on alcohol
23. Expectations for cleanliness around the house and for personal hygiene
24. What is or is not appropriate with friends of the opposite sex
25. How much to tell others about our personal life and about one another
26. How much time to spend with other couples/how much time alone together
27. Where and when to go to church
28. How important is prayer life
29. How much will ministry be a part of our lives
30. How to spend our money
31. Whether to spend money or save it
32. How to invest our money

33. How much money to spend on personal things (clothes, books, etc.)
34. What kind of car to buy
35. How often we will eat out
36. Where to go on vacation
37. How to decorate the house
38. Who should have what chores
39. What kind of birth control to use

How Much Do You Know About Yourself and Your Future Spouse?

Each engaged person should be able to answer the questions below and talk about them with his or her future spouse. If a question cannot be answered now, they should be able to discuss why and how to deal with that in the future.

1. Are you a complete person without your future mate?
2. Do you have a daily prayer life?
3. Does your future mate have a daily prayer life?
4. Have you dealt with your past?
5. Are you ready to break emotional ties with your parents?
6. Do you have similar values?
7. Have you discussed children, visiting in-laws, and finances?
8. If your future mate never changes the way he or she is, will you be willing to accept him or her without change?
9. Have you fasted in regard to God's will in your life with your future mate?
10. Have you or your future mate been involved at all in pornography or in sexual relationships?
11. Does your future mate forgive easily?
12. Is your future mate revengeful?
13. Do you treat yourself as well as you treat your future mate?
14. Do you argue more than two times a week?
15. Is your future mate more positive or negative? How about you?
16. (HIM) Are you willing to lay down your life for your mate? (HER) Do you trust him so much that you will support his decisions?
17. Do you truly understand male/female differences?
18. Do you know your future mate's top five needs?
19. Is your future spouse critical of you?
20. Does your future mate "listen" to you?

21. Have you decided if both will work? Have you discussed jobs in the home?
22. Who is better with money?
23. How do you resolve fights?

What the Bible Has to Say

A Study of Marriage*

Both of you should work on this study together and complete it before the first session. It will provide you with some basic scriptural information plus give you an opportunity to be in the Word together.

MARRIAGE UNDER THE CARE AND COVERING OF GOD

Marriage tends to compound our problems, for in marriage we must learn to share our life with another person who also has needs and personal problems. This study is to encourage our hearts as we face a life together. This sharing of life is enhanced because: I. God created marriage, II. God protects marriage, and III. God redeems marriage.

I. God Created Marriage
   A. According to Genesis 2:18-25, what is the one thing about man that God said was not good?
   B. According to verse 20, what was all the rest of creation unable to be for the man?
   C. In light of verse 24, what is implied by the woman being made from a man's rib?

II. God Protects Marriage
   A. In Matthew 19:1-9 what does Jesus say about God's intention for marriage from the beginning of creation?
   B. According to verse 8 why did Moses allow divorce?
   C. How does God feel about divorce, according to Malachi 3:16?

III. God Redeems Marriage
   A. What did God do for Adam and Eve after they sinned, according to Genesis 3:21?
   B. According to Proverbs 18:22, what is promised to a man who finds a wife?
   C. Read John 2:1-11 and see how Jesus' first miracle might be an encouragement to any marriage in trouble.

---

*Written by Dan Stewart, president of Life Pacific College. Used with permission.

Notes

1. Rose M. Kreider and Jason M. Fields, "Number, Timing and Duration of Marriages and Divorces: 1996" (U.S. Census Bureau Current Populations Reports, February 2002), 18.

2. David Blankehorn, Steve Bayme, and Jean Bethke, "Rebuilding the Nest: A New Commitment to the American Family," *The Abolition of Marriage* (Milwaukee: Family Service America, 1990), 97-98.

3. John Gottman, Ph.D., *Why Marriages Succeed or Fail and How You Can Make Yours Last* (New York: Simon and Schuster, 1994), 72.

4. Ibid., 57.

5. Jeff Kemp, *Building Marriage in the New Millennium*, Executive Director (July 2003).

6. Ibid.

20 — MARITAL HELPS

Helping a couple having marital problems may mean working through several areas of their lives. Problems can range from misunderstandings and stress to intimacy and sexual issues. Many of these matters are explored in this chapter, with guidance to assist you in the helping process. Included is a list of ten common marital problems, a discussion about the root of marital problems, and information about the lack of sexual desire among women. Although no homework for the helpees is given in this chapter because so many kinds of marital issues are discussed, other features found in previous chapters—Steps to Assist the Helpee, Books for the Helpee, and so on—are provided for your use.

Ten Common Marital Problems

1. Failure to pray together as a couple. One of the few differences between the divorce rate of Christians and non-Christians comes from the couples who pray together. You cannot pray with someone when you are angry.
2. Failure to learn true intimacy. Few men understand what intimacy is to women as well as some women do not understand the need of sexual intercourse to men.
3. Failure to talk things out (hold resentments). Lack of communication is a greater problem than communicating with misunderstandings.
4. Failure to prioritize (allow time and stress to rule) and by that fail to make the other one's life better. This is really letting stress rule one's life.

5. Failure to understand difference or needs (don't value differences, don't meet needs, don't value what is truly important to spouse).
6. Failure to apologize humbly to one another.
7. As men—failure to take the spiritual leadership. This is vitally important to women. It is a part of protection to her.
8. As men—failure to protect wife from people and situations.
9. As women—failure to show respect and give admiration.
10. As women—failure to express self, instead expect spouse to be a mind reader and become angry when he can't.

The Root of Marriage Problems

CBS News cites a study on spouses called "Bad Relationship Bad for Heart" and why couples can develop hardening of the arteries. This coincides with God's Word to husbands to love their wife and wives to honor their husband. We will see how this fits with a man's need to protect his wife and a woman's need to admire her husband.

CBS referred to the study of March 2006 that showed the effects of hostility and controlling behavior on spouses' hearts. It was found that if a wife's husband was hostile toward her, she would develop hardening of the arteries. If the husband's wife was dominant, he would be more likely than other men to have hardening of the arteries. Let's look at this finding, viewing it through the Word of God.

The apostle Peter acknowledged wives' need for protection when he wrote, "Husbands, in the same way be considerate as you live with your wives, and treat them with respect as the weaker partner and as heirs with you of the gracious gift of life, so that nothing will hinder your prayers" (1 Pet. 3:7). This is showing that women do need protection as the weaker partner physically and sometimes emotionally.

In Eph. 5:33, the apostle Paul admonishes the church regarding marriage, "Each one of you also must love his wife as he loves himself, and the wife must respect [another translation—honor] her husband." It is vital that women value their husband by admiring him.

If a man is protecting his wife from many of life's frustrations, he is definitely loving her as himself and being considerate of her being the weaker partner (this will be described below). You can't be angry with someone and protect him or her at the same time. Most often anger from a husband gives the wife fear and anxiety. Fear is quite the opposite of safety.

Hostile husbands not being able to protect due to anger = wife with hardening of the arteries.

In the same way, if a woman is admiring and honoring her husband, she cannot be controlling at the same time. Control from a woman causes resentment and anger in a man. Honor is showing great deference and awe, quite the opposite of control.

Controlling wives not being able to admire and honor due to their control = husband with hardening of the arteries.

The same basic root of discord intertwines most all the couples I counsel: she does not feel protected and he does not feel admired. Although we often hear about these two basic elements, I believe we do not address them because we do not understand how they are manifested in real life. Here is an example of a couple facing a lack of protection and admiration.

The silence was tense as I sat with Bob and Kathy,* watching their faces crumple alternately with frustration and despair. This was my second session with them, and I was finally starting to see the root of their problem. The couple had come with the complaint that they "just weren't getting along anymore" and divorce had been mentioned. Kathy sat on the edge of her seat, chewing on her lower lip as she tried to formulate her next sentence. "I feel like a pressure cooker," she said finally. Her rigid posture and tight voice supported this idea. "I just feel all this weight closing in on me from all sides, and I know that one day soon I'm going to explode!"

I turned my attention to Bob, whose face reflected genuine confusion and concern mixed with intense frustration. "I don't get it," he began gruffly. "I work long hours every day to provide for her and our kids. I try to give her nice things whenever she wants them. I have never hit her, called her names, or been unfaithful to her. What else could she possibly want?" Kathy looked confused, too, like she felt that Bob's list should be enough to make her happy, and she was upset with herself that she wasn't. She stared at the floor for a few moments, then looked up into his eyes before quietly saying, "I just thought when I got married, someone would have my back, you know? That I would be covered. Instead, I feel like I am living life alone." As tiny, silent tears began to leak from Kathy's tired eyes, I let her words sink in. When the couple first came into my office, I had suspected their deeper

---

*Not their real names.

issue, but with Kathy's statement about living life alone, I knew Kathy did not feel protected.

When we hear the word "protection" we automatically think of physical protection. However, with most couples this is not the case. There is no abuse involved, and both partners know that the other would die for them if necessary. But there are other areas where a woman needs to feel protected, and the happiness of any marriage can be greatly increased if these areas are identified and addressed.

The Need of Protection for a Woman

1. *Protection from the stress she experiences from her internal world*

Let's look at where "weakness" needs protection.

Daily hassles can build up into monstrous stress for women. These can be things as simple as fighting traffic on her daily commute or as difficult as getting the kids ready for bed. Merely by asking his wife about such hassles and doing his best to relieve some of them, a husband can make her feel protected.

Women also live under the stress of too much to do. In today's society, a woman is often responsible for a job, raising the kids, keeping the house, and looking good while doing it! A husband can protect his wife from this type of stress by pitching in and helping around the house without being asked. A wife does not feel protected when her husband lives by the idea that "a woman's work is never done."

A woman's home is an extension of herself, and when projects go unfinished or things are broken, the woman tends to feel undone too. Her husband can help by seeing these needs around the house and fixing them without waiting for a reward. It also helps for him to be aware of his wife's physical limitations and her inability to do some of the chores around the house. Men can also protect their wives from stress by taking care of the "little things," such as being the one to get the waiter's attention at a restaurant or pumping her gas for her.

2. *Protection from people*

It is not uncommon for women to need protection by their husband from relatives. If a family member (on her side or his side) insults the wife, it is her husband's duty to stand up for her. He protects her from her relatives by putting her first and letting her know that she is more valuable to him than his extended family. With people in general, a man can protect his wife by spending focused time with her at a social gathering, by defending her against people who may insult her, and by showing public affection for her so everyone sees that he is proud to be with her.

3. *Protection from the pressure of outside forces*

Pushy salesmen, bill collectors, problems with credit cards . . . these can put unnecessary pressures on a woman. Her husband needs to understand that to a woman some of these issues are more easily fixed by a man and he needs to take the initiative. Money pressures are also common for many women. Making financial decisions together helps relieve such pressure from a woman. One way men sometimes cause their wives to feel unprotected in this area is when they spend too much money or change jobs and put their family under financial pressure.

4. *Protection from her husband's immaturity and irresponsibility*

Husbands need to protect their wives from their own selfishness by keeping their promises or by not spending so much time watching TV or on the computer and instead spend time with the family. Husbands need to be affectionate with their wives at times that don't lead to sex. A wife also needs protection from her husband's immaturity. He can make progress in this area by being open to talk with her about things that he doesn't understand, by being willing to admit when he is wrong, and by refraining from doing things that embarrass her.

The husband must make an effort to make decisions with his wife instead of leaving them all up to her. He can also help her by having a plan for the future, which will bring security. Spiritually, a husband needs to be the leader of the home. He can protect his wife in this area by modeling a prayer life, including praying with her, and by expressing interest in his wife's personal and spiritual growth. Finally, a woman needs protection from her husband's needs and desires overwhelming hers. He can show that he values her needs and desires by showing enthusiasm about her job and other activities, by cherishing her womanly characteristics and sensitivity, and by refraining from comparing her to other women. It might help to treat her as though the words "Handle with Care" were stamped on her forehead!

In Eph. 5:33, the apostle Paul admonishes the church regarding marriage, "Each one of you also must love his wife as he loves himself, and the wife must respect [another translation—honor] her husband." In many marriages, the problem of a wife feeling unprotected is not a one-sided issue. I have recognized that in this type of relationship the wife is often failing to respect her husband, as Paul exhorted wives to do. When a man does not feel respected and admired, he often stops protecting his wife. As such, when a woman does not feel protected, it is almost impossible for her to bring herself to admire and respect her husband. This easily spins into a miserable cycle that produces resentment and anger. Some women, especially those who grew up in a home with an absent father, do not know how to show respect or admiration for their husbands.

The Definition of Respect for a Man Includes These Four Aspects

1. *Honor—Mark of Distinction or Revering*

Honoring a husband is about valuing him and regarding him highly, including communicating personal gratefulness for him in front of others. A wife can honor her husband by making herself as beautiful as possible. She can also honor him by refraining from comparing her husband to other men. She can honor him by not always having to be right or prove a point but instead learn to let some things go. A woman who obviously shows loyalty to her husband above friends, relatives, and work honors him. Wives who honor their husbands also learn to be content in their present circumstances, even if they are not ideal.

2. *Love—Be Devoted to, Find Irresistible*

Many women love their husbands dearly but do not know how to show it in a way that he will receive. One way that a woman can show her love for her husband is by paying more attention to him than to others, especially at social gatherings. Also, she can express her love for him by accepting and returning his physical affection, which is a man's most common way of showing love.

"The husband should fulfill his marital duty to his wife, and likewise the wife to her husband. The wife's body does not belong to her alone but also to her husband. In the same way, the husband's body does not belong to him alone but also to his wife" (1 Cor. 7:3).

In order to show her love for her husband, a woman must not use withdrawal of sex as a punishment for his insensitivity or wrong actions. When they disagree, a wife can display her love in a gentle, respectful spirit toward her husband.

3. *Admire, Praise, and Adore—Think Highly of and Be Crazy over Your Husband*

Men love to receive praise and adoration from their wives. It is so important for a woman to express unconditional acceptance of her husband, as well as to give him her approval and encouragement. A wife can do this by making an effort to gain appreciation for her husband's occupation, and by expressing enthusiasm for his achievements. She can also use her womanly sensitivity to detect his personal goals and then lend her support as he pursues those goals. A man will feel adored by his wife if she brags to other people about him and refrains from discrediting or criticizing him.

4. *Defer to Him*

"Now as the church submits to Christ, so also wives should submit to their husbands in everything" (Eph. 5:24).

Submission has become a hot topic in some circles today, but a woman's deferment toward her husband is essential to her respecting him. This includes valuing his opinions enough to give hers up if necessary and a willingness to listen to his advice. A woman who defers to her husband expresses confidence in him and shows loyalty and support in spite of the wrong decisions he may make. Submitting to her husband also means being willing to admit when she is wrong and making a point to value his input in front of their children. Submission is not being a doormat but instead knowing when to say, "Honey, I will support you on that decision."

Many of these ways for husbands to protect their wives and for wives to admire their husbands are easier said than done and include a great deal of self-sacrifice. However, once the cycle has started, it takes one person to start making sacrifices to change things. This is God's way to a healthy fulfilling marriage.

Coping with the Lack of Sexual Desire Among Women

As a helper, I often wish I could give the gift of sexual desire to female helpees. Although this area is a private part of our lives, it is also a vital part of marital health and fulfillment. Even with helping, the degree of happiness and contentment in this area is sometimes difficult to ascertain. However, statistics demonstrate that at least one half of all marriages are lacking any sexual fulfillment. I'm convinced from years of helping and teaching on marital issues that part of the problem is faulty information and part is lack of information. I have found that few people chose to teach on this issue partly because of the discomfort of talking about sexual intimacy and partly because it is easy to be caught in the snare of your own words. Misinterpretations come easy in any group of people, especially when it involves something so private and personal.

We are bombarded daily in a society that is confused about the meaning of sexual love in a marital relationship. Women say they sometimes feel that they "are to be vapid virgins prior to marriage and then secretly be hot stuff in bed, returning in daylight to the role of a 'nice wife.'"[1] With this kind of confusion and lack of information women first need a clear road map to find clarity in their sexual relationship with their husband.

10 Reasons Women Withdraw Sexual Love from Their Husbands

1. **Stress.** Often considered the number one factor that robs a couple of intimacy. It would be easy to daily let stress take control of our lives. Stress can be defined as our body's natural response to any extra demands placed on it. In an average day, we encounter stressors several times. We often let the immediate stressors outweigh our priorities to our family and take up our time. We react to life by surviving through the stress rather than making our own choices. The first thing to go is most often intimate time together.

    Note: There is no extraordinary way to resolve stress issues. It is simply a choice to change priorities.

2. **Communication.** Husband and wife are unable to communicate their needs to one another. We often hear that communication is the biggest problem of a marriage. Actually it is more the lack of communication and misreading signals. It is imperative that there is a safe atmosphere to express needs.

    "The essence of sexual intimacy lies not in mastering specific sexual skills . . . but in the ability to deeply know and to be deeply known by one's partner. So simple to articulate, so difficult to achieve, this ability of couples to really see each other, to see inside each other during sex, requires the courage, integrity, and maturity to face oneself and, even more frightening, convey that self—all that one is capable of feeling and expressing—to the partner."[2] This depth of communication requires maturity and a great amount of unselfishness from husband and wife.

3. **Hormones.** The amount of testosterone that a woman has can determine her sexual drive. Women have one-ninth the amount of testosterone a man has. Therefore, if the wife loses one-half of one-ninth, there isn't much sexual drive remaining. It is common during the menopause years for testosterone to start diminishing; however in recent years research has shown women as early as their thirties may experience this loss.

    Note: Testosterone replacement therapy may be helpful.

4. **Unresolved issues.** Women particularly are good at hoarding and remembering the hurts of the past. Anytime there are unresolved hurts, it will be difficult for a woman to participate freely in sexual love-

making. She will feel "used." Everything flows together for a woman, therefore if something is wrong, it affects every area of her life.

The equity theory says that if a woman doesn't feel she is getting satisfaction out of her marital relationship, she will let her appearance go, refuse to have sex, or be neglectful in the marriage.[3]

Resolving differences is a must for the marital temperature to be healthy.

5. **Erroneous thinking.** Erroneous thinking says:
   - That being sexy for your husband is wrong. We are bombarded daily in a society that is confused about the meaning of sexual love in a marital relationship.
   - That it is up to your husband to initiate the degree of intimacy that you need. The wife needs to initiate intimacy. She understands her own needs of intimacy and what that involves. Communication begins with the wife expressing her needs in a loving manner.
   - If he doesn't give you intimacy, you can withdraw. This is where it is vitally important for the woman to understand and value the differences in her husband.
   - That all your husband wants is sex. A man is motivated by sight; however, the faulty thinking is that sex is all he wants. He is demonstrating to you his self-worth, attractiveness, manhood, and love. He is giving you his deepest love.

6. **Media influence.** The display of sex in the media has led us to believe that people are far more sexually active than studies demonstrate.
   - The media fantasizes sex, giving false beliefs that women should be perfect in body. Sexual fulfillment is highly influenced by one's self-concept. It is vitally important for a person to feel good about his or her body in order to enjoy someone else being close to and touching his or her body.[4]
   - The media influences women to believe they must be experts in bed. Only your husband can communicate to you his needs. Be willing to be creative in meeting his needs. Dr. Don Dunlap's *Twenty Ways to Become Your Husband's Dream Wife*[5] may be very beneficial to your sexual lovemaking.
   - The media influences women to believe they must have orgasm in order to be fulfilled. Women need to recognize that there isn't just one standard. Much popular literature about sex has

focused on the simultaneous orgasm as the sexual ideal, which often leads people to believe that their sex lives are lacking unless this ideal is achieved.[6]

According to Darling, since fewer than 50 percent of women consistently have orgasm during coitus, only those women who feel it interferes with personal satisfaction should seek some kind of therapy.[7]

7. **The wife initiates sex and the husband refuses.** If a man initiates and the woman refuses, he may simply attribute it to her lesser sexual appetite, whereas if the woman initiates and the man refuses, she has no stereotype to rescue her.[8] These factors give the man a much easier way to deal with refusal than a woman. Feelings of rejection can escalate and transfer later into lovemaking.

8. **Lack of intimacy and closeness.** When the wife feels she doesn't have intimacy (oneness) and physical closeness outside of sex.

    In a study written by Stephen Arterburn in *Every Woman's Desire*, these alarming statistics were given:
    - "84 percent of women feel they don't have intimacy."
    - "83 percent of women feel their husbands don't even know the basic needs of a woman for intimacy."[9]

    There are many books that demonstrate the need of men and women to understand each other's needs. Harley in *His Needs, Her Needs*, depicts the top need of a woman as affection. Without this, he says, the man is depleting her energy and desire for him.[10] Affection along with times of sharing inner feelings will help develop intimacy. I have seen few women who will not respond to a caring and loving husband who understands her needs.

9. **Abuse or a bad experience with sex.** Some statistics say that at least one out of every four women in the United States has been sexually molested by age eighteen. The effect of childhood trauma often appears more in adulthood as a woman becomes involved in intimate relationships. Even a one time bad experience can bring back memories during sexual lovemaking. Often the sexual relationship suffers and emotions escalate.

    Barshinger's book *Haunted Marriage* provides insight into healing into the lives of those touched by sexual abuse.

10. **Not understanding her husband's physical need.** *Every Man's Battle* says that most men desire release about every seventy-two hours.[11] Few women understand their husband's desire for sexual

intercourse on this level. A woman will benefit greatly by understanding her husband's needs by fulfilling his desires before he starts his day.

How Can You Start Changing the Sexual Temperature of the Marriage?

1. **Learning to talk about sex with your spouse.** Be comfortable with your own sexuality. To understand the needs of your spouse, you must understand yourself first. Do you have any biases? How much do you understand about the sexual differences between men and women? It is all about being willing to be vulnerable by opening your heart to your spouse.
2. **Understanding the differences in your spouse's needs.** Men need to understand what emotional and spiritual intimacy means to a woman. A man needs to view the needs of his wife in a holistic way—that every need and desire flow together. One need cannot be fully met if the others are ignored. Much of a woman's fulfillment comes from feeling a sense of oneness in the relationship. The book *Every Man's Marriage* by Arterburn is an excellent source for understanding the needs of women.

    A woman needs to understand the sexual needs and fantasies of her husband. She needs to understand the heart of her husband and highly prize what is important to him. *The Act of Marriage* by Tim LaHaye is a great source for understanding the needs and heart of a man. As a woman values her husband's needs, she will most likely see him responding to her with a greater depth of intimacy.
3. **Meaningful helping for couples** to freely express their frustrations and desires can be a great way to encourage freedom in discussion of the couple's sexual needs and will start the healing process. Many let preconceived ideas about helping stop them from pursuing what could result in awesome sexual fulfillment.

    It has been said that if the sexual temperature in a marriage is good, then sex is 10 percent of the relationship. If the sexual temperature in a marriage is on the downswing, it becomes 90 percent of the relationship. Since the need of a healthy sexual relationship is a necessary part of a good relationship, a couple must change their thinking by knowing the truth about sexual intimacy, start a dialogue discussing their needs and desires, and continue to take small steps daily toward bettering their lives together.

Steps to Assist the Helpee in Healing from Marital Problems

1. Be aware of your own issues. Be informed and well-read about information on the opposite sex. Be sure you can be objective and fair.
2. Let each spouse tell their scenario of why they are coming. Be sure to validate each one's feelings. Whether or not one of them is right or wrong is not important. They need to see you have some understanding of the issue.
3. Ask yourself, what is the real issue? Is the husband protecting the wife's feelings and caring about her hurts? Is the wife willing to honor her husband? Is the husband the spiritual leader? Is the wife willing to support her husband's leadership? You need to find out what is at the bottom of their arguments or their lack of communication. What are their hurts?
4. What is their goal in coming? Do they talk over their issues? Are they in denial about what is going on?
5. What does each one need to change in order to feel hope in the marriage?
6. Are their desires of change possible? What is each one's attitude like? What have they tried and failed? Converse with them establishing why they have come. (KEY: How willing are they to work on these issues? Only if both are willing to put 100 percent into this process will it work.)
7. Is forgiveness involved from one or both? Help each one in looking at his or her own issues. Give them each one or two things to work on until the next meeting.

Suggestions for Them to Work On

- Pray each night together—even a minute or two is a beginning.
- Read *Safe Haven Marriage* together and answer the questions at the end of each chapter.
- Work on individual issues if needed. See various roots and fruits for help in this area.
- Practice communicating with understanding. One may need to repeat in his or her own words what the other one said. They need to practice saying, "I feel _____ when you do that." Not, "You made me feel _____." They may need to learn how to validate each other, not give advice.

Suggested Questions for First Interview with a Married Couple*

1. What brings you here and which one was concerned about coming?
2. Often when people come for helping they are experiencing some kind of pain. What is the pain that you are experiencing in this relationship?
3. Who do you feel is contributing to this pain and in what way?
4. What efforts have been made to eliminate this pain and what has happened?
5. Describe what you want to have in your marriage.
6. How much time do you have to work on your marriage?
7. What is your dream that you had for your marriage? What has happened to it?
8. What would it take for you to be satisfied with your spouse? What would it take for him or her to be satisfied with you?
9. If your marriage were really good tomorrow, how would you know?
10. What do you want from your marriage and what are you willing to do to get there?
11. If I were to ask you the question, "What are you doing to mess up this marriage?" after you recover from the shock of such a direct question, what would you say?
12. In what way do you complement each other?
13. What are your needs? Is your spouse aware of how to meet them?
14. Let's think about the goals you have for helping. What would it be like if the helping were completely successful?
15. What is the worst possible thing that could happen in helping? What do you fear the most?

Books for the Helpee

Marriage

Arterburn, Stephen. *Every Woman's Desire*. Colorado Springs: Waterbrook Press, 2001. (MEN)

Chapman, Gary. *The Five Love Languages*. Chicago: Northfield Publishing, 1995.

Cloud, Henry, and John Townsend. *Boundaries in Marriage*. Grand Rapids: Zondervan, 1999.

---

*Dan Stewart, president of Life Pacific College, Counseling Course Materials, 2003. Used with permission.

Collins, Gary R. *Family Shock: Keeping Families Strong in the Midst of Earthshaking Change*. Wheaton, Ill.: American Association of Christian Counselors, Tyndale House Publishers, Inc., 1995.

Evans, Debra. *Blessing Your Husband*. Wheaton, Ill.: Focus on the Family, Tyndale House Publishers. (WOMEN)

Hart, Archibald, and Sharon Hart Morris May. *Safe Haven Marriage*, Feb. 2003.

Rainey, Dennis and Barbara. *Building Your Mate's Self-Esteem*. Nashville: Thomas Nelson, 1995.

Communication

Wright, Norman. *Communication: Key to Your Marriage*. Revised and updated edition. Ventura, Calif.: Regal Books, 2000.

Parenting

Cloud, Henry, and John Townsend. *Boundaries for Kids*. Grand Rapids: Zondervan, 1999.

Dobson, Dr. James C. *Bringing up Boys*. Carol Stream, Ill.: Tyndale House, 2005.

——————. *The New Strong Willed Child*. Carol Stream, Ill.: Tyndale House, 2007.

Smalley, Gary. *The Keys to Your Child's Heart*. Waco, Tex.: Proven Word Books, 1984.

Sexual Intimacy

Dobson, James. *Romantic Love*. Ventura, Calif.: Regal Books, 2004.

Focus on the Family. *The Passionate Marriage*. Ventura, Calif.: Gospel Light, 2003.

Gardner, Tim Alan. *Sacred Sex: A Celebration of Oneness in Marriage*. Colorado: Waterbrook Press, 2002.

LaHaye, Tim, and Beverly LaHaye. *The Act of Marriage*. Grand Rapids: Zondervan, 1976.

Leman, Kevin. *Sex Begins in the Kitchen*. Grand Rapids: Revell, 1999.

Scriptures for the Helpee

For Wives

Ephesians 5:22-24
Wives, submit to your husbands as to the Lord. For the husband is the head of the wife as Christ is the head of the church, his body, of which he is the Savior. Now as the church submits to Christ, so also wives should submit to their husbands in everything.

Titus 2:4-5
Then they can train the younger women to love their husbands and children, to be self-controlled and pure, to be busy at home, to be kind, and to be subject to their husbands, so that no one will malign the word of God.

For Husbands

1 Peter 3:7 (NLT)
In the same way, you husbands must give honor to your wives. Treat your wife with understanding as you live together. She may be weaker than you are, but she is your equal partner in God's gift of new life. Treat her as you should so your prayers will not be hindered.

Colossians 3:19
Husbands, love your wives and do not be harsh with them.

1 Timothy 3:2
Now the overseer must be above reproach, the husband of but one wife, temperate, self-controlled, respectable, hospitable, able to teach.

1 Timothy 3:12
A deacon must be the husband of but one wife and must manage his children and his household well.

Titus 1:6
An elder must be blameless, the husband of but one wife, a man whose children believe and are not open to the charge of being wild and disobedient.

For Both

1 Corinthians 13:4-7 (NLT)
Love is patient and kind. Love is not jealous or boastful or proud or rude. It does not demand its own way. It is not irritable, and it keeps no record of being wronged. It does not rejoice about injustice but rejoices whenever the truth wins out. Love never gives up, never loses faith, is always hopeful, and endures through every circumstance.

Notes

1. Charlotte Kasl, *Women, Sex, and Addiction* (New York: Ticknor and Fields, 1989), 13.
2. D. Schnarch, "Inside the Sexual Crucible," *Networker* (March/April 1993), 40-48.
3. Janet S. Hyde and John DeLamater, *Understanding Human Sexuality*, 6th ed. (Boston: McGraw Hill, 1997), 325.
4. David Knox and Caroline Schacht, *Marriage and the Family* (Belmont, Calif.: Wadsworth, 1999), 48, 194.
5. Dr. Don Dunlap, "Eight Sure Ways a Wife Can Ruin a Marriage" (1998). http://www.electro-net.com/~dondun/Wife%20Ruin.htm.
6. J. D'Emilio and E. B. Freedman, *Intimate Matters: A History of Sexuality in America*, 2nd ed. (Chicago: University of Chicago Press, 1998), 267-68.
7. C. A. Darling, J. K. Davidson Sr., and D. A. Jennings, "The Female Sexual Response Revisited: Understanding the Multiorgasmic Response in Women," *Archives of Sexual Behavior*, 20 (1991), 527-40.
8. Hyde and DeLamater, *Understanding Human Sexuality*, 318.
9. Stephen Arterburn, Fred Stoeker, and Mike Yorkey, *Every Woman's Desire* (Colorado Springs: Waterbrook Press, 2001), 61.
10. Willard Harley, Jr., *His Needs, Her Needs*, 15th ed. (Old Tappan, N.J.: Baker, Revell, 2001), 182.
11. Stephen Arterburn, Fred Stoeker, and Mike Yorkey, *Every Man's Battle* (Colorado Springs: Waterbrook Press, 2000), 64.

21 – LEGAL AND ETHICAL ISSUES

Knowing the legal and ethical risks and responsibilities that come when working with a helpee is essential. The guidelines, questions, and information found in this chapter are designed to assist you in these matters. Areas of risk, knowing when to make a referral, and legal and ethical dilemmas are among the topics covered. Having a sound understanding of these issues will help provide a safe and healthy experience for both you and the helpee.

Areas of Risk[1]

1. Interpretation and using psychological tests unless qualified.
2. Belief that there are "simple spiritual solutions [for] complex emotional and psychological problems."
3. "Belief that pastoral and lay [helpers] need only biblical training to solve such severe problems as neuroses, psychoses, and suicidal intentions."
4. "Belief that sincerity and good intentions are the major ingredients in pastoral and lay [helping]."
5. "[Helping] psychotic and suicidal individuals."
6. "[Helping a] mentally incompetent person."
7. "Advising against medical or psychological treatment."
8. "Denial of the existence or severity of a psychological or psychosomatic disorder."
9. "Improper care of records" or no records at all.
10. "Failure to give credence to violent intentions or statements." Failure to follow through by contacting police and following policy of your state.

11. "Misdiagnosing psychotics as demon-possessed."
12. "Misrepresenting [your] title, position, degree, or abilities." *Do not call yourself a counselor* if you aren't licensed by your state.
13. "Poorly supervised lay [helpers]."
14. "Recommending divorce" for any reason.
15. "Sexual relations with a counseled" person.
16. "Violation of confidentiality."
17. Not understanding when confidentiality can be broken (see page 283, "Authorization to Release Information").
18. Telling one spouse that his or her mate has AIDS when that fact was told to you in confidence.
19. Not knowing the laws in regard to child/elder abuse. Generally you have thirty-six to forty-eight hours to report if you suspect physical or sexual abuse.
20. Not knowing how to deal with a battered woman/man—who to call. You need to have the numbers available for abuse, battered women's homes, rape crisis centers, suicide hot line numbers, doctors, psychiatrists, and other professionals available to know information before and when needed.
21. In case of possible suicide, keep the person with someone, call the police, and call your suicide hot line number and whatever else is asked of you. This person needs to be referred out.
22. *Know when to refer* to other professionals.

What Every Pastor Should Know

Helping can be very rewarding and can also be emotionally depleting. How you as a pastor balance the demands and needs of a congregation and keep yourself from legal hassles is of utmost importance.

1. **Learn the wisdom of referral.** You need to know when something is beyond you—when it entails too many sessions or is too complex. For example, when any type of abuse is involved, you should have available a list of Christian helpers, psychiatrists, and so forth, to whom you can make a referral.
2. **To protect yourself, limit your sessions to three.** Not only is your time valuable, but if the person needs more than three sessions, he or she should be referred out.
3. **Assign homework.** If you are "working" on the person's situation by giving your time, he or she needs to work also. This will sort out

those who just want to vent and not change. Tell the person that when he or she does the assigned work, you will see him or her.

Examples of assignments:

Self-esteem. Have the helpee read *Telling Yourself the Truth* by Backus and write down his or her negative self-talk each day and then refute it, keep a journal of his or her devotional life, and read the scripture passages you have given. An alternative book might be *Boundaries* by McCloud and Townsend.

Rejection. Have the helpee read *The Root of Rejection* by Joyce Meyer. Possibly another book would be *The Art of Forgiveness* by Smedes. Have the person write out behaviors that he or she wants to change and choose one of the behaviors to work on each day.

Sexual addiction. Refer the helpee to a men's or women's group (at another church if you don't have one). If the helpee is a man, have him read *Every Man's Battle* by Stephen Arterburn or *Pure Desire* by Ted Roberts. A woman helpee will benefit from reading *Addicted to Love* by Arterburn, *Every Woman's Battle* by Arterburn and Shannon Ethridge, or *She Has a Secret* by Douglas Weiss.

Divorce. Read *Growing Through Divorce;* work on some of the listed questions in the back of the book.

If the helpee doesn't follow through on the assignment, don't see him or her again. If the helpee isn't willing to work on getting better, why should you? This way you weed out those who aren't serious about changing from those who want to change. Your time is valuable.

4. **Learn to validate.** Validation is merely acknowledging verbally what you are hearing the person say and what he or she appears to be feeling. You can "see the pain." Sometimes you can simplify your life when you learn to truly validate after a person speaks of pain. That in itself can be a healer.

Example: I can see you have been through a lot of very difficult situations. I can see you are experiencing great pain. I can't even imagine how difficult it might be to go through something like that.

Protect Yourself from Legal and Ethical Dilemmas

1. Keep a list of phone numbers for:
   a. Suicide hotline—different states have different guidelines.
   b. Abuse (for children and elderly)—find out the time limit to call, and so forth.
   c. Domestic violence hotline (know where to call for shelters).
   d. AIDS prevention

   If the person you are seeing is going to harm someone else, in some states you must call the police and the person that might be harmed. In other states you can only call the police. Know your state's policies.

   Keep a written plan for each of the above. Keep the numbers and plans available to whoever is at the church taking messages.

2. Always document each part of your plan for the above mentioned as you carry it out. Write down the dates, times, who you called, what was said, and then your next step. You need to know beforehand the best plan for each of the four: suicide, abuse, domestic violence, and AIDS. You as a helper at a church can be held liable.

3. Keep records of each person you see. It is good to keep simple records stating the person's name, why they came in, and briefly what was said. Example: A person is considering divorce. You give him or her pros and cons of a divorce, you show him or her Scripture, but *you don't make any decisions for him or her.* Even if the person is being battered, or the husband is a homosexual, and so forth, don't suggest that the person get a divorce. Keep the information of what you said well documented for your own protection. Keep all records in a confidential place.

4. As a pastor, if you are not a licensed helper, don't call yourself professional, helper, and so forth. Simply say that you will *minister* to their needs.

5. Don't give advice outside of God's Word. Helping is not advice. It is showing the alternatives and giving the helpee the keys to learn to cope and make his or her own decisions. Simplistic advice such as ways to help someone parent is different from a life-altering decision.

6. Don't help anyone under eighteen unless you have written permission from his or her parents. It is really in your best interest to refer him or her. A youth pastor could spend time with a teen. If there is more than one time that the teen asks to talk to the youth

pastor, then it would be wise to talk to the parents. Remember, you are still held to confidentiality. You need to check with your state's guidelines for children, their ages, and so forth.
7. If you are in a dilemma about what to do, call a helper, doctor, psychiatrist—or whatever you have to do and document your call. Example: If a person tells you he or she has AIDS but refuses to tell the spouse. What do you do? In most all states, it is unlawful for you to disclose to anyone that the person has AIDS. You can recommend the person tell the spouse. You can tell him or her that you are uncomfortable with the fact that he or she won't tell the spouse, but you cannot tell anyone. It would be wise to call an AIDS hotline and without using any names, ask their procedures. Document the call. Call a medical doctor—ask what he or she would do (without using any names). Document the call.
8. Don't counsel the opposite sex unless you have an office with a window in the door and you know that someone is in the area outside your office at all times. Even then, unless there is at least a twenty-five-year gap between your ages, it isn't a wise idea.
9. Keep all information confidential (even from your spouse) unless of course the helpee would be in harm to himself or herself or others, abuse is involved, or you have been asked to go to court to testify on this information. Have each person sign a waiver form stating he or she knows the exceptions to confidentiality.
10. When and if you feel yourself being attracted to a helpee, stop helping him or her. If you are only seeing the helpee three times, this won't be difficult. Take your spouse with you on the last session if you need to see this person again. From a survey of four major denomination, 90 percent of pastors admitted to being sexually attracted to at least one helpee. Eighty-three percent of adulterous relationships state it began in a helping session.[2] Guard your heart. Dr. Dobson says that the biggest downfall of pastors is thinking that it will never happen to them.

Most important of all, keep in prayer and let the Lord give you His wisdom. "If any of you lacks wisdom, he should ask God, who gives generously to all without finding fault, and it will be given to him" (James 1:5).

Adultery and Helping

- Seventeen percent of pastoral helpers admitted to having sexual contact with helpees.

- Eighty percent of those who reported to crossing the boundary did so with more than one helpee.
- More than 58 percent of pastoral helpers have been sexually aroused during helping session.
- Ninety percent of pastoral helpers admitted to being sexually attracted to at least one helpee.
- Nearly 75 percent of pastoral helpers have had sexual fantasies about a helpee.
- Findings from four major surveys showed that 44 to 56 percent of helpers report having treated a patient formerly abused by another helper.
- From a survey of four denominations, 23 percent reported sexual physical contact with a church member.
- Twelve percent stated they had sexual intercourse with a church member.
- Ninety percent of pastoral helpers reported to having a constant struggle with sexual temptation.
- Forty-six percent of pastoral helpers reported having sexual problems within their own marriages.
- Eighty-three percent of ministers who began adulterous relationships state it began in a helping session.[3]

Concerns for Helpers

Evaluate yourself (the helper) and answer the following questions. Which ones do you need to work on? It is important as a helper to evaluate yourself yearly using these questions.

1. Do I know the laws of my state regarding those who help?
2. Which helpees do I enjoy seeing more than others? Who? Why?
3. Am I using virtually the same forms I did years ago?
4. How do I hear the inner prompting of the Holy Spirit?
5. Am I consistently praying for helpees?
6. How are my personal devotions?
7. Am I applying the things I'm sharing with helpees to my own relationships?
8. What characterizes my relationships outside of helping?
9. What is my walk with Christ like?
10. Do I have a handle on my emotions?
11. Am I aware of what my issues are?

12. Are any of my needs (especially those tied to my issues) being met by my helpees? Which needs? And which helpees?
13. Am I following my treatment plans legally and ethically every time? What do I think about that?
14. What is the major lesson God is teaching me presently in my life?
15. Do I know when I'm getting close to burnt out? Am I?

Notes

1. Nos. 1-16 adapted or quoted from Thomas L. Needham, "Areas of Risk" in Ted Roberts and Kathy Rodriguez, *Pure Desire Workbook* (Gresham, Oreg.: East Hill Church, 2006), sess. 10, app. C.

2. John Kie Vining, *Pastoral Care/Counseling Never Includes Sex* (New York: Cummings and Hawthaway, 1995), 16-17.

3. Taken from ibid.

22 – SUPPLEMENTS

What follows are several supplements to assist you in the counseling (helping) process. The first, "Understanding Self," is a form for the helpee to fill out to aid in his or her assessment. Coming next is "Prayers for Helpees," a collection of prayers to encourage the helpee. Finally, a set of useful documents is included in "Helpful Forms for Legal Protection."

Understanding Self

This form is designed to help a helpee search his or her past for clues of possible hurt in order to discover what has come about in his or her heart. This could be used before you decide to talk with someone. It could give you clues as to what direction you need to take. Perhaps this person must be referred to another source and not see you at all. Always safeguard yourself and the person needing help by making the best decision.

UNDERSTANDING SELF

- List the positive and negative characteristics of your dad.
- List the positive and negative characteristics of your mom.
- List as many significant negative and positive experiences as you can from the first time you can remember.
  1.
  2.
  3.
  4.
  5.
  6.
  7.
  8.
  9.
  10.
- Were there arguments in your home? If so, how were they handled? Example: We sat down and talked about it. Or, my dad blew up and mom tried to calm him down. We didn't talk about it. Others . . .
- How often did you sit down with one or both parents and talk about how you felt about something?
- How often did you express emotions? Why or why not?
- What emotions were not expressed?
- How often did you express your opinions? Were they valued?
- Which one of these has the closest fit for you: the favored child, the least favored child, the dependable child—always helping, the lost child, the family hero, the clown of the family, the caretaker of one parent (in some ways), the least attached to the family?
- Go back to the characteristics of your parents. Which of those characteristics do you have?
- Which of those characteristics does your spouse have?
- How often do you express feelings to your spouse (or someone close)? Why or why not?
- What would you like to change as a result of this information?

Prayers for Helpees

Sometimes people are so discouraged they feel they can't or don't know how to pray. A prayer that would fit their situation can be helpful until they are better able to deal with issues.

Prayer for When You Are Stuck in the Mud

Dear God,

I don't always feel like talking to You but I will. I am trying to make the right choices because it is the only road to freedom. Please help me with this.

I am making a choice to let go of all the pain I have had in my life. Please help me to mean this. Help me to choose today to forgive You and make the right choices to trust You.

Help me to forgive _____ if I am holding anything against him (her). Help me to see him (her) the way You want me to see him (her). I am asking for You to bless him (her). If there is anyone else in my life that I might have unforgiveness toward, please help me to forgive.

I am making a choice to let myself off the hook. I don't want to have to deal with all of this anymore. Please help me to forgive myself if I am being too hard on myself. Please help me to stop putting up walls and be willing to see what is inside. Let me be willing to let go of the *things* that are keeping me from being close to You, the things that are keeping me from truly touching others. Free me from their holds!

Help me to choose to love You and to love myself. Help me to praise You when I don't feel like it. I will choose to praise You even when I don't feel like it.

Help me to be content as I am as I grow closer to You. Help me to delight myself in You. Stir me up that I will feel excited about serving You.

Help me to discover the things that are holding me back from going forward in my life. Help me work out my relationship with You and others in the right way.

I am choosing to praise You each day! Please help me to choose to be happy and choose to praise You no matter what.

I am asking You for peace. I am asking You that my prayers will start reaching You. Help me to trust You that You will now be able to take care of me. I have tied Your hands and I am asking for a *release* from the pain and anger. *I am choosing to forgive. Help me to mean it. Help me to be patient with myself and with you.*

In Jesus' name I pray. Amen.

Prayer to Be Renewed in the Lord
Dear God,

I am coming to You now to ask for Your help with my life. I want You to pull down any strongholds in my life that are hindering me from being close to You. The only way I can be totally free is to have You remove *all* the areas that are hindering my walk with You. Please show me the areas that need to be removed. Help me in getting them out of my life. Please forgive me where I have failed You and have not made the effort I needed to serve You.

I am asking that You will help me to forgive myself for the past. I want to be free from that. Help me to see myself as You see me. Help me in forgiving _____. Help me to see the areas that I need to forgive and let go of. Open my eyes to see any anger or unforgiveness toward other areas in my life that I may not even recognize. I want to make the right choices so I will praise You for these circumstances as they are now. I want all unforgiveness rooted out.

Help me to delight myself in You and desire only what You want. Renew my vision for ministry and for others. Use me to bless others each day. Help me in my prayer life to seek You every day.

I am asking You to help me to praise You every day for all things. I am asking for peace in my life. Help me to be the person of God that You want me to be. Help me to want to be as close to You as I can and be willing to do what You want.

In Jesus' name I pray. Amen.

Needing to Love and Forgive Self
Dear God,

I don't feel like talking to You, but I will. I am trying to make the right choices because it is the only road to freedom. Please help me with this.

I am making a choice to let You off the hook for all the pain I have had in my life. I am asking You to forgive me for being so angry at You. Please help me to mean this.

I am making a choice to let myself off the hook. I don't want to suffer anymore. Please help me to forgive myself for what I felt I did. Please help me to stop being angry with myself.

Help me to choose to love You and to love myself. Help me to praise You when I don't feel like it. I will choose to praise You even when I don't feel like it.

I am asking You for peace. I am asking You that my prayers will start reaching You. Give me the strength to make the choice to forgive _____—to forgive him (her) and turn him (her) over to You. Help me to trust You that You will now be able to take care of me. I have tied Your hands and I am asking for a *release* from the pain and anger. *I am choosing to forgive. Help me to mean it. Help me to be patient with myself and with You.*

In Jesus' name I pray. Amen.

Helpful Forms for Legal Protection

The forms on this page and the next are for use in the helping process.[1]

HELPEE'S RIGHTS AND RESPONSIBILITIES

As a helpee of the *(name of your church)* and helpee of the *(name of your center)*, you have certain rights.

1. You have the right to dignity and respect as an individual human being.[2]
2. You have the right to loving care. "Therefore, regardless of how we respond to and challenge harmful attitudes and actions, Christian counselors *[in this case, ministers or helpers]* will express a loving care to any client *[in this case, helpee]*, service-inquiring person, or anyone encountered in the course of practice or ministry, without regard to race, ethnicity, gender, sexual behavior or orientation, socio-economic status, education, denomination, belief system, values, or political affiliation."[3]
3. You have a right to be provided with respectful care in the perimeters of our ministry here at *(name of church)*.
4. You have the right to confidentiality with those who minister help. You "may direct the mental health counselor *[in this case, minister or helper]*, in writing, to release information to others. The release of information without the consent of the client *[you]* may only take place under the most extreme circumstances. The protection of life, as in the case of suicidal or homicidal clients, exceeds the requirements of confidentiality. The protection of a child, an elderly person, or a person not competent to care for themselves from physical or sexual abuse or neglect requires that a report be made to a legally constituted authority."[4] There may be other possible exceptions to confidentiality. The laws of the state must be followed.
5. You have the right to know how we see the issue you are dealing with and the right to have resources made available to help improve this issue.
6. You have the right to refuse coming to this ministry. Even though your helper may strongly suggest you seek help here, you may choose not to follow the helper's advice.

Along with these rights go certain responsibilities. These are:

1. To be honest, open, and willing to share your concerns about your life and about this ministry with your helper.
2. To recognize that this is a ministry, not a counseling service, and that there are many limitations to this ministry.
3. To ask questions when you need clarification or don't understand.
4. To discuss any reservations you have about your ministry time with your helper.
5. To follow the homework agreed upon.
6. To recognize that because this is a ministry and not a counseling service we may refer you to a professional counseling service if we feel we are not qualified to help after a small number of meetings with you.
7. To attend this church regularly as we provide you help.

If a dispute should arise between you and the ministry team, we ask that you agree to solve this dispute through mediation and, if necessary, through the arbitration services of the Christian Legal Society.

Remember that you are responsible for your thoughts, feelings, actions, and your growth. We are here to help you become the best person you can be.

Please sign below indicating that you have read and understand your rights and responsibilities.

I have agreed to the above information, and I will not in any way hold *(name of the church)*, their agents, or their employees liable for my actions.[5] I will abide by the aforementioned requests.

Signature: _____ Date: _____

Print: _____ Date: _____

AUTHORIZATION TO RELEASE INFORMATION

I, the undersigned, agree that information I may have disclosed in my voluntary participation in ministry at *(the name of your church)* may be released to appropriate authorities and persons on a "need-to-know" basis whenever, in the discretion of *(the name of your church)*, the information presented is deemed as "reasonable cause" to believe that there may be a threat of harm to self or others, child abuse, elder or dependent adult abuse, or a need for hospitalization, or the information has been made an issue in a court action or poses a threat of harm to the ministry of *(the name of your church)*.[6]

Confidentiality is essential but not absolute.
Exceptions
- The helpee poses a threat of harm to self or others.
- A helpee under the age of 16 is the victim of abuse, or information is given that pertains to evidence of child abuse.
- There is evidence of elder or dependent adult abuse.
- The helpee needs to be hospitalized.
- The information is made an issue in a court action.
- The helpee requests a release of record.
- Information that poses a threat of harm to *(name of church)*.

I willingly release and hold harmless *(the name of your church)*, their agents, employees and volunteers of *(the name of your church)*, from claims of loss, damage, and harm that may arise as a result of the disclosure of the above information.

Signature: _____ Date:_____

Print: _____ Date:_____

Notes

1. Before designing a legal form for your church, check with the American Association of Christian Counselors (AACC) Code of Ethics (http://www.aacc.net/about-us/code-of-ethics/). For laypeople, the code states the following:

> Lay helpers minister only under the supervision of the church or a Christian counseling organization. Lay helpers seek out and secure supervision and spiritual-ethical covering by pastors and professional clinicians. Independent, unsupervised, and solo practice or ministry by lay and unlicensed helpers and non-ordained staff shall be avoided due to its excessive risk for legal, ethical, spiritual, interpersonal, and ecclesiastical trouble ("The Y2004 Final Code" developed and drafted by the AACC Law and Ethics Committee, George Ohlschlager, chairman, "4-220 Lay Helping Under Supervision of the Church," 24).

2. On the Net Counseling, "Client's Bill of Rights and Responsibilities" (ONTHENET, INC., 2008), https://onthenetcounseling.com/index.php?file=sp&fn=Client%27s_Bill_of_Rights_and_Responsibilities.

3. American Association of Christian Counselors, *AACC Code of Ethics*, "1-101 Affirming the God-given Dignity of All Persons," p. 6, http://www.aacc.net/about-us/code-of-ethics/.

4. *Code of Ethics of the American Mental Health Counselors Association*, "Principle 3: Confidentiality" (2000), http://www.amhca.org/code.

5. *Handbook for the Operation of Foursquare Churches*, "Pastoral Care Policies," pp. G-1, G-2, http://www.foursquare.org/.

6. Ibid.

BIBLIOGRAPHY

Arterburn, Stephen. *Addicted to Love.* Ann Arbor, Mich.: Vine Books, 1991.

―――. "Freeing the Sex Addict." *Christianity Today, Inc. Leadership Journal,* 1995.

Arterburn, Stephen, and Fred Stoeker. *Every Man's Battle.* Colorado Springs: Waterbrook Press, 2000.

Arterburn, Stephen, Fred Stoeker, and Mike Yorkey. *Every Woman's Desire.* Colorado Springs: Waterbrook Press, 2001.

Bales, Norman, ed. *All About Families Newsletter.* "Coping with Shame and Guilt." Believers Organization—http://www.believers.org/believe/bell47.htm

Black, Claudia. *Changing Course: Healing from Loss, Abandonment, and Fear.* Center City, Minn.: Hazelden Foundation, 2002.

Blankehorn, David, Steve Bayme, and Jean Bethke. "Rebuilding the Nest: A New Commitment to the American Family." *The Abolition of Marriage* (Milwaukee, Wis.: Regnery Publishing, 1990.

Blumstein, P., and P. Schwartz. *American Couples.* New York: Morrow, 1983.

Bradshaw, John. *The Family.* Deerfield Beach, Fla.: Health Communications, Inc., 1996.

Bray, James. *Stepfamilies: Love, Marriage, and Parenting in the First Decade.* New York: Broadway Books, 1998.

Carlson, Dwight L., M.D. *Christianity Today* (Feb 9, 1998), Vol. 42, No. 2.

Carnes, Patrick. *Facing the Shadow: Starting Sexual and Relationship Recovery.* Carefree, Ariz.: Gentle Path Press, 2001.

―――. *Out of the Shadows: Understanding Sexual Addiction.* Center City, Minn.: Hazelden, 1992.

Carter, Les, and Frank Minirth. *The Freedom from Depression Workbook.* Nashville: Thomas Nelson Publishers, 1995.

―――. *The Anger Workbook.* Nashville: Thomas Nelson, 1993.

Chadwell, David W. "The Foundation of Evil." *Repentance: Teacher's Guide.* http://www.westarkchurchofchrist.org/chadwell/repent/teaching/y2004ql1.htm (accessed July 21, 2009).

Cloud, Dr. Henry, and Dr. John Townsend. *The Mom Factor.* Grand Rapids: Zondervan, 1996.

Collins, Gary R. *Christian Counseling.* Dallas: Word Publishing, 1977.

―――. *Christian Helping: A Comprehensive Guide,* rev. ed. Dallas: Word Publishing, 1988.

―――. *Family Shock.* Wheaton, Ill.: Tyndale House Publishers, Inc., 1995.

Collum, Jason. "Reality Check Time Comes Before 'I Do.'" *American Family Association Journal* (June 2003).

Cook, Jerry, with Stanley C. Baldwin. *Love, Acceptance, and Forgiveness.* Ventura, Calif.: Regal Books, 1979.

Coon, Dennis. *Essentials of Psychology*, 9th ed. Belmont, Calif.: Thomson Wadsworth, 2003.

Corey, Gerald. *Theory and Practice of Counseling and Psychotherapy.* Pacific Grove, Calif.: Brooks/Cole Publishing Co., 1986.

Darling, C. A., J. K. Davidson Sr., and D. A. Jennings. "The Female Sexual Response Revisited: Understanding the Multiorgasmic Response in Women." *Archives of Sexual Behavior*, 20 (1991).

Deal, Ron. *The Smart Stepfamily: Seven Steps to a Healthy Family.* Ada, Mich.: Bethany House Publishers, 2002.

D'Emilio, J., and E. B. Freedman. *Intimate Matters: A History of Sexuality in America.* New York: Harper and Row, 1988.

Dunlap, Dr. Don. "Eight Sure Ways a Wife Can Ruin a Marriage." (1998) http://www.electro-net.com/~dondun/Wife%20Ruin.htm

Engel, Beverly. *Healing Your Emotional Self: A Powerful Program to Help You Raise Your Self-Esteem, Quiet Your Inner Critic, and Overcome Your Shame.* Hoboken, N.J.: Wiley, 2006.

_____. *The Right to Innocence: Healing the Trauma of Childhood Sexual Abuse.* New York: Ivy Books, 1989.

Flach, Frederic F. *A New Marriage, a New Life.* New York: Hatherleigh Press, 1998.

Forward, Susan, Ph.D., with Craig Buck. *Toxic Parents: Overcoming Their Hurtful Legacy and Reclaiming Your Life.* New York: Bantam Books, 1989.

Genung, Mike. "How Many Porn Addicts Are in Your Church?" Crosswalk.com Director of blazinggrace.org.

Glass, Shirley, Ph.D., "Shattered Vows." *Psychology Today* (July/Aug. 1998).

Gottman, John, Ph.D. *Why Marriages Succeed or Fail and How You Can Make Yours Last.* New York: Simon and Schuster, 1994.

Harley, Willard, Jr. *His Needs, Her Needs.* 15th edition. Old Tappan, N.J.: Baker, Revell, 2001.

Hart, Archibald. *The Sexual Man: Masculinity Without Guilt.* Grand Rapids: Zondervan Publishing House, 1994.

Hayford, Jack. "Why Sex Sins Are Worse than Others" (audiotape). Van Nuys, Calif.: Living Way Ministries, CO179 and 180.

Hyde, Janet S., and John DeLamater. *Understanding Human Sexuality.* 6th ed. Boston: McGraw Hill, 1997.

Jeffress, Robert. *Guilt Free Living.* Carol Stream, Ill.: Tyndale House Publishers, Inc., 1995.

Kasl, Dr. C. *Women, Sex, and Addiction.* New York: Harper and Row, 1990.

Kemp, Jeff. *Building Marriage in the New Millennium.* Executive Director (July 2003).

Knox, David, and Caroline Schacht. *Marriage and the Family.* Belmont, Calif.: Wadsworth, 1999.

Kreider, Rose M., and Jason M. Fields. "Number, Timing and Duration of Marriages and Divorces: 1996." U.S. Census Bureau Current Populations Reports (February 2002), 18.

LaHaye, Tim. *Understanding the Male Temperament.* 2nd ed. Grand Rapids: Fleming H. Revell, 1977, 1996.

LaHaye, Tim, and Bob Phillips. *Anger Is a Choice.* Grand Rapids: Zondervan, 1982.

Lechner, Cathy. *I'm Trying to Sit at His Feet: but Who's Going to Cook Dinner?* Orlando, Fla.: Creation House, 1995.

Lofas, Jeannette. The Stepfamily Foundation, 1975. http://www.stepfamily.org.

Mallinger, Allan, M.D., and Jeannette De Wyze. *Too Perfect: When Being in Control Gets Out of Control.* New York: Clarkson Potter Publishers, 1992.

Mayer, Adele. *Incest: A Treatment Manual for Victims, Spouses, and Offenders.* Holmes Beach, Fla.: Learning Publications, 1983.

McMillen, S. I., and David E. Stern. *None of These Diseases: The Bible's Health for the 21st Century.* Old Tappan, N.J.: Fleming H. Revell Company, 1984.

Meyer, Joyce. *The Root of Rejection.* Tulsa: Harrison House, 1987.

Minirth, Frank, M.D. "Minirth on Depression." *Christian Helping Today*, Vol. 10, No. 4, 2002.

Minirth, Frank B., M.D. and Paul D. Meier, M.D. *Happiness Is a Choice: A Manual on the Symptoms, Causes, and Cures of Depression.* Grand Rapids: Baker Publishing Group, 2007.

Moses, Ken. "The Feeling Stages of Grief." Carbondale, Ill.: Department of Education, Southern Illinois University.

National Committee for the Prevention of Child Abuse, 1987; http://www.safechild.org/childabuse3.htm

Niolon, Richard. *Resources for Students and Professionals.* www.psychpage.com

Oliver, Gary Jackson, and H. Norman Wright. *When Anger Hits Home.* Chicago: Moody Press, 1992.

Papernow, Patricia. *Becoming a Stepfamily: Patterns of Development in Remarried Families.* New York: Gardner Press, 1993.

Pittman III, Frank, M.D. "Beyond Betrayal: Life After Infidelity." *Psychology Today* (May/June 1993).

Roberts, Ted. *Pure Desire: Helping People Break Free from Sexual Struggles.* Ventura, Calif.: Regal Books, 1999.

Rubin, Theodore I. *The Angry Book.* New York: MacMillan, 1969.

Schaumburg, Dr. Harry W. *False Intimacy: Understanding the Struggle of Sexual Addiction.* Colorado Springs: NavPress, 1997.

Schnarch, D. "Inside the Sexual Crucible." *Networker* (March/April 1993).

Sgroi, Suzanne M. *Handbook of Clinical Intervention in Child Sexual Abuse.* New York: Simon and Schuster, Inc., 1982.

Simpson, Paul, Ed.D. *Treating Sexual Compulsive Disorders: A Training Seminar for Mental Health Care Professionals,* 2004.

Smalley, Gary. *Making Love Last Forever.* Dallas: Word Publishing, 1996.

Smalley, Gary, and John Trent, Ph.D. *The Gift of the Blessing.* Nashville: Thomas Nelson Publishers, 1995.

_____. *The Language of Love.* Pomona, Calif.: Focus on the Family Publishing, 1988.

Smedes, Lewis B. *The Art of Forgiveness.* Nashville: Moorings, 1996.

Smoke, Jim. *Growing Through Divorce.* Eugene, Oreg.: Harvest House Publishing, 1995.

Stewart, Dan, president of Life Pacific College. Instructor Material, 2005.

Swindoll, Charles. Insight for Living. Radio and audio Bible teaching ministry.

Taylor, Glenn, and Rod Wilson. *Helping Angry People.* Grand Rapids: Baker Books, 1997.

Thompson, Carroll. *Possess the Land.* Dallas: Carroll Thompson Ministries, 1977.

Warren, Neil Clark. *Making Anger Your Ally.* 3rd ed. Colorado Springs: Focus on the Family Publishing, 1990.

Weeden, Larry K. *Feeling Guilty, Finding Grace.* Ann Arbor, Mich.: Servant Publications, 1993.

Wegscheider-Cruse, Sharon. *Learning to Love Yourself: Finding Your Self-Worth.* Deerfield Beach, Fla.: Health Communications Inc., 1987.

Weiss, Douglas. *Sex, Men and God: A Godly Man's Road Map to Sexual Success.* Lake Mary, Fla.: Charisma House, 2002.

_____. *She Has a Secret: Understanding Female Sexual Addiction.* Fort Worth: Discovery Press, 2000.

Wright, H. Norman. *Crisis Care: Hope for the Hurting.* Richardson, Tex.: Grace Products Corporation, 2002.

www.ingramcontent.com/pod-product-compliance
Lightning Source LLC
Chambersburg PA
CBHW050855160426
43194CB00011B/2165